Education for Changing Unions

I was inspired by this book and I thank the authors for providing an antidote to the creeping cynicism that has been infecting my professional life as a union educator. It's a very readable text and one that I can use as a catalyst for dialogue on the education program within my own organization.

—Trisha Sadoway
labour educator, Kingston, Ontario

Education for Changing Unions is full of insightful labour educational "union moments." Written by a remarkable collective of five diversely experienced, thoughtful labour educators who critically examine their own practice, the book defies the notion that "wisdom cannot be told." To read this book is to engage in a learning experience which can enlighten both the novice as well as the experienced union educator.

—Elaine Bernard
Executive Director, Harvard Trade Union Program & Labor and Worklife Program at Harvard Law School, Cambridge, Mass.

There are so many exercises I want to try. Thanks for the thoughtful, clear expansion of the spiral model and for the guidelines on worker educators. *Education for Changing Unions* helps labor educators think more critically as we meet our training goals and contributions for our changing labor movement.

—Carol Anderson
Assistant Education Director, American Federation of State, County and Municipal Employees, Washington, D.C.

We welcome wholeheartedly *Education for Changing Unions*, a new book from our Canadian sister and brother educators. The clear, straightforward writing blends concrete union education ideas and important basic principles with vision, a sense of humor, a collective spirit, inspirational stories and a toughness clearly born of years of education practice within unions. It will be an important text for unions and grassroots groups throughout the United States.

—Suzanne Pharr

Director, the Highlander Research and Education Center, New Market, Tennessee

Bravo! A lovely read, engaging, and highly useful. The chapter on worker educator programs makes the important links between education, democratization, and leadership.

I was awed by the respect, admiration, and love for union learners that just radiates from this book. That spirit, as much as the techniques and activities presented, reminds me that union education is not a performance by the facilitator, but a complex engagement and relationship with peers (the participants) who are as affected by how a course is facilitated as by its content.

—Adriane Paavo

Staff Representive and labour educator, Grain Services Union, Regina, Saskatchewan

Education for Changing Unions

Bev Burke

Jojo Geronimo

D'Arcy Martin

Barb Thomas

Carol Wall

Between the Lines

Toronto

Education for Changing Unions

First published in Canada in 2002 by
Between the Lines
720 Bathurst Street, Suite #404
Toronto, Ontario M5S 2R4
1-800-718-7201   www.btlbooks.com

Distributed in the USA by
SCB Distributors
Gardena, California

National Library of Canada Cataloguing in Publication

Education for changing unions / Bev Burke ... [et al.].

Includes bibliographical references.
ISBN 1-896357-61-X

1. Labour unions and education—Canada.
2. Working class—Education—Canada.   I. Burke, Bev, 1943-

LC5054.E38 2002   374'.971   C2002-903380-2

Cover, text design and illustrations by Margie Adam, ArtWork

Frontispiece: Sherwin Modeste / photo—Barb Thomas; background photo—Deb Barndt
Part 1 title: Linda Delp / photo—Dorothy Wigmore; background photo—Deb Barndt
Part 2 title: Lawrence Angeconeb / photo—Barb Thomas; background photo—Deb Barndt
Part 3 title: Jackie Edwards / photo—Barb Thomas; background photo—Deb Barndt

Printed in Canada by union labour

Between the Lines gratefully acknowledges assistance for its publishing activities from the Canada Council for the Arts, the Ontario Arts Council, and the Government of Canada through the Book Publishing Industry Development Program.

CONTENTS

Foreword....ix
Acknowledgements....x

Introduction....1
A Word about Words....6

Part 1 THE JOB OF UNION EDUCATION

1   The Union Educator: What's the Job?....12
2   Working Inside: Navigating the Union Culture....18
3   Union Education in a Globalizing Economy....28

Pause   "Where Are We Five Coming From?"....39
        Traditions Shaping Our Educational Practice....46
        A Gift and a Challenge by WUT-TUN-NEE (Tim Brown)....53

Part 2 THE CRAFT OF UNION EDUCATION

4   Designing the Program....56
5   Making Activities Work....78
6   Our Favourite Union Education Activities....90
7   Facilitation....132
8   The Power of Co-Facilitation....159

Part 3 MAKING OUR PRESENCE FELT

9   Evaluation for Impact....172
10   Worker Educator Programs....191
11   Strategic Planning....215
12   Staying the Course....228

Appendix: More of Our Favourite Union Education Activities....241
            Resources and Sources....273

To all those who have endured our union education programs
over the years we offer

our gratitude for all you have taught us;
our amazement that you have asked us to write it down;
our readiness to stand together in future struggles.

In memoriam:
Marlene Green,
who accompanied and challenged us
through many stages of our education for social change;
Jim Counahan,
worker educator and union activist.

Our deepest fear is not that we are inadequate.
Our deepest fear is that we are powerful beyond measure.
It is our Light, not our Darkness, that most frightens us.

Nelson Mandela

I want to see ordinary people feeling their own worth
and seeing the same worth in other people.
This cannot be done from the top down,
but only by ordinary people imbued with their own power.

Doris Marshall

FOREWORD

M Y FAVORITE ICE-BREAKER at the beginning of a class with union leaders is an exercise called "union moments." The class forms pairs, and each participant takes five minutes or so, to tell their partner about a personal union moment. What's a union moment? Well, people join unions and get involved in the labour movement for all sorts of reasons and through many paths. Most people didn't set out to become a union activist or leader. But a union moment isn't a story about how and why people join unions. Rather, it s about experiencing unions, developing a community of interest among a group of workers, and engaging in collective deliberation and concerted action. A union moment is an incident that has a profound effect on the individual and demonstrates to the participant (often for the first time) the power of democratic, collective action.

As the class shares their various narratives, we note that in spite of the diverse personal histories and stories, there are common elements to all the tales. They are all accounts of groups in action dealing with issues of economic and social justice and dignity. The exercise ends with a challenge to the group to consider how to reorganize the activities of their unions to create more participatory, empowering union moments for all of their members so that they too can experience what it really means to be union. It's these very personally experienced, union moments that breathe life into an organization. It's these experiences that transform members into activists and build unions numerically, and qualitatively.

Education for Changing Unions is full of insightful, labour, educational, union moments. Written by a remarkable collective of five, diversely experienced, thoughtful labour educators who critically examine their own practice, the book defies the notion that wisdom cannot be told. There is wisdom and insight on each page. To read this book is to engage in a learning experience which can enlighten both the novice as well as the experienced union educator.

One third labour education tool kit, one third autobiography, and one third reflective conversation on the craft of union education, this book engages the reader in a thoughtful exploration of designing and delivering education for transformation. Each author has taken a different path to labour education, but all have come to recognize the pivotal significance of a class-conscious labour movement and the role of education in building such a movement. They are unapologetic about the fact that labour education is advocacy. There is no pretense of ideological neutrality. *Education for Changing Unions* is about creating more powerful, democratic unions that fight for economic and social justice and equality.

The authors embrace the teaching of Paulo Freire, though thankfully, their writing is much more engaging and accessible for the activist educator. Of course, many in the North American labour movement today embraced popular education, but too often I fear, in practice, it has been little more than a compendium of games, exercises, and stimulating forms of delivering a pre-packaged message. Be forewarned, *Education for Changing Unions* is focused on the real power of popular education, its critical thinking and action-oriented content. The authors share the perspective that popular education is about transformation. Like any type of genuine, critical education it will shake things up, often in unintended ways. They don't mind discussing some of the more difficult educational situations that they've encountered, mistakes they've made, and lessons they've picked up along the way.

Education for Changing Unions models the method it seeks to teach. It's reflective practice at its best.

Elaine Bernard
Executive Director, Harvard Trade Union Program &
Labor and Worklife Program at Harvard Law School

ACKNOWLEDGEMENTS

TWO OF THE CO-AUTHORS, Bev Burke and Barb Thomas, co-ordinated the writing and production phases of this project respectively. The contribution of WUT-TUN-NEE (Tim Brown) added a richness for which we are eternally grateful—especially because, as we acknowledge in the book, our knowledge of Aboriginal teachings and traditions is limited. While we want to avoid any appropriation of voice, we recognize the importance of the Aboriginal contribution, which is too often missing from our work. We would also be amiss if we did not acknowledge the many influences on our work by all those who courageously work in advocacy and social justice organizations in Canada and internationally.

We also want to acknowledge the unions across Canada with whom we have worked and from whom we have drawn our inspiration, in particular, the Canadian Labour Congress (CLC); Fédération des travailleurs et travailleuses du Québec (FTQ); the Federations of Labour in Ontario (OFL), Saskatchewan (SFL), British Columbia (BCFL), and New Brunswick (NBFL), and their affiliate unions; British Columbia Government and Service Employees' Union (BCGSEU); Canadian Autoworkers Union (CAW); Communications, Energy and Paperworkers Union of Canada (CEP); Canadian Union of Public Employees (CUPE); Canadian Union of Postal Workers (CUPW); Hotel Employees and Restaurant Employees Union (HERE); Industrial Wood and Allied Workers (IWA); Office and Professional Employees International Union (OPEIU); Ontario Public Service Employees Union (OPSEU); Public Service Alliance of Canada (PSAC); Service Employees International Union (SEIU); United Food and Commercial Workers Union (UFCW); and the United Steelworkers of America (USWA). We also want to acknowledge our work with the American Federation of State, County and Municipal Employees (AFSCME), which sharpened our thinking on worker educator programs, and with the Public Service International (PSI), which enriched our global gender analysis.

Fortunately for us, many of our colleagues were willing and able to give us instructive feedback on the manuscript; among them were Carol Anderson, Barb Byers, Sue Carter, Johanne Deschamps, Bob Hatfield, Nancy Roscoe-Huntley, Amber Hockin, Maureen Hynes, Denis Lemelin, and Denise Nadeau. We thank them all. Rob Fairley, Adriane Paavo, and Mary Rowles provided detailed comments that helped us greatly in the final draft. Gail Nye not only helped out as a reader but also sent us the Chinese symbols, which we use as graphics in CHAPTER 1.

We owe a debt of gratitude to Paul Eprile and Peter Steven of Between the Lines for their belief in this book. Two tireless friends once again took on the final production of the words and pictures: our thanks to Robert Clarke for editing and Margie Adam of ArtWork for illustration and design. Thanks also go to our comrade and colleague Elaine Bernard for her generous comments.

All photos and visuals are credited where they appear. Particular thanks go to artist and friend, Deborah Barndt, to the Centre for the Study of Education and Work at OISE/University of Toronto, and to the Public Service International. Funding support provided by the Ontario Arts Council has been instrumental in producing this book. Any royalties from sales will go to the authors' choice of charities, social justice networks, coalitions, or organizations engaging in popular education.

Bev Burke   Jojo Geronimo   D'Arcy Martin   Barb Thomas   Carol Wall

Introduction

THIS BOOK IS OUR EFFORT to put on paper what we've learned collectively in decades of union work, and shared in two years of intense dialogue. We feel it is time to move this conversation out of our living rooms.

For many years now educators working in Canada's labour movement have been talking informally about the beauty and the strain of our work. As five people engaged in very different ways in union education, we have discussed in ones and twos why we love the labour movement and how it drives us crazy—what we find that works and doesn't work in our courses and meetings, in our conferences and conventions. Often these conversations have involved other activists who promote learning in the labour movement (though many of them might not think of themselves as educators). In this text we are responding to the wide interest in the labour movement and its social allies about methods of increasing participation, mobilization, and democratic practice. The book represents our effort to pull together what we have learned both separately and together, and then to turn that learning into a wider public discussion.

ABOUT THIS BOOK

THIS COLLECTIVE WRITING PROJECT builds on the experience of *Educating for a Change*, published in 1991. (Three of us were among the five authors of that book, which presents a popular education approach to the strategy, design, and facilitation issues that face politically progressive adult educators.) To a large degree, this book reflects the same values as the earlier one, but applies them to a specific part of the broad movement for economic and social justice: the labour movement. It reflects what all of us have learned from our successes and failures in the past decade.

The title?

Education for Changing Unions consciously plays with the word "changing." This book celebrates the unions that are using education as a strategy for change and offers tools to further their work. We also know that there are many educators, inside and outside the labour movement, who are working to increase the will and capacity of unions as instruments of social and economic justice. In both these senses, our book aims to support activists in bringing the practices of our social movements closer to their declared goals.

Who are we anyway, who presume to write this book?

Readers will find out lots about us in the pages that follow, but it may be helpful up front for us to put our cards on the table, to save readers some time. Please remember that no individual is the sole author of any part of this book, but you will certainly find some individual personalities shining through on occasion.

Bev Burke brings to the group many years of international solidarity education, especially in Latin America. Her special focus has been on the design of union education programs, and on teaching potential worker educators. She has worked on contract with a range of unions, including the Steelworkers, Autoworkers, and Postal Workers.

Jojo Geronimo, with his mix of experience in several parts of Asia and deep roots in Toronto's immigrant and refugee community, has a flair for policy analysis and strategy. He works in the Ontario Public Service Employees Union (OPSEU), with specific responsibility for the educational component of the "Network for Better Contracts" Program.

D'Arcy Martin, a former Canadian education director in three different unions, brings a sense of organizational issues and union democracy. He works on contract with several labour bodies, especially in Quebec and Saskatchewan, and is co-ordinator of the Centre for the Study of Education and Work at the University of Toronto.

Barb Thomas worked initially in community settings in Canada and the Caribbean, then on contract at all levels of the labour movement, and later as a staff member of the Service Employees International Union. She brings to our discussion particular strengths in anti-racism work, facilitation, and worker educator programs. She now works on contract for several unions.

Carol Wall worked for years in the newspaper industry and sharpened her social justice perspective through various volunteer positions within the labour movement before becoming a union staff rep for the Communications, Energy and Paperworkers Union of Canada (CEP). She continues to design and lead courses as the first Human Rights Director of the CEP.

IN WRITING THIS BOOK, we have had to deal continually with our different locations or identities as educators. We can't be reduced to those identities, but certainly our views and interests are shaped by them. Three of us are women, and two are men; three of us are white, and two are Canadians of colour. English is a second language for only one of us, although all of us have learned at least one other language. We are all straight, over forty-five years old, physically mobile, and living in Ontario. Two of us have jobs in unions, and three of us are contract workers. These conditions shape our histories and responses to social justice work. The process of writing this book required us to negotiate our differences and find common ground.

As individuals and as a group, we have plenty of limitations. We continue to be surprised and humbled by what we don't know. Day after day we experience wakeup calls of different sorts in our courses. One time, for instance, one of us pushed a lively discussion into the lunch break–not recognizing the protests of a participant who turned out to be diabetic, with strict eating requirements. Other times we have begun an activity without realizing that a participant with a physical disability would be excluded from it. We have used terms that exclude and upset people. We know we have missed out on wonderful union education initiatives in affiliates and various regions of the country because none of us has the necessary continuing contacts there.

That is why this book doesn't claim to be THE story, why we don't give our opinion on every issue facing the labour movement. We don't pronounce here on matters like Quebec's right to self-determination, or the structure of international unions, or methods of organizing unions in Aboriginal communities.We especially recognize our limited personal knowledge of both the richness and horror of the Aboriginal experience in the Americas, and the great need to amplify the contributions that Aboriginal people can and do make to the union culture.

WHAT'S OUR AGENDA? THE SIX THREADS

Community

Democracy

Equity

FOR ALL OF THE WRITERS OF THIS BOOK, six threads hold together the fabric of our work: community, democracy, equity, class-consciousness, organization-building, and the greater good.

For us, **community** means building connections between different people for a common purpose. We are aware of the often flabby use of the term. We want to reclaim the word to denote the intentional goal of building solidarity, often across differences in power based on social identity. What we have in mind is a community based on a sense of common humanity and a bond of shared experience and values that goes beyond tactical agreement on a particular political priority or struggle. This is community forged by deep listening to difficult differences in order to build more trust and shared power.

But community is also developed through creating a sense of ease in a group, dealing with issues of exclusion and conflict, sharing stories, humour, and food. These are not peripheral "soft" issues, to be endured while waiting for the "real political discussion" to start. In our experience, building community is part of building a social movement—a precondition to healthy politics—particularly given the individualistic culture of Canada in the twenty-first century.

By **democracy**, we mean genuine participation by a broad range of members in labour movement decision-making. We recognize that there are times of crisis when leaders cannot consult, and times of deadlock when leaders need to propose a personal vision for the path ahead. Most of the time, though, unions are strengthened by increasing member involvement. Despite efforts to move from servicing to mobilizing and organizing models of unionism, this participation is far from integrated throughout our movement. We cannot continue to call for worker empowerment in the workplace while blocking it in the union. Democratic participation is a heated issue inside unions, and the focus of courageous and sometimes futile struggles. It is also a complex issue, because the very character of our unions will shift as new forms of participation emerge and new internal alliances develop.

By **equity**, we mean recognizing and challenging the historically built-in barriers experienced by some groups and the privileged position of others. This is not comfortable and tidy work. It means exploring white supremacy (what W.E.B. Dubois referred to as "wages for whiteness"), considering how images of union activism assume men to be the norm and women to be "a problem," and so on. The struggle for equity recognizes unequal starting points and unequal power in a society in which classism, racism, sexism, ableism, ageism, and heterosexism shape the "normal" ways of doing things.

Equity is both an agenda for unions to advance in our society and a challenge within unions themselves. Equity highlights the need to broaden the range of social identities reflected in union membership and leadership. "Too male, too pale, too stale" was a criticism made of the U.S. labour movement leadership just a few years ago. Within Canada we have seen these divisions widened by resentments among groups who should logically be labour supporters, and even activists. The union structures we have inherited were built, largely, by white men. We continue to need their creativity and courage as Canadian unions develop the leadership of women, young people, racialized workers, and others to build a movement that advances the interests of all working people.

By **class-consciousness**, we mean understanding, as workers, the differences between those who rule the economy and those employed in it. As a famous political poster by Press Gang Publishers puts it, "Class consciousness is knowing which side of the fence you're on. Class analysis is figuring out who is there with you." Of course, oceans of ink have been spilled to argue that such a line no longer exists in advanced industrial economies, that workers have become conservative and passive in the face of prosperity. A disturbing variant of this worn-out cliché is that the divisions by gender or race or other social identities have become primary, eclipsing the importance of class. Most labour activists can smell the trap in such thinking, the playing of class against other equity struggles to the benefit of the establishment. Most workers with whom we have learned and taught are quite capable of carrying both equity and class awareness into their union work. Is it easy? Of course not, but it's a challenge we take up in this book.

By **organization-building**, we mean working to increase the collective strength of unions. Raising individual social awareness is a noble task, but our commitment is to building organizations that can "fight the boss," that can help to change power relations across communities, regions, and countries. It is a serious business, sometimes downright scary. Union education is a careful knitting of networks of trust, renewing the structures that have emerged from years of struggle. Workers take a risk when they step forward as activists, and they deserve respect for themselves and the organizations they have built. Good labour education develops strong individuals with strong collective supports, equipped to work for justice over the long haul.

By the **greater good**, we mean to emphasize a constant insistence that the labour movement serve more than its current, employed, and dues-paying membership. When we deal with a local union, we try to link them with their national and international structures. When we deal with a national or international union, we try to link them with their central labour bodies and the labour movement as a whole. When we are working with the Canadian Labour Congress or the Fédération des travailleurs et travailleuses du Québec, we try to link them with the international labour movement. Anywhere in the labour movement, we emphasize links with actual and potential allies, especially in the community and the academy.

Both inside and outside their working hours, union members are residents, citizens, taxpayers, and neighbours. They live in families, are active in sports and hobbies, try to lead spiritual lives. They are caregivers and artists as well as activists, and they quite properly expect their unions to address the full range and complexity of their lives. Effective opposition to the naked corporate power grab called "globalization" will require more than workplace action to turn it back. In thinking about a greater good, we are drawn back to our commitment to community, the first of our six threads.

Although these six threads tie our book together, we will not try to convince readers to adopt them. We are simply coming clean. Many books are available to promote individualism, authoritarianism, bigotry, class blindness, narrow self-interest, and union-bashing—though many of them are clothed in the guise of moral or social "neutrality." We don't claim to be neutral. We have taken sides, with the labour movement and with these values. Many complex and contradictory issues arise as a result—certainly enough to fill a book.

Education for Changing Unions

Class-consciousness

Organization building

Greater good

WHAT'S IN THIS BOOK?

EDUCATION FOR CHANGING UNIONS addresses three dimensions of union education: the job itself, the craft involved, and the many ways of making its presence felt. The "PAUSE" after the first section is for those interested in the sources and experiences that have inspired us.

PART I describes the job of union education and situates it in the union culture, that special workplace for progressive adult educators. Like other workplaces, it has been shaken up by the neo-liberal offensive.

In PART II we share what we have learned about the craft of union education, beginning with designing structured events, whether or not they are called courses. (Later, in both chapter 6 and an appendix, we offer up some of our favourite activities, and we fully expect that some experienced educators will go directly to those pages in search of new ideas and activities.) We have included a chapter on the art of facilitation, and another that explores the arguments for co-facilitation and the challenges of doing it well.

PART III deals with how education might strengthen democracy and participation across our unions, looking at organizational practices rather than individual courses and events. Here we consider a framework and strategies for evaluating our work, as well as ways of developing worker educator programs. We look at strategic planning initiatives and how education can strengthen them. We conclude with some thoughts about doing this work over the long haul without burning out.

In the end our biggest hope is to make at least one small contribution to the great joint efforts of working people, made over so many years, to promote learning for economic and social justice.

Working together in English and French, the Regina Labour Educators' Exchange, October 2002.

A word about words

Affiliate — a union that is a member of a central labour body or group of unions.[1]

Anti-harassment policy — policy set by the union, or jointly with management, to deal with harassment of members by each other, or by management. Harassment is unwelcome behaviour that can include name-calling, jokes, graffiti, insults, threats, discourteous treatment, or written, verbal, or physical abuse. Harassment is usually an abuse of power that violates human rights, based on prohibited grounds such as racial background, ethnicity, place of origin, sex, age, religion, sexual orientation, and language. Some union anti-harassment policies now have provisions for "personal harassment" as well.

Business and social unionism — two approaches to unionism representing two different political perspectives; business unionism focuses on immediate economic concerns of the current membership, while social unionism links the well-being of the members to social justice in the broader community.

CLC (Canadian Labour Congress) — a central labour body, representing over 80 per cent of organized labour across Canada.

Central labour body — brings together affiliates in a geographic area, such as a district labour council, a provincial federation of labour, or a national umbrella organization of unions (for example, the CLC).

Certification — the official designation of a union, by a labour relations board or similar government agency, as sole and exclusive bargaining agent, following proof of majority support among employees in a bargaining unit.

Collective agreement — a contract between one or more unions—acting as a bargaining agent—and one or more employers, covering matters such as wages, hours, working conditions, fringe benefits, rights of workers and unions, and procedures to be followed in settling disputes and grievances.

Collective bargaining — a method of determining wages, hours, and other conditions of employment through direct negotiations between the union and employer. Usually, in Canada, the result of collective bargaining is a written contract, a collective agreement, which covers all employees in the bargaining unit, both union members and non-members.

Demand setting — a stage preceding actual negotiation, in which the membership determines the priorities for this round of bargaining.

---

1. Thanks to the following, on whose work we drew for some of these words about words: Bishop, *Becoming an Ally*; Barndt, ed., Women *Working the NAFTA Food Chain*; Canadian Labour Congress, *Glossary of Labour Terms*. For full references, see "RESOURCES AND SOURCES."

Federation of Labour — one of twelve federations chartered by the Canadian Labour Congress, grouping local unions and labour councils in a given province or territory.

FTQ (Fédération des travailleurs et travailleuses du Québec) — the largest central labour body in Quebec; it works on a basis of sovereignty-association with the CLC.

Grievance — a complaint against management by one or more employees or a union, concerning an alleged breach of the collective agreement, or an alleged injustice. The procedure for handling grievances is usually defined in the collective agreement. The last step of a grievance procedure is usually arbitration.

International union — a union that has members in Canada, Quebec, and the United States.

Labour Council — an organization composed of locals of CLC-affiliated unions in a given community or district (in Quebec, referred to as a regional council or *conseil regional*).

Local executive (or executive board) — the officers elected by the membership to run the local. The president, vice-president, and secretary-treasurer sit on the executive.

Local union — the basic unit of union organization. Trade unions are usually divided into a number of locals, which have their own bylaws and elect their own officers. They are responsible for the day-to-day administration of the collective agreements covering their members, and they name delegates to conventions of their affiliates and central labour bodies.

"Mobilizing/organizing" and "servicing" models of unionism — represent two approaches to unionism. The *mobilizing/organizing model* seeks active participation of members at all levels of union life, as the basis of union power in relation to the employer. The *servicing model* emphasizes handling individual cases of conflict with the employer by union staff and officers, through the collective agreement.

National union — a union whose membership is confined to Canada or Quebec only.

Paid educational leave — a provision of the collective agreement negotiated between the union and the employer, whereby the employer deposits an amount per paid hour into a fund for the education of members; the fund is controlled by the union. With such a fund, unions can develop and provide intensive courses for activists, worker educator training, and supports to participation such as day care.

Staff representative — a full-time employee of a national or international union whose job is to service and mobilize the members, in co-ordination with elected officials at all levels.

Steward — a member elected to represent a specific group of members within the union and to management. Stewards handle workplace problems and serve as communicators and mobilizers of the membership.

ABOUT EDUCATION

Content and process — represents the tension between what people learn and how they learn. As social change educators we try to pay attention to both elements, as two sides of one reality.

Energizer — a short activity, often playful, used to restore participants' ability to focus and accomplish the content goals of a course or meeting.

Facilitation — see p.152.

Popular education — a translation of the Spanish *educación popular*, and a form of social change education with roots in Latin America. It starts with the experience of oppressed people, links new knowledge to what people already know, and leads to an expression of that knowledge through collective action for social change. Paulo Freire, a Brazilian educator, pioneered its theory and practice. See p.46.

Social change education — the term we use to describe the work of union or popular education in general. It signifies an approach to education that is in the interests of oppressed groups. It involves people in the process of critical analysis so that they can act collectively to change oppressive structures and practices. The process is participatory, creative, and empowering.

Spiral model — a tool for planning social change education, which goes through the following phases: starts with people's experience, identifies patterns in these experiences, adds and deepens information and theory, practises new skills, and leads to action. See p.57.

Worker educators — union members who facilitate and teach educational courses and other union events.

ABOUT PEOPLE, POWER, AND POLITICS

Aboriginal — a term referring to the first inhabitants of what is now Canada, and their descendants. The term as used in Canada includes First Nations peoples who have negotiated treaties or have status under the Indian Act; Métis peoples, whose heritage includes European as well as Aboriginal ancestry; and Inuit people. We understand that these terms are used differently elsewhere, particularly in the United States and Australia.

Accommodation — a set of measures designed to remove barriers to people with disabilities, in institutions and workplaces.

Ally — refers to a member of a dominant group who works to end a form of oppression that gives her or him privilege. Examples include a white person who works to end racism, or a man who challenges sexism.

Class-consciousness — see p.4.

Community — see p.3.

Democracy — see p.3.

Equity/equity lens — *equity* names the struggle to recognize and challenge positions of privilege and historically built-in barriers experienced by some groups. It recognizes unequal starting points and unequal power in a society in which classism, racism, sexism, ableism, ageism, and heterosexism shape the "normal" ways of doing things. (See p.3.) An *equity lens* is a critical eye on our work that looks for the ways in which we may be unconsciously reinforcing these systems of barriers and privileges.

Gender analysis — *gender* refers not to the physical characteristics that make someone male or female, but to socially defined traits of men and women: appearance, attitudes, roles, preferences, work, for example. *Gender analysis* examines how men and women are "gendered" and how power works in this process.

Heterosexism/homophobia — *Heterosexism* refers to the social structures and attitudes that favour one kind of loving—between one man and one woman in a monogamous marriage with children—over all others. Heterosexism oppresses gay, lesbian, bi-sexual, and transgender people, single people, one-parent families, unmarried couples, childless couples, and others who do not fit this mould. *Homophobia* is a reaction of hatred, fear, or discomfort, acted out through discrimination and violence against gay, lesbian, bisexual, and transgender people.

Maquila/maquiladora — An assembly or parts plant in Mexico, originally situated along the US border, that produces for export. These plants are a form of sweatshop because they are unregulated, exploit a primarily female workforce, and undermine labour standards in Mexico and across North America.

Marginalized/Marginalization — describes groups that have historically experienced oppression and exploitation and the process which pushes them further and further from the centres of power in a society.

Neo-liberalism — a recent, extreme form of traditional liberal values. *Liberalism* comes from the time of liberal revolutions, especially in France, Britain, and the United States, which brought a merchant middle class to power and overthrew the older monarchical systems. Its key traits are a belief in individual freedom and commerce. In the late twentieth century *neo-liberalism* extended traditional liberal values to an extreme of privatization and deregulation. By reducing the role of the state in social matters, it sought to increase the power of business in an unregulated market economy. Its values are individuality, efficiency, profitability, and productivity. Since this agenda was promoted by conservative regimes in Britain, New Zealand, Canada, and the United States beginning in the 1980s, it is sometimes also referred to as "neo-conservatism."

North/South — a division of the world that results from centuries of colonialism. The Northern countries, particularly in Europe and North America, fuelled their industrialization by exploiting the resources and labour of Southern countries in Asia, Africa, Latin America and the Caribbean, and the Pacific. This inequitable relationship continues today through economic and trade practices promoted by the World Bank, International Monetary Fund, and World Trade Organization (sometimes referred to by critics as the "axis of evil").

People of colour — people who suffer colour-based racism in Canada because of their Asian, Latin American, African, Southern European, or Middle Eastern origins. The term originated in the United States to denote a common experience of racism across national and ethnic ancestry. (See "racialized.")

People with disabilities — this large and varied group of people face a common form of oppression, often called *ableism*. However, there are huge differences in how people with disabilities experience this oppression. Those who move with the aid of wheelchairs face discrimination differently from those who suffer chronic pain, those who are deaf, or those whose mental abilities are different from the majority.

Racialized — a fairly recent term referring to the ways in which racism makes groups of people identifiable or "raced" because of their physical characteristics. It is a helpful word because it validates the experience of some people who are treated as if they belong to "another and inferior race," and it rejects the false notion that race is a biological reality.

Sovereignty-association — a political relationship between states that includes the right of each state to make decisions over agreed-upon areas, and the integration of some functions of governance. The Fédération des travailleurs et travailleuses du Québec (FTQ) and the Canadian Labour Congress (CLC) have a form of sovereignty-association agreement between them, in the sense that the FTQ is recognized as having a national authority in Quebec similar to the CLC's authority in Canada; the financial relations between them reflect this agreement.

Transgendered/transphobia — *transgendered* (or trans for short) describes individuals who are not comfortable with, or who reject, in whole or in part, the gender they were assigned at birth. A transgendered person may be gay, lesbian, bisexual, or heterosexual; there is no direct connection between gender identity and sexual orientation. *Transphobia* is the irrational fear and hatred of cross-dressers and transsexuals. Like all prejudices, it is based on negative stereotypes and misconceptions that are used to justify and support hatred, discrimination, harassment, and violence.

White people — refers to people belonging to the dominant racial group in Canada. Definitions of "whiteness" vary in different countries, depending on the history of colonial relations and racism, and in that sense "white" is not a static term.

White supremacy — a system based on assumptions of the "rightness of whiteness," in which the "normal" way things work results in white people having more privilege and power than peoples of colour and Aboriginal peoples. The term "white supremacy" is often associated only with societies in which racism is overt and violent. But white supremacy can be seen in any society, including Canada, where there is a racial hierarchy with whites at the top.

The Job of Union Education

Part 1

The Union Educator: What's the Job?

CONTENTS

WHY IT MATTERS....12

WHAT DOES IT TAKE?....15

*When I dare to be powerful, to use my strength in the service of my vision,
then it becomes less and less important whether I am afraid.*

Audre Lorde

AN EXAMPLE

WHY IT MATTERS

I was co-facilitating a pilot workshop with a small group of women. I vividly remember one participant who began the week with a tiny voice and bowed head. As we went over the objectives of the course she squirmed in her seat. When we did introductions, she was very apologetic for what she perceived as her inexperience.

By mid-week she was actively participating and leading a report-back. In a quiet conversation with me, she explained that for the first time her experience and contribution had been validated, and she felt that it was okay to make mistakes. In that context, she found the new knowledge, enthusiasm, and experience of others inspirational rather than intimidating.

ON OUR GOOD DAYS IN UNION EDUCATION, we have the privilege of watching whole groups of workers, like this sister, develop self-confidence and courage to act. We are awed by the possibilities in people, and by the energy generated through working together. This is what sustains us through other less-than-perfect moments in the trenches. In turn it helps us to develop our own self-confidence and courage to act.

This chapter provides a job description for the "union educator" that we elaborate on throughout the book, as well as some thoughts on keeping our full humanity on the job (a theme we return to in the final chapter).

Wanted: A Union Educator

Responsibilities:

➡ design courses, meetings, and conferences, sometimes on the fly

➡ create inviting learning environments, occasionally in seedy motels

➡ facilitate learning by starting with the participants' knowledge and experience

➡ begin from a working-class analysis by asking, "who benefits?"

➡ expose themselves as learners as well as teachers

➡ encourage political, cultural, economic, and social analysis

➡ help participants to "name their differences and identify their common interests"

➡ develop workers' capacity to challenge inequitable power relations in their workplaces and communities

➡ build a sense of community in classrooms, meetings, and on picket lines

➡ shine an equity lens on all activities, integrating an analysis of class, race, and gender

➡ support solidarity links between workers locally and globally

➡ encourage collective action against the inequities in the workplace and the world

➡ use education to strengthen the organizational capacity of the union.

Necessary qualifications:

➡ good listener

➡ thinks with feet on ground, with eyes on blue sky

➡ preserves emotional and physical stamina

➡ flexible and capable of contortions as required

➡ will challenge, because one cares; cares, and so must challenge

➡ has a "life" outside of union education—can say no occasionally

➡ can see and avoid political pitfalls

➡ passionately committed to labour ideals

➡ willing to stretch both heart and mind

➡ can take control when participation gets too chaotic

➡ crazy enough to think that all of this is fun.

Suitable candidates would also be willing to take on any other duties required by union members, and local and national union leaders, which of course means just about anything.

The Popular Labour Educator

WHAT DOES IT TAKE?

Dᴀʏs ᴀʀᴇ sʜᴏʀᴛ, ᴅᴇᴍᴀɴᴅs ᴀʀᴇ ᴍᴀɴʏ, ᴀɴᴅ ᴡᴇ'ʀᴇ ᴊᴜsᴛ ʜᴜᴍᴀɴ. It's a tall order to work with our six guiding threads.

To frame the challenge, we draw on six elements in traditional Chinese thinking. Those of us raised in the West have been trained in the classical Greek perspective—that the world is made up of four elements: air, earth, fire, and water. Because we have done work with unions in the forest and metalworking sectors, we feel comfortable in broadening our view to include two elements in the Chinese tradition: wood and metal. These six elements offer one way of expressing what our work takes, and what we need to sustain ourselves.

Earth

This is the connection to the ground, to the possibilities and limits of being in a human body, in working conditions shaped by human beings, on a planet where one action influences everything else.

Earth reminds us, as educators:
- to remain humble, knowing the limits in ourselves;
- to stay connected to the individuals around us and to the realities of the union organizations that we are building; to check the limits of our situation rather than becoming perfectionists and wearing ourselves out;
- to resist going off on ideological or personal tangents to the point of alienating others and reducing our effectiveness;
- to gauge the weight of our opponents, the employing class, and, in "union judo" fashion, use that momentum against them;
- to take up our responsibility to care for the earth, to ensure that our generation does its share to pass the earth along with minimal damage to the next generation.

Water

This is the fluidity in us, our capacity to work with uncertainty and to adapt to challenges as they emerge, in our courses and the movement as a whole.

Water helps us, as educators:
- to work with the unexpected in our education programs;
- to stay with the members in all their diversity;
- to find the laughter and sense the absurd in the world around us and in our own efforts;
- to work not just in the light but also in the shadow of our emotions, not just in courage and honour but also in fear and doubt;
- to listen to other people's caring even when we don't share their opinion;
- to work with our own passion, even when we don't know the answer (as one participant said in a tense moment of a course, "I don't care what you know until I know that you care");
- to soothe the dryness of our daily toils and heal the wounds inflicted by injustice.

Wood

This is the fuel that keeps us warm inside, the root that sustains us in moments of frustration, powerlessness, and despair.

Wood helps us, as educators:
- to renew and nourish ourselves so we can offer our best to those around us (for many union educators, it isn't easy to take a rest, to read some fiction or humour, to follow a hobby, to relax with friends outside the movement, so that when we are "on stage" we are whole people);
- to remember there are seasons—"a time to build up, a time to break down; a time to laugh, a time to mourn";
- to encourage balance and wholeness in others, without which the members learn that becoming an educated union militant means to burn out slowly;
- to stay in for the long haul, with the patience of a tree sinking roots in uneven ground over years.

Fire

This is our rage against injustice, our passion for dignity and peace.

Fire helps us, as educators:
- to inspire others with the conviction that what they do matters;
- to act to defend ourselves and others against bullying and unfairness both outside and inside our movement;
- to keep passion in our work rather than marching through course manuals;
- to support daring action for justice, even when we're not sure it will work;
- to channel our anger while refusing to hate (as Audre Lorde says, anger is full of energy and information, while hate carries neither);
- to generate light from the heat of critical debate.

Metal

This is courage. It is a recognition that we need to define our principles, as people and as unionists, and be ready to pay a price for them.

Metal helps us, as educators:
- to know where we stand so we don't fall for just anything;
- to be hard when necessary;
- to support a frightened member who has finally found the courage to do something;
- to deal with the hurts, disappointments, betrayals, the personal wounds from internal union struggles.

Calligraphy by Gail Nye

Air

This is imagination and spirit. It is the vision and creativity that give vitality to the labour movement.

Air helps us, as educators:

- to recall those who went before us in the struggle for economic and social justice and imagine ways of interpreting their spirit in the present conditions (as Stanley Grizzle of the Brotherhood of Sleeping Car Porters likes to say, "We walk on bridges that others have built");
- to call on and honour the spiritual dimension of our work;
- to think big in the face of cynicism (for example, Quebec's largest central labour body, the Fédération des travailleurs et travailleuses du Québec, dared to train member worker educators on a large scale, secured a training tax on employers, and built a massive investment fund under union control);
- to imagine mobilizing despite establishment and media efforts to paralyze us (one such occasion was the 1998 Ontario Days of Action, with labour and community demonstrating together and shutting down Ontario cities; the tens of thousands of marchers glimpsed what is possible when standing in solidarity).

All six of these elements help us in the best moments of union education.

Are you ready to apply for the job?

Asia-Pacific Regional Womens' Workshop, Seoul, Korea, 2001.

Working Inside: Navigating the Union Culture

CONTENTS

A SENSE OF OWNERSHIP AND LOYALTY....18

NOSE TO NOSE WITH POWER....20

UNCERTAIN AUTHORITY....22

HEAVINESS OF SPIRIT AND A REBEL STREAK....24

ON THE FLY, JUST IN TIME....25

The strength and the vulnerability of unions have the same source: the trust that members place in their representatives.

Jean-Gérin Lajoie

A UNION EDUCATOR HAS AN OUTSIDE AND AN INSIDE JOB. The outside job requires staying attuned to the larger world, connecting union education and activity to movement-building (see CHAPTER 3). The inside job means working creatively with the organizational structures to build the union.

To do the insider job effectively the educator needs to recognize a number of important dynamics of union culture. While each union is different, certain dynamics occur in some form in all unions, and they all provide challenges for the educator as well as possible openings.

A SENSE OF OWNERSHIP AND LOYALTY

SEASONED LABOUR ACTIVISTS have learned not to expect much from management. They remain open to pleasant surprises—for instance, when a competent and fair employer creates the space for workers to grow and contribute within the workplace. But normally they make do with large management egos and small abilities, large claims and small accomplishments.

However, activists have huge expectations of union leadership, and the range of forgiveness for error is small. That's because people put their hearts into their unions, and there is a smaller margin of tolerance for human frailty.

In part this is because the drama of union life is played out on a stage of voluntary involvement and commitment. It is a high compliment to be described as one who can be counted on to show up steadily, without pay or glory, where there is work to be done. People who feel patronized in their children's school, or disrespected and silenced by the boss, come into their own in their local union, with a sense of entitlement, belonging, and voice. This feature creates an enormous loyalty and identification with the union.

Challenges and openings

Ownership and loyalty help members identify with key demands in bargaining, contract enforcement, and mobilizing on the shop floor. These elements are also an absolute prerequisite for cultivating a collaborative approach to learning, an approach that lies at the heart of our vision of a democratic and equitable union. For example, the education program in one union directly reached over five thousand members in Canada each year during the early 1980s, yet the bulk of the teaching was done by over one hundred committed volunteers trained and coached by the education staff. The volunteers worked on weekends, without pay, to build their union.

This sense of ownership has its vulnerable spots; it can also turn into an overwhelming need for control. While generous in giving, unionists can also be grudging in letting go, in venturing into the unfamiliar and leaving the cocoon of the tried and tested. For example, if teachers or facilitators try to rearrange the sitting arrangement in the middle of a session, participants may tend to hold on to their seats like sovereign territory. Participating in creative educational activities can feel, to some, like abandoning solid ground.

Sometimes this strong sense of ownership and loyalty takes a defensive position against possible threats from other unions, as well as from the boss. More unpleasantly, it can express itself in competition and blunt bashing of other unions. To deal with the odds against them, workers have always had to fight and create at the same time. The challenge for the educator is to work with this sense of ownership and loyalty for the betterment of the union and the movement.

AN EXAMPLE

A course was aimed at preparing union members for a representation vote against another union. The vote had been made necessary by the merger of two employers in the public sector. The members in the room began by putting down the other union, although clearly neither union had created the conflict. As it turned out, much of the negative information about the other union had come from managers. The challenge for the two facilitators was to redirect the anger away from the other union and towards the government and the employers that had reorganized in a way that forced two groups of workers into a single bargaining unit.

At first the discussion centred on how and where the union was weak vis-à-vis management. The members repeatedly brought up the split of full-time and part-time workers, though neither of the facilitators picked up on this issue. As other topics kept adding fuel to the competitive fire, participants began to recognize that this same split had occurred, as a deliberate management strategy. Without much optimism, the facilitators went with the theme, as the least damaging at hand.

At one point, as a way of exploring the four interests identified, the participants were asked to move chairs around to form groups: "management" was in one group, "full-time workers" in another, "part-time workers" in a third, and "union stewards" in the fourth. In response to questions from the steward group, people in the first three groups stated what they liked most and least about the current situation. It turned out that "management" was quite happy with the dynamic, because it gave them maximum flexibility. The "full-time" and "part-time" groups were unhappy, but both agreed that the situation could be eased if the union and company together defined a level of hours after which part-time workers would have the option to become full-time. With that suggestion, people in the steward group became quite excited, and the energy in the room shifted.

Discussion of this common wish among the workers showed that it would also be in the best interests of providing a high-quality public service. This issue could become a public campaign, supported by clients and their families. Then discussion focused on how to get such a campaign underway. Participants noted that a mobilized and campaigning union, clearly responding to a key concern of members, would also be more likely to win a representation vote. Now, instead of bashing the other union, the members became engaged in a constructive debate over the tactics of facing management. The day, which had begun with lethargy and blaming, turned out to be full of positive energy and momentum.

Experiences like this keep us in the trade. We get to turn the negative energy around, to bring a group of workers to a deeper level of unity, to combine fighting with creative thinking, and to draw on the positive strengths of that sense of ownership and loyalty.

NOSE TO NOSE WITH POWER

EXPERIENCING EMPLOYER POWER and analysing how it works are two different things. Unions were formed as a response to the hugely unequal power of workers and bosses. But of course unions have never equalized power in the workplace; a quick glance at a management rights clause makes this clear. While the struggle continues, unions focus on limiting the arbitrary exercise of that power.

A key here is a grasp of how class power works in Canadian society. Many Canadians talk of "class," if they talk about it at all, as though it just means a vague difference in income rather than a sharply different location in the power structure. But most workers have a very direct experience of class: the power of the company (or government ministry or department), the ownership, the management, is in their faces and on their backs every day. Even apathetic union members want the union to do something about "the way the employer treats workers." Occasionally an employer does something disrespectful enough that even the workers who have never been active want to do something. Workers may not want to hear union "rhetoric" about collectivity and evil bosses, but they want protection. This need, or recognition, produces a rich educative challenge: how to turn the raw experience of "classism" into an analysis of class oppression.

Indeed, research indicates that members identify as their number one priority for union action, the "protection of employees against the abuses of employers." When Gregor Murray and Christian Lévesque, two professors of industrial relations, researched the attitudes of Quebec unionized and non-union workers, they found that both groups alike identified the "protection of employees against employer abuse" as the highest need. That item had twice as high a priority as improving salaries and benefits. Those research results stand in sharp contrast to much conventional wisdom. For instance, when participants in a leadership class were informally polled to identify their members' top priority, two-thirds of them said their members wanted better salaries and benefits.

Challenges and openings

The expressed desire for protection from employer abuse provides an opening for educators, even when the members are disenchanted and hostile. Education can help workers build strategies to curb the arbitrary exercise of employer power, beginning with an analysis of how that power works.

AN EXAMPLE

The union's goal was to get the employer back to the table, to renegotiate an expired contract. The task required mobilizing the members, including getting them ready for a possible illegal strike, to a degree never done before. It also involved co-ordinating actions with another union, which represented a comparable number of workers in the sector. This group had not previously shown a high degree of militancy, but the levels of disrespect and overload in the workplace had mounted to such a degree that now workers who had always leaned towards accommodation with employer demands were outraged. A new level of "class anger" was directed against the employer.

Deb Barndt

An educator was asked to participate in the first campaign meeting to help develop strategy. The union officers decided to:

- use the campaign as part of a larger union-building strategy;
- develop modules on civil disobedience, strike issues, strike administration, and public relations; these modules could then be used or not, depending on needs in each area;
- conduct a survey of members that each local executive could use as a basis of planning;
- train worker educators—by that point, a total of five pairs working with local officers—who would in turn train stewards;
- have the worker educators deliver one-day training sessions to all stewards to coach them through the issues they would need to discuss with or present to members;
- provide half-day training classes for all members, to be facilitated by the stewards.

In the three months of this campaign, the union educators reached more union activists, and broadened the receptivity of more members, than they had previously done in all the regularly scheduled courses in their formal educational calendar.

York University Faculty Association strike, Toronto, 1997.

UNCERTAIN AUTHORITY

MANY UNIONISTS THEMSELVES have ambivalent relations to power. They are more likely to have experience in the arts of resistance than of command. But in the face of the larger power of the employer, they have become seasoned in reading between the lines of formal documents. They are sensitive to pretentiousness of any kind and skilled in undermining organizational initiatives without opposing them formally.

Most activists apply to union operations that same keen smell for the exercise of employer power. Their resistance reflex questions the authority of elected officers who sound too much like the boss; casts a critical eye on the too-formal chairing of a meeting or conference; tunes out the distracted educator. Questioning authority is part of union culture. Like any other aspect of union culture, it is a tricky function, and it offers rich possibilities to educators.

Challenges and openings

At every turn, educators face limits to their authority. When activists feel ownership of their union, they may consider themselves to be the employer of the educators. When elected officers have a message to transmit to members, they may well insist that the educators carry it, out of loyalty to the union, its leadership, or themselves personally.

The complexity of the educators' authority and role shows up, for instance, in courses for local union treasurers. These are workers formal legal responsibility. They usually volunteer for that job because they are comfortable with detail, systems, and precision. They sign all the cheques, which means they worry about making mistakes. They also can feel undervalued, because they monitor the revenue and expenditure in a culture that values the orator, the vision of justice, the informal bond among workers. The flow of generalizations drives these union activists nuts.

Educating treasurers, then, provides a delicate challenge. Educators can't talk to treasurers about social justice until the educators are at peace with double-entry bookkeeping, and until the treasurers know that they have the educators' respect. It is not the educators' organizational position that gives them authority, but their capacity to listen, to work respectfully in the treasurers' (and others') terrain, and to help unionists do their jobs effectively for the larger good of the organization.

As educators, we all have found a form of personal and cultural authority that allows us to lead educational events in a movement owned by all participants, all members. Our authority must be different from the formal, marks-based authority of the school system, because so many activists carry scars from their school experiences. In this context of uncertain authority, we need to find our unique space of influence; to be able to "teach" without being an expert; to be an educator and not possess a monopoly of knowledge; to be transparent in our uncertainty, and not lose the group's confidence.

This is where equity, one of our guiding threads, resurfaces. The tools of authority are not evenly distributed amongst us. Our unions, like any other social institutions, internalize the systemic biases of dominant groups, amplifying the voices of some people (particularly white, able-bodied men) over those of other people (such as young people, new unionists, women of colour, Aboriginal people, and disabled people). These biases mean that some of us are "naturally" listened to, accorded authority, simply because we "fit." Others among us have to push our words forward in order to be heard at all. This is not something to be surprised or guilty about; it is a challenge to action.

Educators seeking to widen the range of practices available to the union risk undermining their already uncertain authority. Still, despite this risk, we need to ask ourselves a number of questions—questions to which some of our readers may well have the answers.

Barb Thomas

SOME QUESTIONS

- When we assess the impact of an action or decision, what would it mean to do strategic planning from the Aboriginal perspective of "thinking seven generations ahead"? How would our conversation work if we adopted the way of the "talking stick"? How would our health and safety programs evolve if they were inspired by the holistic approach to body, mind, and spirit as practised by First Nations people? How, indeed, would our unions look and how would they work, if we began to give rightful place to the original dwellers of Turtle Island?

- When one educator is from a more-dominant social identity than the other—for example, when one is a person with a disability, and one is able-bodied—how does the dynamic of uncertain authority and inequity influence co-facilitation? It takes time and patience on both sides for a pair of educators to work through the differences in their social power, and to plan sessions so that both can make their optimum contributions to the benefit of the course participants. It also takes political will—a conscious choice by the union leadership—to ensure that non-dominant voices get to teach at all.

Regina Labour Educators' Exchange, October 2002.

HEAVINESS OF SPIRIT AND A REBEL STREAK

UNIONISM IS NOT FOR THE FAINT OF HEART. Many people's work lives are monotonous and humiliating, and they bring a certain misery into the union. Many people's experiences of management have been toxic, and they bring that poison into the union. Cumulatively, unions can pick up a climate of "heaviness," of anger turned inwards. This feeling co-exists with the defiance and rebellion that built the union in the first place.

The heaviness can show up in courses, especially when educators read out answers to questions that nobody has asked. It can show up in tiny union gatherings, in the control of who speaks and under what protocol, when most people would prefer an open discussion. It can show up in the educators' lack of humour when the trouble-makers we are developing make trouble for us too. And it can repel the rebel in people, keep them out of union activism, which, to be truly effective, ought to be subversive and daring, playful and inventive, light and expansive.

Challenges and openings

An important part of the educators' role is to call on the rebel in workers, to work against the deadly seriousness of what we're up against, and do it playfully. A serious but light rebellious tone appears in bumper stickers that say "The labour movement: the people who brought you the weekend." The joy of music in union courses is not only about reviving the classics of past campaigns but also about inventing new and satirical songs—as composed, perhaps, by participants in week-long courses. The very art of songwriting can be a powerful energizer in courses, lifting spirits and putting people back in touch with their own creative, rebellious power.

In our courses, the time for socialization and getting together is as much a learning experience as the classroom discussion; the storytelling is as important, if not more so, than the rigorous analysis. In our exercises the seemingly childish drawings and sketches depicting workers' struggle are as powerful expressions of resistance and counter-resistance as any case study. The use of the humble "stickies" (those self-stick notes) or index cards, a seemingly pedestrian but handy tool to display each participant's ideas on walls or flip charts, can be a fun and colourful display of democracy in action. They are a tool that allows the less articulate, the timid, and the slow-on-the-draw to join the conversation on an equal footing with the verbally fluent and seasoned "public speaker," facilitating the formation of group consensus.

Why do most workers read the cartoons on the union bulletin boards, and not the earnest, yellowed papers on health and safety? Why do many working people prefer Harlequin romances or science fiction novels or tabloid newspapers to their union's publications? Perhaps it has something to do with lightness, with tapping into the font of creative and impish disrespect inherent in all of us.

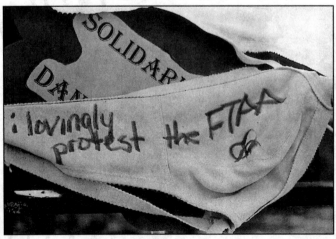

Graffiti bra on the security fence at the Economic Summit, Quebec City, 2001.

Deb Barndt

AN EXAMPLE

In a Thunder Bay hospital in late 1999, the game of "Bargaining bingo" (based on an Internet game) was used as a mobilizing tool. During a time of heated negotiations, the hospital management was aggressively publicizing its budget limitations, and the constraints imposed by government regulations and cutbacks. The participants in a local union executive workshop developed a list of management slogans designed to limit union demands. The local union issued bingo cards, placing management cost-saving clichés in the squares: "We have to do more with less" and "If each of us saves a little, we can all save a lot," for instance. The union offered prizes for people who overheard a manager use several of the indicated phrases. The members had the option of having witnesses initial that they had heard the phrase, or if they had the nerve they could ask the managers to initial the phrase themselves.

The effect of this "light" tactic was to silence management. Their pat phrases were ridiculed, their campaign was undermined, and the morale of union activists was greatly raised. While management continued to push at the table, they had lost control over the climate of the workplace and never regained it in the months it took to reach an agreement. (See CHAPTER 6 for another way of using "Bingo.")

Taking people's pain seriously doesn't mean being captured by it.

ON THE FLY, JUST IN TIME

UNIONS ARE ALWAYS REACTING to some new direction or strategy initiated by the employer, and inevitably they have only been given partial information about it. Chronically under-resourced, limited in how much detailed, long-term planning they can do, constantly on the defensive to do something in too short a time, unions have developed a creative capacity for action on the fly, just in time.

Challenges and openings

The ability to pull things together quickly at the last minute can turn into a liability if it becomes the only or the main way of functioning.

AN EXAMPLE

You are asked to give a weekend leadership course in three days' time for a local in another city that you've had little contact with. In addition to thoughts about reorganizing your current workload, you have a number of things running through your head as you put down the phone after receiving the request.
- Who is asking for this course and why? How will this course make a difference for them?
- Who is expected to attend this course: people from composite, newly merged, just organized, or long-established locals? And who's the local leadership? Are they mostly men, mostly white people? What's the percentage of new versus long-time officers?

- What are the workplace issues, and how will they shape participants' expectations? Are members stressed out by unreasonable workloads? Are they winning most of their grievances? Are they expecting another round of cutbacks or fending off the dire consequences of some harsh piece of anti-union legislation?
- What is the membership like—tightly knit and well connected to the leadership, or distant and unconnected? Is there a solid core of activists, or is the core of activists being hollowed out?

You are also trying to sort out what might be the relevant objectives of and scope for the weekend course. On top of this, you are expected to work with another staff person and/or member from the region—someone with whom you have big political difficulties.

Luckily for you, there is somebody else assigned to notify employers so that participants can get leave from their regular jobs, to deal with hotel accommodations for out-of-town participants, and to look after the travel arrangements, the meals, and other logistics. But that person also wants to know what information to send out, if you need an overhead projector, and what kind of seating arrangements you prefer. You make a mental note: "Please don't get me a training room with no windows; and yes, we need lots of wall space for our flip charts."

What's the big deal? Haven't you done a similar course before? Write a couple of objectives, throw in a small-group discussion here and a role play there, photocopy a few handouts, pull out your handy little bag of markers, masking tape, and sticky notes, and voila! Off you go to another successful educational event. What's your problem?

Indeed, being able to do things fast with no preparation can become a badge of honour in a culture in which rapid response means survival. It highlights the precarious status of education, which is often the first thing to be cut when budgets get really tight.

Dorothy Wigmore

Ruth Needleman,
Montreal Labour Educators' Exchange, April 2002.

A "just in time" course design is an oxymoron in the context of transformative education. Having said that, we still deal with "just in time" demands every day. What are some practical ways in which educators can work creatively with this aspect of union culture at the same time as we advocate for a more strategic way of providing education?

- Keep records of your designs and materials, so you don't have to reinvent everything every time.
- Develop a tool kit with supplies and materials you always use, that's ready to hit the road any time.
- If you can reach them, talk to the president and/or other officers of the local to make sure you understand their priorities. Agree on the focus or objectives with them. If they will be present, get them to introduce the session, its purpose, and why they've asked you in.
- Develop contacts, people you can call to brief you on pertinent issues—to answer all the questions that ran through your mind after you accepted the job.
- Keep your eye on creating a respectful climate for the participants and not on some abstract perfection of design. (Remember the element of "earth.")
- Work with the spiral (see CHAPTER 4), and keep it simple.
- Develop as much of a rapport with your co-facilitator(s) as you can ahead of time. If you can, plan things over the phone or by e-mail. If you can't contact the person, leave messages about any plans that you are making or considering.
- Keep looking for ways to link every course to the broader priorities of the locals (or sector) involved and to the long-term goals of the union. That way, one course builds on the next and you maintain continuity.

(See also CHAPTER 9, "Evaluation for Impact," CHAPTER 10, "Worker Educator Programs," and CHAPTER 11, "Strategic Planning.")

In choosing how to respond to the immediate union context, then, educators need to apply a combination of art and heart. The union culture requires educators to pick up the cues empathetically, and then to act with more courage than they sometimes feel. For educators to understand what is going on in a union, they can't just read formal policy statements, hear speeches from the leadership, and deduce the appropriate path for educational work. Rather, they need to watch and listen carefully—to catch the signals of member alienation, ownership, and loyalty; to discern the current struggles with employer power; to tap into the openings of a rebel streak; to hear the multiple voices that surround them—and then they can find ways of responding, and taking action.

Union Education in a Globalizing Economy

CONTENTS

WHY THE GLOBAL PICTURE MATTERS....29

THE CHALLENGE FOR THE UNION EDUCATOR....31

PUTTING A GLOBAL LENS ON UNION EDUCATION....32

THE FUNNEL: A TOOL TO CONNECT WORKERS' LIVES TO
    GLOBAL FORCES....35

CANADIAN UNIONS HAVE LONG RECOGNIZED THEIR INTERNATIONAL LINKS with brothers and sisters in other countries and the inherent interconnectedness of workers' lives across the globe. Several unions have humanity funds that link struggles of Canadian workers to their global union family and are used to develop courses to bring the world into the Canadian union classroom. International visitors at conventions, newly emerging globalization courses, and mobilizations aimed at boycotting sweatshop corporations help members live out the principles of international solidarity.

Unions are linking more and more internationally as they awaken to the reality of how work has been reorganized and fragmented, and how workers in one country have been pitted against those in another. Most importantly, this global phenomenon challenges us to understand more acutely how "underdevelopment" in the South is a necessary condition for the "development" of the North, and what this means in terms of unionism today.

Analysing and monitoring this process are important tasks for union educators. As transnational corporations spread their economic and political tentacles across the globe, educators have an additional task: to integrate these wider concerns into the everyday life of union education.

In this chapter we present the case for thinking globally; we offer some guidelines for applying a global lens to all aspects of union education; and we outline a tool we have found useful in connecting workplace issues to the global economy.

WHY THE GLOBAL PICTURE MATTERS

WRITER JACQUES ROBIN has succinctly described a necessary communications project for our times:

> An anguish has begun to take root in a large number of citizens, as a result of living in our society of fear, of competition, of hierarchy and of egoism. It's a matter of extreme urgency for humankind to construct a culture oriented towards sharing, service, and community. This project presupposes an enormous educational effort in time to avoid being overwhelmed by an acceleration of war, of hate, and of the narrowed identities which are already flooding our societies.[1]

Canadian union education is well placed to make a contribution to this global effort. Each year over 120,000 members participate in Canada and Quebec in some form of union education.[2] We believe that our education must be attuned to this global picture for a number of reasons.

Solid information has been even harder to get since September 11, 2001

To ease any doubts we may have about the war in Afghanistan and the continuing wars in other states that "harbour terrorists," the Pentagon has been busy diffusing information to "influence public opinion and political leaders as much in friendly countries as in enemy states."[3]

In the responses to the attacks on September 11, 2001, governments of the larger world powers have rescued global capitalism on a huge scale. In addition to the Pentagon's project, a veritable industry of persuasion has stepped up efforts not only to convince the world that neo-liberal globalization will contribute to the greater good but also to oppose other economic and social models. Examples are the active collaboration of universities, research institutes like the Heritage Foundation and Fraser Institute, and large media like CNN, the *Financial Times*, and the *National Post*. The daily press offers virtually no accounts of resistance or of alternatives that people are creating in Canada and all around the planet. Challenging this continuous disinformation is a crucial role for union education.

September 11 memorial, Manila, Philippines, 2002.

BAYAN

---

1. Robin, "Les contours d'un autre monde," p.26.
2. Spencer, "Workers' Education for the 21st Century."
3. Cited by Ignacio Ramonet, "L'axe du Mal," *Le Monde Diplomatique*, March 2002.

Neo-liberalism undermines the workplace and workers' rights

A major election, the signing of a new free-trade agreement, a sharp increase in use of the security apparatus, racial profiling, a government decision to go to war: these events and trends have a direct impact on our members' well-being.

In the last decade, corporate globalization has widened the gap between rich and poor in our communities, our country, and across the globe. (It could take some one hundred and fifty years for a Bolivian worker to earn what a CEO of a major corporation earns in a day.) Workers now face an increasing concentration of economic power in the hands of transnational corporations, a declining influence of governments on the economy, cuts to public services because of slashed public spending, privatization and deregulation, increased underemployment and unemployment, and an erosion of their rights as workers and citizens as they have become reduced to passive "consumers" or "taxpayers." If people aren't to be overwhelmed or paralyzed by the momentum of this corporate offensive, they need space to discuss and skilled leadership.

The global community in Canada is being further divided

One dramatic and direct impact of a restructured global economy is in who shows up in Canadian workplaces. The demographics of unionized workers in Southern Ontario or the Lower Mainland of British Columbia have changed drastically. Migrations of people, pulled and pushed by global inequities, have changed the proportion of British-descended people in Toronto from two-thirds to less than one-third in a generation. By 1996 people of colour made up 6 per cent of the population of Quebec and 12 per cent of the population of greater Montreal.

Yet the new search for enemies has intensified ethnic and racial scapegoating. In certain circles and media, new immigrants and refugees become portrayed as threats to our security, our health, our jobs—to our very way of life. Our members need information and tools to resist labelling their neighbours as potential terrorists, and to build unions that include us all.

Corporate values influence our members

Dorothy Wigmore

The values of justice, equality, and social responsibility find little echo in an increasingly right-wing media, so that union activists are made to feel "out of it" much of the time. This means that our thinking as workers and citizens is often infiltrated with views that directly contradict our deeper values—resentment of "welfare bums," "aggressive feminists," "lying refugees," and "lazy government bureaucrats."

At a cultural level, the corporate media have widely transmitted a persuasive message that the "market" is more reliable than "rigid government" for generating and distributing wealth. Oddly enough, "shopping" has become a substitute for political engagement: the authorities urge people to get out and shop as a way of reviving the economy and displaying their patriotism. At a workplace level, managers try to convince workers that management rule is natural and inevitable, and that resistance is unrealistic. All of these features have a direct impact on union capacity to mobilize members.

Judith Marshall, Montreal Labour Educators' Exchange, April 2002.

THE CHALLENGE FOR THE UNION EDUCATOR

EDUCATION IS ONLY ONE STRATEGY of the union movement to challenge the neo-liberal offensive, but as educators we know it's a critical one. Union education can help:

- counter the increasing individualism and isolation amongst our members;
- build solidarity and inclusion towards a stronger and less divided social movement;
- demonstrate that what people do can make a difference, and that apathy is the best friend of neo-liberalism;
- support workers to understand how global power functions;
- provide a taste of real democracy in a world where that word is increasingly confused;
- strengthen the imagination and capacity of union activists to initiate effective alternatives to savage capitalism in their own communities and workplaces. For example, in Argentina they are organizing the unemployed and in California the undocumented workers.

Union education "for another world" is not just about alternative information, then. It must build community, develop democratic practice, strengthen class consciousness, advance equity, reinforce union capacity, and link union struggles to the common good—globally.

If we start lecturing people about the importance of the global picture, the odds are pretty good we'll be met by the glazed eyes of most participants. Many activists already have plenty of ideas about the bigger picture. Some of them are involved in community struggles; they have family in other countries, relatives in the military or in political parties; they have friends trying to survive on family farms or in high-tech jobs in California. When we move beyond issues related to the immediate workplace and internal union dynamics, our task is to bring out already existing knowledge, surface opinions and test those opinions against solid information. This can create a climate of discussion that allows people to move past prejudices and divisions to reflection and action.

Our job is to offer a "framework" for analysing global forces that takes in personal experiences at the workplace. Our education work can help to hone workers' collective ability to link workplace struggles with the global movement for social justice.

PUTTING A GLOBAL LENS ON UNION EDUCATION: SOME IDEAS

Draw on the expertise of the members

Increasingly we have participants in our courses who have come to Canada from other countries. Often they have had rich experiences in organizing, and those experiences can provide inspiration and ideas in Canada. They have fought oppression in the form of military regimes and exploitative transnational corporations (and many of the corporations have their headquarters in Canada and the United States).

Connect personal priorities to global issues

Sometimes people are concerned about violence among their children's generation, favouritism in awarding government contracts in their community, or the loss of good public parks. For educators it is a waste of time to insist on the union's definition of an issue—or of what the issues are—as the only legitimate starting point for a conversation. Rather, if we have confidence in the value and purpose of the union's perspective, we can engage first with the issues as the course participants define them. We can trust, for instance, that a discussion about community violence will lead to a conversation about government cutbacks, that talk about government practices will lead to the issue of privatization, that concerns about public parks will lead to the subject of deregulation. In all of our discussions we should be able to move towards a common "basket" of issues—a basket that will hold the concerns of everyone present.

Reflect the globe back on workers' lives

In the global economy workers are both producers and consumers. Their employers are often transnational corporations—and today most of the goods we buy, or the services we purchase, come from transnational corporations. In its educational work, Maquila Solidarity Network (MSN), which connects workers' struggles internationally, has participants examine the labels on their clothes as a way of beginning a discussion of the wages and working conditions facing sweatshop workers.[4] An introductory activity for a course on economics might ask participants to make a list of all the transnational corporations they have dealt with in the past twenty-four hours, or of all the "foreign" workers who contributed to what they ate for breakfast.

Use the international resources in your union

Your union or central labour body probably hosts visitors from time to time for courses, conventions, or policy conferences. For example, the Canadian Labour Congress has invited labour activists from Colombia to its winter school to speak about the heroic struggle of unions and communities against state repression and U.S. complicity in the so-called "war on drugs." Union members sometimes participate in tours and exchanges with workers in other countries.

Some unions have initiated sectoral exchanges with counterpart unions in other countries. The CLC, Fédération des travailleurs et travailleuses du Québec, provincial labour bodies, and many unions have produced materials for use in union courses. The Maquila Solidarity Network produces excellent educational materials; as does Common Frontiers, which mobilizes energies in cross-border coalitions against the excesses of

---

4. See the RESOURCES AND SOURCES for an excellent resource kit from the MSN, with lots of ideas for educators.

free-trade agreements; and many other organizations do similar work. (See the BIBLIOGRAPHY for other examples.) Educators can find ways of using these kinds of resources in courses or meetings.

Link local analysis to the impact on workers in other countries

A powerful means of exploring the impact of changes in jobs and social programs on women can be to look at how some of the same issues are facing women in Latin America and Asia. Our friend and colleague Deborah Barndt has developed a photo-story linking the lives of a Mexican woman who plants tomatoes, a migrant worker who harvests tomatoes in Ontario, and a union member who works at a checkout counter at Loblaws selling this produce.[5]

As an educator, you might focus on how the latest strategy of a transnational employer is affecting members of your union as well as workers in other countries. You might look at the impact on Canada and other countries of a U.S. company such as United Parcel Services (UPS). In recent years UPS has been fighting the Canadian postal service, citing "Priority Post" as "unfair competition."

Or you might choose to use at least one case study in a course on toxic chemicals to show the impact of chemicals on workers in a similar sector in another country. For instance, you might examine how the operations of Placer Dome, a Canadian mining firm operating in the Philippines, killed the Boac River and destroyed the livelihoods of 31,000 farming and fishing families, and consider the options available to the local union in that situation.

At the People's Summit in Quebec City in April 2001, a union convened a conference of workers from several countries. The participants worked at Cominco, Noranda, and other mining companies in Canada and Quebec, Peru, Brazil, Chile, and Mexico. They spoke to each other in four languages of the stories, past and present, of their struggles in workplaces, so far from each other and so similar in their oppressive working conditions—exchanging strategies and raising hope that workers across borders could bring about a different kind of globalization.

Find resource materials from different perspectives and backgrounds

One simple, but effective, practice is to ensure the participant materials reflect different perspectives. For example, when a group considers the aftermath of September 11, the discussion should examine a range of viewpoints, including some from the Arab world. In a course on organizing, you might use a story about the Coca Cola workers in Guatemala—people who have long survived as a union, in part thanks to their leadership and alliance-building strategies in the face of sustained repression.

Several solidarity organizations send frequent updates of these struggles through the Internet. Making the various perspectives clear (identifying, for instance, who wrote an article and in what context) also tells people that a certain perspective is only one among many.

------

5. Barndt, *Tangled Routes.*

Bring a wider lens to familiar issues

Most issues in union life have been with us for a long time: pay equity, discrimination at work, full employment, and workplace injuries or hazards, among others. These remain critical issues for many of our members, and we continue to need to find new strategies for dealing with them.

For example, to bring a fresh perspective to organizing we might look at how the Argentinian unions work with the unemployed, or how in Texas they attempt to organize undocumented workers, and how educators in the community and university in Southern California helped in the organizing of 75,000 home-care workers.

Often we look only for information under our own noses when we could, for instance, be searching out international resources that would add new insights to our knowledge and campaigns. For example, in 1964 Canada signed an international convention on full employment, an agreement that is little known and little used here in Canada, as far as we know—and something that the Canadian government has clearly forgotten. As another example, the International Labour Organization (ILO) is doing education to promote the concept of "decent work," which includes not just working conditions, but reconciling work and family, providing children with decent education and ensuring hope for the future.

Think global when we analyse the forces for and against us

The people's summits in Porto Alegre, Brazil, in 2001 and 2002 and in Quebec City in April 2001 were events that brought together participants with different global visions, people who came from all over the world. They came from unions, community organizations, solidarity groups, faith groups, universities, Aboriginal organizations, environmental groups, and seniors and youth organizations. But sustaining these links beyond single events continues to be a challenge.

In our union struggles we often have more allies than we think, but our relations are strained or undeveloped with these "outsiders." Union educators have an important role to play in assisting a careful analysis of possible links. The clearer we are on our common ground, as well as on what divides us, the more creative we can be in creating bonds that last with the majority of people who want justice.

Publicize the work of allies

We can bring the work of allies directly into our union education. That work provides inspiration; it builds hope. For example, workers in Libya held a work slowdown in support of a strike of Petro-Canada brothers and sisters in Canada. A couple of unions in Canada allocate part of their Paid Education Leave Fund to supporting their members' participation in community events. The Ontario Coalition Against Poverty, in solidarity with unions, advocated for the rights of refugees threatened with deportation from Canada; they also organized a rally in support of the Korean Confederation of Trade Unions, fighting for the rights of undocumented workers in Korea. We need to learn about many more of the inspiring actions and creative strategies of unions and their allies.

Dalit rights activists, UN World Conference against Racism, Durban South Africa, 2001.

Ahmad Saidullah

THE FUNNEL:
A TOOL TO
CONNECT
WORKERS' LIVES
TO GLOBAL
FORCES

THERE IS NO SHORTAGE OF "POLITICAL ACTION" course manuals in the Canadian labour movement. We would like to build on the work of colleagues and friends (see BIBLIOGRAPHY) by offering a tool we've found helpful, informally known as "the funnel." It aims to anchor the discussion of globalization in the workplace.

The funnel is suited best to a two-day workshop, with the early sessions working to establish a sense of the union's history and accomplishments in the particular work area. That kind of initial grounding will mean that the discussion of broader issues is better linked to concrete experience and more likely to lead to concrete action.

To bring veterans and new members into a common picture, first we do a little reconstruction of the local's history. To begin, we use the "historical timeline" (see CHAPTER 6); and to develop a profile of our membership, we use "membership mapping" (also described in CHAPTER 6). We divide the information into the content and the objectives of what we're trying to do in the opening activities.

CONTENT	OBJECTIVES
Our union: the history of our local, affiliate, labour movement	• reconstruct the key moments of our history • link issues and events among our various locals • name the key issues and major trends we face • analyse our major recent gains and losses • connect past and present struggles/campaigns
Our members: their interests, values, and identities	• map out our membership profile: who are we? • name the basis of our unity and recognize our diversity • explore how management exploits our differences • assess the impact of our similarities and differences on our strategy in all phases of the bargaining cycle

After establishing a grounding in the union's history and profile, we move to the funnel, which helps us connect, to a larger employer's agenda, the specific techniques that management uses against us in the workplace. It then relates this agenda to global trends and forces.

THE FUNNEL

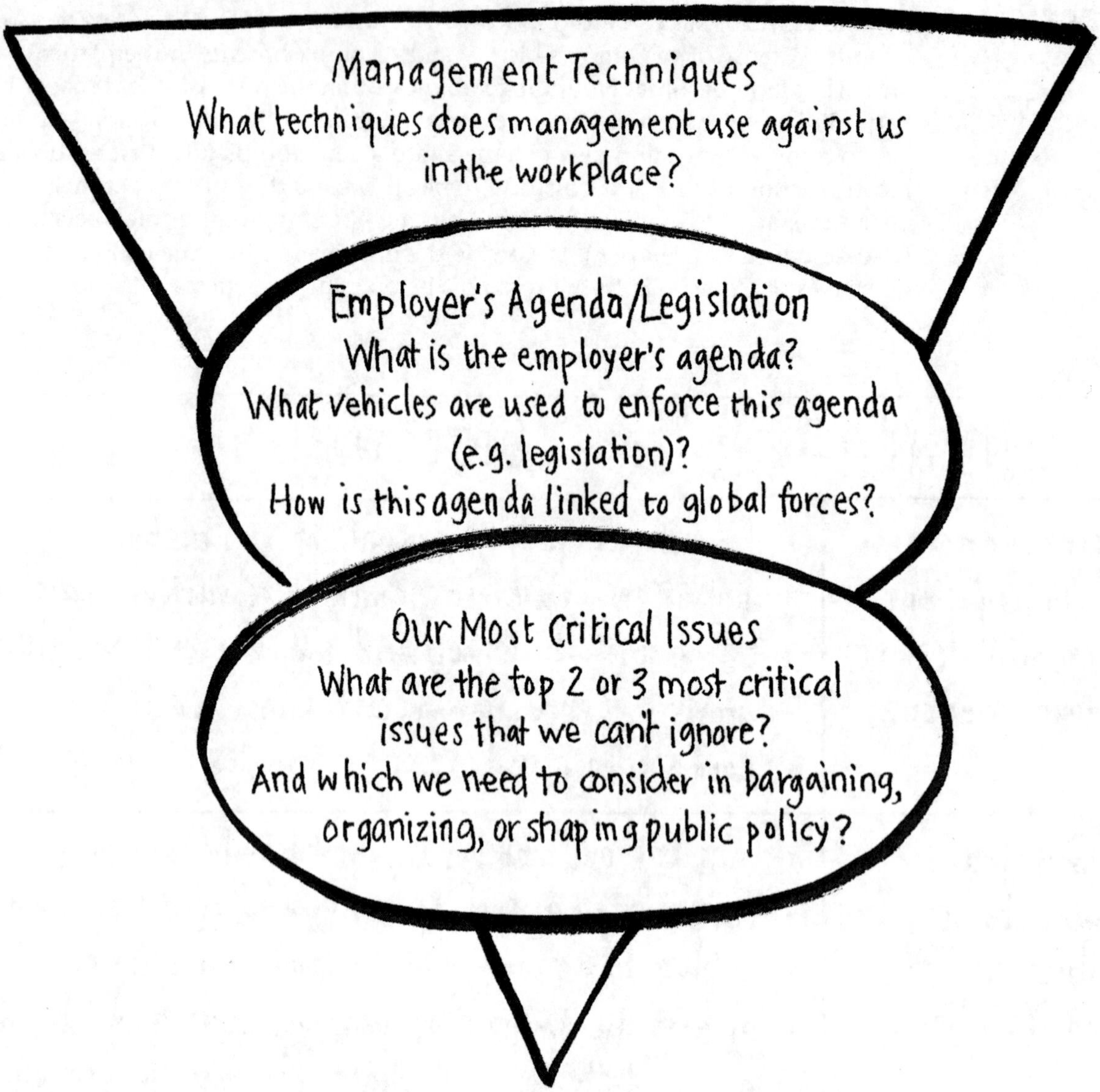

Management Techniques
What techniques does management use against us in the workplace?

Employer's Agenda/Legislation
What is the employer's agenda?
What vehicles are used to enforce this agenda (e.g. legislation)?
How is this agenda linked to global forces?

Our Most Critical Issues
What are the top 2 or 3 most critical issues that we can't ignore?
And which we need to consider in bargaining, organizing, or shaping public policy?

THE TOP 2 OR 3 MOST CRITICAL ISSUES FOR OUR UNION ARE:

▶

▶

▶

Participants first share stories about management techniques used against them in the workplace (bullying, contracting out, sweet-talking, divide and conquer tactics, for instance). They then look for patterns in these techniques and determine what policy agenda of the employer drives these practices (cut cost or weaken the union, for instance). In doing this they locate the impacts of globalization on an everyday level—through their own experiences of contracting out, restructuring, mergers, divestments, and various forms of work organization that deny workers respect, job security, and decent working conditions.

The funnel provides a basis for further discussion and research

A discussion could, for example, examine how the current political climate has legitimized a blatant promotion of corporate values. Competitiveness is now the norm, even in non-profit organizations funded by the government. Productivity and efficiency are the standards of measurements; and doing "more with less" is the mantra. The gap between rich and poor widens steadily. Unionized workers are somewhere in the middle, between rich and poor, struggling to sustain their incomes and living conditions.

Another possible direction for discussion is the role of government and the private sector. In recent years the public taxation of private corporations has declined steadily, and the resulting shortfall has been passed onto citizens in the form of higher taxes and reduced services. Governments engage in deregulation, privatization, and a downloading of services. The result is more and more precarious employment (contract, part-time, and temporary workers) both in government and the private sector. The existing work takes place amidst lower environmental and health and safety standards in workplaces, and with increasing violation of union rights. The greatest impact of these decisions and conditions falls on women, workers of colour, and Aboriginal workers (see, for instance, *Canada's Creeping Economic Apartheid,* by Grace-Edward Galabuzi).

A discussion could also explore the links between organized and unorganized workers, especially in a legislative environment that pits the two groups against each other and lowers the floor of workplace standards for both.

The funnel brings the real employer to the surface—an employer often hiding behind the mask of immediate bosses. The real employer, who drives the anti-union,

anti-public service agenda, is a network of transnational corporations.

In many workplaces governed by arms-length agencies, boards, and commissions (for example, boards of education, hospitals, and community-based service agencies), the ghost at the bargaining table is the government ministry that holds the purse strings or dictates the funding formula.

In all of this, when the task feels too great, let's remember the people who went before us, who knew this was long-term work, who settled in for the long haul. Part of the benefit of thinking globally is the amazing range of human endeavour to give us inspiration. Here's just one example:

AN EXAMPLE

The year 2000 marked the twenty-fifth anniversary of the end of the Vietnam war. When Dien Bien Phu fell to the North Vietnamese in 1954, the French military forces could not believe how a ragtag army could defeat the nation that was heir to the military genius of Napoleon Bonaparte. But in battle after battle the proud French soldiers had to accept defeat, leading one general to remark, "If they can defeat us so consistently, they must have a *concept...*"

Indeed, two basic concepts were essential to the North Vietnamese struggle for liberation: the strategy of serving the people and guerrilla tactics. This strategy was implemented years before a battle started—political cadres went into the village one or two years before the first shot was fired, educating and organizing the people. They were everywhere; they were nowhere. They mingled with the people; the enemy could not separate them from the people. A peasant by day became a fighter by night; a rickshaw driver one moment became a spy the next; a student or a professor in the classroom became an organizer among the rice paddies.

When the battle began, the French became amazed at how they were surrounded from all sides—when for weeks before they had not seen one enemy in the village.

The tactic on the battlefield varied—adapting to the terrain, the season, and the enemy, whereas the French (and later the Americans) were trapped by their own heavy armour and technology. With the coming of the monsoon rains, which is the timing for major offensives, landmarks on the French map were erased, but they remained clear in the memories of the local Vietnamese; heavy tanks became stuck in the soft mud and machine guns jammed.[6]

This example reminds us of people's capacity to resist and actually defeat more powerful adversaries. It shows one way in which the global picture matters to union education. An inward-looking union education is inconsistent with the broader goals of both effective union education and progressive unionism; in powerful North America, it is more important than ever for Canadian and U.S. workers to see the common ground between their lives and the lives of workers in India, Africa, the Middle East, the Philippines—wherever corporate employers do business and dictate to governments. With these points in mind—and with our ideas for a "global lens" and a tool like the funnel—we are ready to move to the nuts and bolts of the craft of the union educator.

---

6. Inspired by the historical novel on U.S. involvement in Southeast Asia, Lederer and Burdick, *The Ugly American*.

Pause

Where are we five coming from?

To acknowledge our own educational roots, we want to identify some of the frameworks and traditions that have shaped our practice. Thus this "Pause"—a moment of reflection on where we've come from.

The Pause begins with five stories in which each of us tries to answer the question "What was a moment in your life that influenced how you do your education work today?" After discussing these stories, we came up with a list of educational traditions that we want to acknowledge, which we identify in the "Traditions Chart." We know there are other valuable traditions that have contributed to union education; but these are the ones that, so far, have shaped us the most. The one exception, again, is "Aboriginal Education." We are still feeling our way in how to draw on this rich educational tradition, which we know has much to offer our future practice of union education; and so the Pause ends with a gift and a challenge from WUT-TUN-NEE (Tim Brown), Spiritual Leader, Six Nations of the Grand, Mohawk; OFL vice-president, Aboriginal Persons Committee; chair, OPSEU Aboriginal Circle.

The "traditions chart" is not intended to be an inclusive summary of each tradition. For more, see the references in the Bibliography.

Jojo Geronimo, Bev Burke, Carol Wall, D'Arcy Martin, Barb Thomas.

Bev During the exciting early days of the Nicaraguan revolution, I participated as an observer in a workshop on the Atlantic Coast of that country, where health promoters were gathering to evaluate their work on a recent anti-polio campaign. The two facilitators were recent graduates from the successful Nicaraguan literacy campaign. The participants included thirty health promoters, who came in by donkey, horseback, and boat from small villages in the area, and two Spanish doctors who had supported the campaign.

A problem arose when the doctors asked to deal publicly with one health promoter who, during the campaign, had not arrived on time with his donkey to transport the polio vaccine, leaving several villages without vaccine. The facilitators decided to ask several participants involved in the incident to develop a short skit to illustrate what had happened. The skit portrayed the doctors as arrogant, as lacking respect for the knowledge and work of the health promoters.

Before the skit the doctors had wanted to dress down the health promoters. After the presentation, the man who had failed to provide the donkey immediately stood up and apologized. He said he had not understood the implications of his lack of discipline. The major discussion, however, focused on the relationship between the health promoters and the doctors. It was these progressive professionals who were most challenged to think about their values and practices and how their link to the people could be sharpened in the next phase of the campaign. Throughout, the facilitators were polite and firm. Their commitment to unified and effective action kept everyone in the meeting and strengthened everyone's will to work better together.

These popular educators, and many others in Central America, challenged me to think differently about my education work. To this day they are a model for me of how to do creative, participatory education that values and draws upon people's experience, challenges power relations, and strengthens organization.

Deb Barndt

Wall mural, Managua, Nicaragua.

Jojo Picture a detention camp in Manila, in the Philippines, in the early 1970s. It holds political detainees from the broad national liberation front fighting the Marcos dictatorship and U.S. imperialism: workers, peasants, indigenous people, students, progressive professionals, and people from the church, community-based, and academic sectors. The issue was how to mark Holy Week in the predominantly Christian country, under the noses of armed guards.

Some activists wanted to "expose and oppose" the hypocrisy and opportunism of the Catholic Church, with its empty Holy Week rituals. Others wanted to transform Filipino spirituality and culture into a liberating tool of resistance. Both perspectives went into deciding how and what to celebrate.

The result was a "passion play" incorporating the pageantry and theology of a traditional Filipino celebration. It also depicted the national liberation struggle for indigenous land, sovereignty, human and workers' rights, peace, and justice. Participants rehearsed with sounds, songs, costumes, and dramatic dialogue; the backdrop was military massacres and armed resistance, land occupation and U.S. military bases, workers' exploitation and their fight against transnational corporations. The audience was the families, supporters, friends of the political detainees coming for a visit, and the military guards.

Through the rehearsals and the performance, a new unity of purpose and commitment emerged in the camp. The faces of my fellow detainees shone that day, as we dared to speak and carve out a free space in both the physical confines of detention and the political environment of a dictatorship. We were raising critical consciousness, but within a traditional format that the authorities would have trouble punishing.

I saw how "popular spirituality," like any other cultural practice, including trade unionism, can both be transformed and transforming. Some fifteen years later the Marcos dictatorship was toppled and people took over the streets, dancing, singing, and celebrating. Our little passion play was one of many rehearsals for that moment.

Jojo Geronimo

D'Arcy

A highlight of my time in Latin America in the early 1970s was studying with a group of community educators called INDICEP, in the highlands of Bolivia. One of their projects involved teaching math as a way of helping people get full value for sale of their crops. To better understand what people already knew about math, they had spent a few days in the local market, watching how the women measured vegetables and calculated the prices.

Unfortunately, the system was so complex that they couldn't codify it for teaching purposes (it involved the colours of vegetables, the weight of coins, and the colours of bills). They worked instead with pebbles, animals, and numbers and large study posters to make representations of how livestock were counted each day.

In the evening literacy workshops, people were excited to see familiar images as the basis for study. They progressed extraordinarily quickly, labelling the quantities in the exercises with numbers. They started from the unit of ten fingers and learned all the numbers up to one hundred before tackling the most difficult quantity in their culture, which was one. Their excitement was in sharp contrast to their previous failures in classes, which had begun with the rote practising of $1 + 1 = 2$.

This was a time of opening for progressive politics and education in Bolivia, as it was in neighbouring Chile under Salvador Allende's government. These learners were Aymara-speaking Aboriginal people, whose culture had been attacked and suppressed through the centuries since the Spanish conquest of the Inca empire. They responded powerfully to being treated with political, cultural, and educational respect. The INDICEP program was shut down by a later military dictatorship.

Those educators and learners are in my mind when I measure my own attempts in the labour movement at courage, imagination, and respectful dialogue.

Margie Adam

Education for Changing Unions

Barb In March 1983, the fourth anniversary of the revolution in Grenada, representatives from across the small Caribbean island met to hear their government present the People's Budget. This budget distilled a year of discussion in all the small communities about whether to allocate scarce resources to building a road or enlarging a fruit-canning business, or repairing the local school—a year of harvesting people's knowledge of what was working and what was needed. Those local discussions were conducted by a newly emerging, young leadership.

Sparrow's song "Capitalism Gone Mad," played by a local band, welcomed us all. The lyrics reminded us that organizing, decision-making, and community-building in Grenada were occurring, not just in the teeth of U.S. opposition, but under the boots of a global system in which this effort by a country of 110,000 people was not supposed to work. What people achieved on that day gave me immense joy and hope.

Later that night, on a moon-lit road, we listened to a crackling radio transmission of U.S. President Ronald Reagan warning the American people that a secret military airstrip in Grenada threatened them—an airstrip on which, that afternoon, we had attended a barbecue to raise money and more volunteer labour for the people's airport. Popular education in Grenada was dangerous work for Grenadians. But the vision and work of this small country inspired thousands of us who had similar dreams in other countries.

Six months later, internal political conflicts resulted in the killing of Prime Minister Maurice Bishop. The U.S. military invaded Grenada. The combat was over in four days, along with the little revolution that had drawn so much hope and energy to its creation.

But the accomplishments of the Grenadian people in those few years stay with me. It is the feeling of working people's entitlement to a future, the conviction that even with scant resources people can create democracy together. I still draw courage and vision from their efforts.

Maurice Bishop and community leaders, Grenada, circa 1981.

unknown

Carol For as long as I can remember our family in Canada has always had an annual family reunion. This is where stories are shared, and we are told repeatedly, "If you don't know where you have been, you won't know where you are going" and "You stand tall, because you stand on the shoulders of your ancestors."

In the early 1990s our family was contacted by an American researching his family tree. Harold Howard explained that as a small boy he had heard stories about a cousin, William Holland, who around 1860 had escaped slavery in Gaithersburg, Maryland, to go to Canada through the Underground Railroad. Back home William Holland had been identified as a "troublemaker" and was going to be sold. Harold said he wasn't sure if this story was true or not, but he decided he should find out. If William had made it to Canada there would be family to meet. If William hadn't made it, Harold wanted to make sure he had a proper gravestone.

Harold was thrilled to discover that there was a thriving family in Canada that had originated with William Holland. I remember the first time we travelled to Maryland by bus. My children were in awe of the fact that their great-great-grandfather as a nineteen-year-old slave could have made this journey on foot, hiding in absolute fear of being caught and killed or, worse, returned. We began a biannual family reunion with the American and Canadian cousins, switching between Maryland and Ontario. At the reunions Harold proudly holds workshops recounting family stories and displaying photos and bills of sale for ancestors. We now refer to Harold as our family historian.

The family reunion is one event that younger family members do not need to be coaxed to attend. They are spellbound by the history told of their ancestors. To me, Harold is a great popular educator.

Crest on the Howard-Holland family t-shirt.

Feminist Education

Anti-Racist Education

Critical Pedagogy

Popular Education

Liberal Adult Education

UNION EDUCATION

Historical Roots of Labour Education and Social Change

Literacy

Quebec Labour Traditions

International Solidarity/Global Development Education

Aboriginal Education

BUILDING UNIONS

Traditions Shaping Our Educational Practice

POPULAR EDUCATION

Aims/Objectives
- ❑ support movements for social change (both attitudes and structures)
- ❑ encourage respectful and committed dialogue

Approach/Methodology
- ❑ respects and builds on people's knowledge
- ❑ links learning to action
- ❑ uses creative, collective methods
- ❑ poses questions more than imposing solutions

Origins/Key Themes
- ❑ Paulo Freire's literacy work in North-East Brazil in the 1960s
- ❑ uses generative themes, consciousness raising, integrates head and heart learning
- ❑ no education is politically neutral

Debates/Tensions
- ❑ class analysis did not address race/gender oppression
- ❑ relationship between practice and theory/education and organizing

Insights for Labour Education Now
- ❑ emphasis on respect for the experience of workers
- ❑ link between education and organizing
- ❑ creative, participatory tools

FEMINIST PEDAGOGY

Aims/Objectives
- ❑ increase the individual and collective power of women
- ❑ integrate feminist analysis into teaching

Approach/Methodology
- ❑ treat women as "normal" rather than problematic
- ❑ personal consciousness raising linked to political campaigns
- ❑ formal university curricula in women's studies programs

Origins/Key Themes

- ❑ Western university women's studies challenging critical pedagogy
- ❑ gender oppression as dominant theme

Debates/Tensions

- ❑ centred in North America and Western Europe
- ❑ challenging structures or only empowering individual women
- ❑ integration of class and race oppression into analysis

Insights for Labour Education Now

- ❑ analysis of gender inequities
- ❑ incorporate women's experience in the home and community as well in the workplace and the union
- ❑ draw on the whole person, including the body

CRITICAL PEDAGOGY

Aims/Objectives

- ❑ develop critical capacity to resist and challenge existing social and political structures

Approach/Methodology

- ❑ explore the hidden curriculum—what is learned is not just the content of courses but the way power works in education

Origins/Key Themes

- ❑ Western universities, 1980s
- ❑ uncovering assumptions about what is "natural"

Debates/Tensions

- ❑ applicability of skills to adult life
- ❑ location and language of academia inaccessible to many
- ❑ strong in critique, weak in proposal

Insights for Labour Education Now

- ❑ power is always at work in learning situations; the need to use power consciously
- ❑ importance of challenging our own biases and assumptions as union educators

CANADIAN LABOUR/SOCIAL CHANGE EDUCATION

Aims/Objectives
- ❏ build class consciousness
- ❏ change relations of power in the workplace
- ❏ promote alternatives to capitalist logic (such as co-operatives)

Approach/Methodology
- ❏ early trade union education emphasized practical subjects for workers
- ❏ adult study groups in the Atlantic provinces linked to action (establishing co-ops and credit unions)
- ❏ radio used to organize rural people in Western Canada (read-listen-discuss-act)

Origins/Key Themes
- ❏ some key programs included: Frontier College (1902); the Workers Educational Association (WEA)—1930s and 1940s; The Antigonish Movement (1932); National Farm Radio Forums (1940s-1950s)
- ❏ links to student movements since the 1960s

Debates/Tensions
- ❏ only recently addressing how social class is raced, gendered, abled

Insights for Labour Education Now
- ❏ test of good labour education is activism in the workplace
- ❏ important to know your history and the bridges you are walking on

QUEBEC LABOUR/ SOCIAL CHANGE EDUCATION

Aims/ Objectives
- ❏ critique of dominant North American values
- ❏ affirming identity in face of national and cultural oppression

Approach/ Methodology
- ❏ starting with lived experience of learners
- ❏ building on a shared popular culture

Origins/ Key Themes
- ❏ influence of Latin American popular education since the 1970s
- ❏ key union role in building nationalist movement
- ❏ sovereignty-association with Canadian labour movement secured 1975-95

Debates/ Tensions
- ❏ role of unions and allies within nationalist electoral coalitions
- ❏ frictions with logic and culture of Canadian and U.S. union educators

Insights for Labour Education Now
- ❏ innovations in a context of high union density (over 40 per cent)
- ❏ ways of broadening economic influence (Fonds de solidarité)
- ❏ ways of working with social democratic government
- ❏ long experience of potential and limits in worker educator programs

INTERNATIONAL/SOLIDARITY/GLOBAL/DEVELOPMENT EDUCATION

Aims/Objectives
- ❏ develop awareness of North-South issues
- ❏ challenge the "charity" model
- ❏ uncover international power relations and assumptions about them
- ❏ make local-global connections and promote international solidarity

Approach/Methodology
- ❏ teach-ins, development of school curriculum and resource materials, community educational events, tours North-South, policy development

Origins/Key Themes
- ❏ international non-government organizations and solidarity groups (1970s)
- ❏ international department of the CLC; the humanity/solidarity funds of some affiliates
- ❏ key themes: development/underdevelopment; South Pacific; demands and programs of people's movements in Africa, Latin America, Asia, and the Caribbean; critique of Canadian and U.S. government policies in the South ("Third World"); more recently, globalization and free trade

Debates/Tensions
- ❏ role of political advocacy
- ❏ support to armed struggles (e.g., African National Congress—ANC)
- ❏ links among local, national, and international issues and struggles
- ❏ analysis of racial oppression "over there" not necessarily applied "over here"

Insights for Labour Education Now
- ❏ importance of international solidarity links among workers to be able to understand and to challenge transnational corporations
- ❏ workers in Canada learning from the struggles of workers in other countries

ADULT EDUCATION (THE LIBERAL TRADITION)

Aims/Objectives
- ❏ education for life: at work, in the community, in society
- ❏ empower the individual learner

Approach/Methodology
- ❏ self-directed learning
- ❏ experiential learning
- ❏ school-community collaboration
- ❏ hands-on/application to life/practical skills
- ❏ tutoring: "each one, teach one"

Origins/Key Themes
- ❏ the Canadian Association of Adult Education (CAAE) brought together social movement groups and professional adult educators from 1935–98
- ❏ the Institut canadien d'éducation des adultes still performing this role in Quebec
- ❏ life-long learning
- ❏ life/work skills

Debates/Tensions
- ❏ improving unjust situations without tackling the root causes of injustice
- ❏ individual more than collective learning
- ❏ education as "neutral"/professional

Pause

Insights for Labour Education Now
- ❏ a set of operational principles (participant knowledge is respected; participants see learning as valuable, can make mistakes, get frequent feedback, etc.)
- ❏ adult learning theory: e.g., adults have a variety of learning styles; adults remember best when they can discuss and apply what they know

---

ANTI-RACIST EDUCATION

Aims/Objectives
- ❏ challenge racism (systemic/structural racism)
- ❏ analyse systemic barriers in organizations
- ❏ expose racism in colonialism mirrored in racism in immigration policy

Approach/Methodology
- ❏ use of personal experience, linked to structural experiences
- ❏ historical context (colonialism, imperialism)
- ❏ analysis of structural/institutional forms/policies

Origins/Key Themes
- ❏ developed in the 1960s in Britain, where communities of colour were organizing to deal with state racism and the rise of the fascist right
- ❏ developed in Canada following immigration law changes in 1967
- ❏ systemic racism
- ❏ race as a social construct
- ❏ internalization of oppression

Debates/Tensions
- ❏ often lacked class or gender analysis
- ❏ sometimes resisted as guilting white people
- ❏ efforts to change organizations from inside often limited by lack of outside pressure

Insights for Labour Education Now
- ❏ need to integrate equity/anti-racism lens into all labour education
- ❏ tools for analysis
- ❏ importance of working connections with community
- ❏ value of recognizing and using privilege

LIBERATION THEOLOGY

Aims/Objectives
- ❏ build Base Christian Communities, learning from and supporting each other
- ❏ engage in actions of "solidarity with the poor" and encourage collective efforts for social change
- ❏ challenge and change the formal church structures

Approach/Methodology
- ❏ use of biblical themes (forces of slavery vs. forces of freedom/empowerment)
- ❏ participatory research/collective analysis of social realities

Origins/Key Themes
- ❏ church-based organizations and local Christian communities, confronted by institutional violence and "revolutionary situations," critically reflected on the role of church institutions in maintaining injustice
- ❏ actively assisted by theologians from Latin America, Central Europe, Spain, and Asia (mainly Philippines, India, and Indonesia)
- ❏ often informed by and actively informing national liberation movements in Latin America, Asia, and faith-based solidarity groups in the North

Debates/Tensions
- ❏ Christian theology vs. non-theists including Marxism
- ❏ the history of Christian churches as active collaborators in colonialism, feudal structures, and other oppressive practices (i.e., racist, sexist, homophobic)
- ❏ how to reconcile traditional Christian values with violence/armed revolution
- ❏ comfort level of activists in integrating spirituality with political action

Insights for Labour Education Now
- ❏ need for collective and critical reflection, as a distinct moment in one's life and work
- ❏ learn from the coalition-building strategies of liberation theology practitioners
- ❏ spirituality (whether theist or non-theist) as a component for personal and collective self-renewal

A GIFT AND A CHALLENGE

The words that follow are from my teachings, and primarily from the teachings of my teacher Blackwolf; in turn they are almost exclusively from the teachings of his teacher, and so on and so on... traditional teachings are of this way, passed on from one to another for the purpose of passing them on to another and to another... thought and discussion are continuously encouraged though this way of teaching, and this type of teaching also gives the teacher ownership only to pass this teaching on, but in doing so it is held in both the hearts as well as the minds of the teacher and the student.

WUT-TUN-NEE (Tim Brown)
in peace, to all my relations

NAMAJI
(pronounced NA-AM-GEE)

THE HIGHEST PRINCIPLE of all Native American peoples' life principles is called Namaji: respect, honour, dignity, and pride.

Respect, honour, dignity, and pride are given and accepted freely. They are the gifts of a true connection to the Spirit World. They are the flowers that bloom of Mitakuye-Oyasin (pronounced mi-TAHK-wee-a-say, meaning "We are all related"). They are the promising buds on the wreath of Life.

This is Namaji: respect, honour, dignity, and pride. From the East Direction to the North Direction, the children need the Elders and the Elders need the children. Namaji is the geyser that lifts all of creation to sacredness. All is elevated and cared for. Namaji beats strong of commitment, responsibility, and accountability. It embraces and nurtures the We of this world. For all is committed, responsible, and accountable to you. Namaji is a mutual Life principle.

Namaji guides us along the Red Road of life. The Red Road is the Sacred Path for living in harmony with the natural order. Red is the colour of our blood. It is the colour of the most sacred Native stone, the Pipe Stone.

We can easily travel from Vancouver to St. John's, driving only at night. The headlights illuminate the dark path before us. This is all we need to see. We focus on a few hundred feet at a time, adding up to thousands of miles. The Red Road, the narrow path between the dark and bright, is difficult to follow within the depths of yourself. Follow the soft glow of the Eternal Light and avoid the dark and bright sides. Travel the Sacred Hoop of timelessness into the sunlight of Ain-dah-ing (pronounced AH-da-ning, meaning "home, the home within your heart").

Dark is the absence of Light. If we veer off into complete darkness, we punish ourselves because Namaji demands accountability. Consequences for indiscretions are self-imposed, for we choose by our actions. Just as the old way was to banish a member from the tribe, so too are we banished from our inner society if we choose to go off the Red Road into the darkness.

The glare of blinding light may also cause us to veer off the Red Road of Life. Complete lightness causes us to become self-righteous, condescending, and judgemental. We start to believe the light that reflects off of us is our own.

Anyone who is dependent on any thing or substance who successfully remains clean and sober walks the Red Road. Without the denial and depression of active abuse,

Barb Thomas

Tim Brown, Labour Educators' Exchange, Toronto, August 2002.

they escape the darkness and the consequences it brings. Without the dilution and grandiosity of self-achievement, they are able to avoid the glaring brightness of judgementalism. By staying clean and sober one beat at a time, they recognize the gift of sobriety and their role in their new way of life. By walking the Red Road, they keep their eyes on the lighted path.

Many people try to make life black and white and conveniently fit all experiences in either camp of brightness and darkness. What colour is Brother Skunk? If you concentrate on the black, with a hard eye (narrow focus), Skunk is black. If you concentrate on the white stripe, again with a hard eye, Skunk is white. But if you concentrate on the whole of Skunk, with a soft eye (wide focus) you see both the black and the white; they combine to make Skunk grey.

Rarely is Life white or black. Certainly there are wonderful white moments, as celebrating a birth. Certainly there are black moments, as mourning a death. But even these mountains and valleys are marked by the overcast of shadows and the silver lining of clouds. We need to live life between the black and white.

Life is bittersweet. For life is not all or nothing. Life is everything on the continuum of experience. Life asks us to feel the fullness of the Red Road, to feel the pain as well as the joy, to feel the anger as well as the forgiveness, to feel the hunger as well as the satisfaction. The blueberries my child and grandchild picked are both bitter and sweet. The children left the woods not only with blueberry juice all over their faces, but with the dozens of wood ticks that accompanied their sweetness. Sacredness encompasses the entire experience. Accept even the most painful experiences in life. Thank the wood ticks for their part of the experience. The Sacred Strawberry Path is in between the black and the white. It is the narrow path between the dark and the bright.

When we walk softly on the Red Road we are peaceful and calm. The heartbeat of life gives our feet the cadence and we joyfully follow the beat. When we feel uneasy, upset, or our emotions cloud our thinking, we are not staying between the ditches of life's road. We need to get back on the Hoop of Life. The ditches are bumpy reminders to get back and recentred, rebalanced and reconnected to the Spirit World.

Walk in harmony. Walk in beauty. Don't cling to the dark or the bright. Look for the rainbow in the puddle, for every negative has within it a positive and vice versa. Be deliberate in your choices and intentions. Follow your heart. Follow your drum beat. Life is a circle and will return to you what you sent out into the Universe.

Abuse returns abuse. Namaji returns Namaji. Life is circular, it will come full circle. You are the designer of your fortune and future.

Softly place your moccasin on the Red Road and you will find your joy. Discover how Earth Mother's energy supports you. Walk gently on your Mother's Back and she will embrace your step. Honour Her and She will honour you. Walk with Namaji down the Red Road of Life.

Part 2

The Craft of Union Education

photo credit: Barb Thomas (inset) Deb Barndt

4. Designing the Program

CONTENTS

THINKING SPIRAL

    The spiral model....57

    Why we have found the spiral model useful....60

    Yes but....61

    What to do and what to avoid in using the spiral....63

THINKING EQUITY

    Barriers to equitable participation....74

    Taking equity into account on the spiral....75

    Tips for equalizing participation in preparation and design....76

YOUR EDUCATION DIRECTOR ASSIGNS YOU THE TASK of developing a new member orientation course. You will also have to revise and update the old stewards course. You aren't sure where to begin.

The labour council asks you to prepare a discussion at the next meeting on developing a joint campaign against the privatization of public services. They give you current campaign materials to help you prepare. There are no notes on how to use them.

An organizer asks you to give a speech at a conference. You see the possibilities for introducing something that is more participatory into the occasion.

All of these situations—and countless others—call for program design or development, for making a plan before the program begins. In our work we use several tools to help address these kinds of situations. One of those tools is the spiral model, which we use to design a course, an activity, or a political action. Other tools help us to apply an equity lens to the design process; and then there are steps we can take to build a course or program that takes into account the six threads outlined in the INTRODUCTION.

The spiral model (outlined in *Educating for a Change*) represents a way of approaching the nuts and bolts of a union workshop or course, a meeting, or a conference. Following are some of our more recent experiences in using the spiral.

Education for Changing Unions

THINKING SPIRAL

THE SPIRAL MODEL IS A FRAMEWORK for putting principles into action in our education work. We also use it as a tool to assist in the design of an educational event. As we get feedback in our work, our thinking about the spiral, our use of it, continues to evolve.

THE SPIRAL MODEL

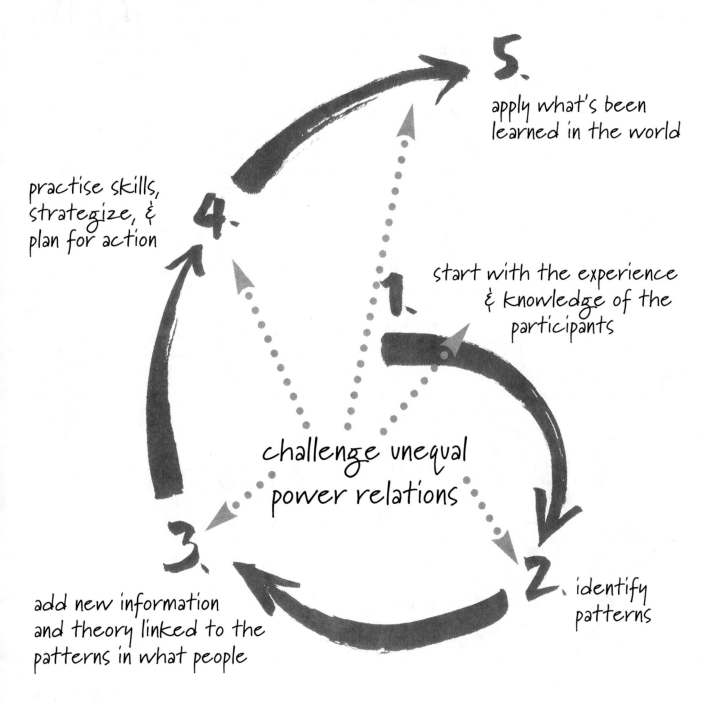

5. apply what's been learned in the world

4. practise skills, strategize, & plan for action

1. start with the experience & knowledge of the participants

challenge unequal power relations

3. add new information and theory linked to the patterns in what people

2. identify patterns

THE SPIRAL MODEL

How it works

1. **The spiral begins with the experience and knowledge of the participants.** When most of us went through school, the teacher would always start with "new information and theory"—as though we didn't know anything. Unfortunately, we often tend to repeat this pattern in our union education programs.

2. After sharing their experience, participants **look for patterns they can use to form a collective picture.** The picture needs to include all of the voices in the room and to recognize differences as well as similarities.

3. **Add new knowledge and theory linked to what people already know.** The analysis includes looking at relations of power—at who benefits most and least from whatever is going on.

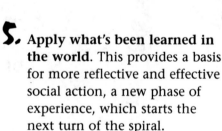

4. Participants then try on what they have learned: they **practise new skills; strategize and plan for action.** In developing an action plan, for instance, participants might name their own power; identify what they can change; and determine who their allies are.

5. **Apply what's been learned in the world.** This provides a basis for more reflective and effective social action, a new phase of experience, which starts the next turn of the spiral.

Education for Changing Unions

Challenging unequal power relations

Beginning with people's information and knowledge can raise some problems. Both participants and facilitators come into the sessions carrying all the misinformation and biases picked up in the larger society. When we are targeted (by racism, or sexism, for instance), we may see the injustice more easily. When we are not the targets, we may have to work harder at understanding what's going on.

An example

> During a women's conference workshop, a woman of colour, who was in the minority in the class, challenged a white woman on how her comments about African women could be interpreted as racist and patronizing. The white woman had said that women in Africa needed to be educated, that they needed to be helped to understand how wrong the practice of genital mutilation is. She went on to criticize African women who wanted to continue the practice in Canada. The other participants mostly rallied to the defence of the white woman. The woman of colour said that many African women were working on this problem and they didn't need to be educated by Canadian women on the issue. She was forced into a mediation session, where she was told she had misunderstood the comments of the white woman and should apologize because the entire class had been disrupted.

This example illustrates many different challenges facing facilitators, and a lack of spiral thinking is just one of them. If a facilitator in this case had been able to think through the situation using the spiral, she or he might have first tried to set a climate in which the two perspectives could have been explored more productively. The facilitator might have asked the participants to consider a couple of questions: "What is your relation to the issue? What are your feelings and concerns about the issue?" The facilitator might have been able to probe those feelings and concerns by asking, "Where are your concerns similar, and where are they different?" The possible result—a "teachable moment"—would, we hope, place a spotlight on the systemic nature of racism, dispel myths, and perhaps add further information on the issue. The facilitator might have gone on to pose other questions: "Who is doing what about this issue? What else do we need to know or find out?" The discussion could provide the woman of colour with an opening to talk about what African women are doing about the issue.

Why we find the spiral model useful

■ The spiral model connects our six threads

The spiral is a democratic model that values and draws upon participant experience and knowledge just as much (or more) than expert knowledge. Everyone teaches and everyone learns in a collective process of creating new knowledge, rather than only the teacher teaching and the students learning. It helps build a sense of community, because individual experience and knowledge are brought together and the group as a whole takes different creative gifts into account. New learning frameworks and new information help workers see how they are linked to workers in other sectors or areas of the world to create a sense of class-consciousness. Ensuring that the learning leads to building the capacity of union members and applying education to action contributes to strengthening the organization—to union building. Education leads to action for social change, to strategizing with others about how to build alliances with other unions and sectors to support the greater good. At all points the spiral model applies the equity lens.

■ The spiral model takes into account how people learn

Think about how you learned your job. Did you learn by doing it? From a manual? From talking with a co-worker? By watching someone else do it? People learn in different ways.

David Kolb developed a theory about learning. He identified four ways of learning: through concrete experience (feeling); logical thinking; reflection or observation (watching); and by experimenting (doing).[1] For example: Two people dismantle a piece of equipment. One, an engineer, puts all the parts in order, screw by screw. The other, a mechanic, throws everything into a pail. He says he can always figure out where it all goes.

Those who learn through concrete experience, like the mechanic, will most likely tune in at points no. 1 and no. 2 of the spiral. Those who learn through logical thinking, like the engineer, will not believe that any concrete learning is happening until they get to a facilitator's presentation or the readings provided in a kit (no. 3). The experimenters won't feel that they've got what it takes until they get a chance to use or practise what they've learned (no. 4).

When we ask workers in our programs how they learned their job—from a manual, from co-workers, or on the job—very few hands go up for the manual. Most people learn their jobs on the job—by doing it or by talking with a co-worker. This experience has other implications for the design of our programs. As doers, workers are often impatient to get on with it and move to action. When they attend a conference or workshop where researchers present graphs and statistics in unintelligible language, they are left wondering how all of this connects to their daily lives. Joint work by researchers and workers can lead to a very different presentation that speaks to workers' reality, backed up by credible research—a powerful combination. Many academics who have worked with the labour movement have learned that while academic knowledge is valuable, it is only one form of knowledge.

---

1. Kolb, *The Learning Style Inventory Technical Manual.*

Designing the Program

■ The spiral model is flexible

Just for fun, we tried to put a number of our workshop, course, meeting, and conference designs into spirals. Some interesting artwork resulted—and what is especially clear is that this is not a linear process.

Sometimes the approach draws out people's experiences related to one aspect of a theme, finds the patterns, and then goes back and draws out another set of experiences about the theme—all before we do any analysis or add new information. Sometimes one activity takes you right around the spiral. You might have a large spiral covering all of a longer course, with many smaller spirals within it as you deal with specific themes. Sometimes when you get to the action stage, you discover that you need to retrace your steps. The spiral serves as a continuing check on the quality and outcomes of your work.

Yes, but . . .

We can hear some of you saying "yes but"—voicing some hesitation and questions about how this approach works in practice. So before moving on to look at the points of the spiral in more depth, we will try to deal with a few concerns that tend to come up when we do this work.

"Yes, but . . . I don't have enough time to use the spiral. The course is short so I only have time to present the information they need."

Using the spiral does not require any specified time-frame. It is a matter of thinking about where to begin and where we want to end up. For example, in a ten-minute workplace presentation to galvanize workers for a campaign, union educators:

■ tried to anticipate, in the planning stage, how the members might support or be hostile to the topic, which helped them decide where to begin the discussion;

■ tried to connect key points they wanted to make about the topic to the experience and knowledge of the participants; and

■ made sure there was something people could do immediately—write or sign petitions, contact their MP, and so on.

"Yes, but . . . this approach would not work in my union. It might be great for other unions and some community groups. But in my union the members are used to presentations. We use a lot of overheads and some videos. Our members wouldn't go for any of this participatory stuff."

Thinking spiral does not assume that you will suddenly begin to do lots of role plays and other exercises participants may not feel comfortable with. Thinking spiral influences how you do your presentation.

- You can consider in advance what experience and/or knowledge your members have on the theme. For example, if the presentation is on the grievance procedure, you might begin by asking if anyone in the room has ever filed a grievance.
- Then you might have the participants line up across the room, depending on how much they know about the grievance procedure: those who know nothing at one end and those who know a lot at the other; others with varying degrees of knowledge somewhere in the middle. Then ask people why they positioned themselves at that point in the line.
- You could try to link the key points you want to make with what people already know and have said in the opening activity.

"Yes, but . . . how is this any different from good adult education? I thought we were talking about social change education here."

Good adult education does incorporate aspects of spiral thinking. Good adult education tries to respect the knowledge of the learner and link new information to what people already know. Good adult education also recognizes that people will retain what they know if they have a chance to practise skills learned. But in addition to those elements, thinking spiral is also collective and critical, and it brings the real world and all of its tensions into the education program. Unlike mainstream adult education, the purpose of union education is not just to understand the world but also to change it. We want our participants to use their learning to develop campaigns and action strategies to tackle the problems they face at work and in their communities.

"Yes, but . . . our education is too technical to use this popular education stuff. People don't have any knowledge of hazardous products. That's why we're doing the course."

We find that workers know a lot more about most issues than either they (sometimes), or we (often) think they do. Most participants will have directly experienced the results of hazardous products in the workplace, the community, and the home. This experience can be the starting point for a course on toxic substances, with new information linked to what people already know. Often technical subjects offer great opportunities for creative ways of learning.

What to do and what to avoid in using the spiral

We hope that some of you are now ready to try the spiral for the first time. We also know that others have been working with the tool for as long as we have. What follows are some questions and tips for working at each point in the spiral, developed with the help of many union and community educators. We hope that you will add to the list from your own experience.

A "spiral worksheet" is an aid in designing a course, workshop, or meeting. In this context the spiral includes two additional elements: "Getting Started" and "Evaluation."

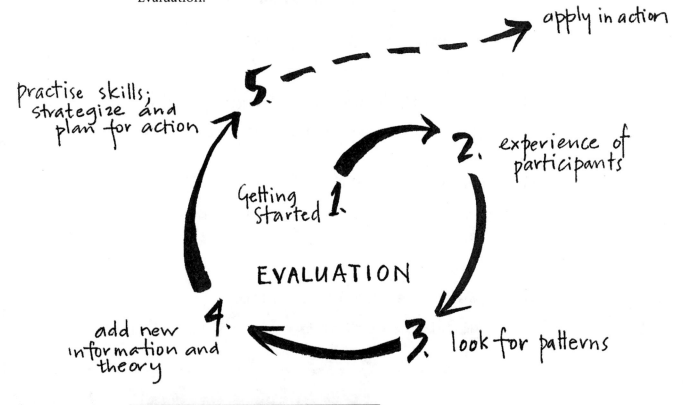

Cathy Lang, The Moment facilitator training, Toronto, 1992.

1. Getting started

Our colleague Rob Fairley calls the step of getting started "creating and maintaining a respectful environment," which underlines the importance of the initial community-building that helps put people at ease and creates conditions in which people feel safer to participate.[2]

Tips for getting started

† Introduce participants and facilitators to each other.

† Get people there mentally as well as physically.

† Establish a comfortable climate for learning and begin to build the group.

† Identify participant expectations and indicate how these expectations will be met through the course.

† Introduce the theme of the course.

† Establish the process that you will be following and indicate how people will be involved in shaping it.

† Clear up logistical details (times to work, washrooms, smoking, etc.).

† Give participants a chance to claim the space in the room.

† Encourage the feeling that participants have something to teach as well as learn.

---

2. See Arnold et al., *Educating for a Change*, pp.48-52, for more ideas about getting started. The appendix here, "More of Our Favourite Union Education Activities," also includes exercises for building participation guidelines and class contracts for helping to create an appropriate environment for learning.

2. Bringing out people's knowledge and experience

Why do it?

Workers often think they don't have anything to say—that they need to listen to the expert. Recognizing people's knowledge and experience helps our members recognize that they do have something to say and that they can learn from each other, not just from the instructor. Starting from people's experience also grounds the process, making it relevant to the participants. It signals a different kind of relationship between students and teacher. At the same time, we (as educators) discover what people already know, which means we won't bore them with old information. In our experience, someone in the room always knows more than we do about a particular aspect of the topic being addressed.

Learning from our successes—things to think about

- **What do people know about the issue?** What we don't want is to make people feel stupid. For example, don't ask new union members about past union history related to a theme. Instead, you might ask them for their experiences with the issue in the time since they joined the union.

- **What diversity of experience do the participants have, and how will we take this diversity into account?** For example, given that there might be someone with a physical disability present, we can ensure that any exercise involving movement can also include that person. Or, in an anti-harassment course, we can take into account how the experience and perspective of women and people of colour are different than those of white men.

- **What experience will get shared where and why?** People have a lot to say about their own experience, which means it is easy to generate more information than you can use. Be careful not to make their participation just a warm-up to the main event—the educator's performance. Ask participants to focus on a few specific questions or on one aspect of their experience.

- **What questions will we ask?** In our experience, this is one of the most difficult things to do: find the right questions. Try to keep your questions focused, open-ended, and clear, and only ask a few. For example:

    What happened? (who, when, where, how, to whom?)

    How did that affect you?

    Can you describe a situation where _____ was an issue for you?

- **What do we want to take up in the full group?** We have all attended sessions where reports-back droned on and on—it's enough to give participation a bad name. We often ask people to report back on only one of the three or four questions they discussed in small groups.

- **How will we organize the data we get back?** Will we write on one flip chart in columns? On several flip charts with different headings? Will we write on cards and then post them on the wall? How will the cards be clustered so we can see emerging patterns? These are decisions to make in advance as you develop your design.

- **Will the discussion have an emotional impact?** For example, with themes related to harassment, violence, or other human rights, some participants will probably have had direct experience of the issues. We need to be ready to support people when needed, and not leave them raw and vulnerable.
- **How does participant experience relate to the topic?** A course on sexism for a mostly male group will be different from one including mostly females. With men, rather than focusing on their experience of sexual harassment, we might place our emphasis on where harassment is an issue for them as union activists, on the impact on member unity, and on how they can help to create an harassment-free environment.

Learning from our mistakes—things to avoid

- **Getting too much data** makes it difficult to find patterns and focus the discussion. It's like flooding the car engine with too much gas—it won't start.
- **Huge numbers of messy flip charts** overwhelm both the facilitators and the participants. We have had workshops where participants got claustrophobia because of all the flip-chart paper generated.
- **Unfocused, general discussion** causes participants to lose interest, especially when the link to workshop goals is fuzzy. You will need to bring participants back on track by reminding them of the workshop goals.

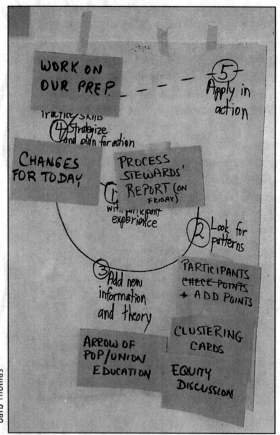

Barb Thomas

In the preparation, try to zero in on the specific objectives or aspects of the experience or issue that you want to focus attention on. For example, you might want to consider using "the parking lot"—a place on the flip chart where you list items for discussion that are not related to the subject at hand, but might be something that participants want to discuss at some later point. It is important to clarify whether topics listed on the parking lot will be either a) incorporated into the workshop at a more appropriate time, or b) dealt with outside of the workshop at a specific time and place.

Flip chart from facilitator training, Saskatchewan Federation of Labour, January 2002.

3. Looking for patterns

Why do it?

Identifying patterns in a discussion is a crucial step that educators often skip to get to the content they want to impart. This leaves participants feeling that the experiential part was a token activity only meant to pave the way to the "real thing."

Sharing patterns in their experience helps people see that they aren't alone, that others have similar problems and concerns. But it also brings differences to the surface, helping us see that not everyone views the world through the same lens. Collectivizing individual experience helps to build a sense of community, which is especially important in union education aimed at building solidarity. This step in the process encourages critical thinking and gives participants the opportunity to contribute "new information or theory" before the facilitator contributes theirs.

Learning from our successes—things to think about

- **How can the patterns be organized visually so that people can see them?** Perhaps one of the most useful tools is card-posting, using large sticky notes, index cards, or half-sheets of paper that participants use to jot down key points. These notes can not only be posted but also moved so that patterns are more easily identified.[3] Also helpful is an overall visual, such as a spiral, triangle, or circle, which you can use to gather information at various points.

- **What insights/patterns will people observe?** You may think of an activity and/or a question that will help bring the patterns into a sharper focus. For example, in a course on benefits, you might look at special leave, if the point is that special-leave provisions have changed and are now more mean-spirited, you might want to arrange people's experience on a timeline. Or you might want them to write the date of a personal experience of requesting leave (or an experience they know of) on cards and post them under headings such as "approved, denied, or other."

- **What questions can bring out the patterns?** Some examples:

    What patterns/themes do you see/hear?

    What does this suggest about . . . ?

    Who else had the same experience? Who reacted differently?

    What strikes you about this picture we've developed?

- **What process will we use to ensure that everyone has a voice?** We often get just one point from each group in the first round of reports-back, which means that the first group will not use up all the time available or deliver all the possible points. Or we ask groups to choose someone to report back who hasn't done it before, which helps avoid having the same people always speaking in plenary.

---

3. See, for instance, the "Stickies" exercise in the appendix, "More of Our Favourite Activities."

Learning from our mistakes—things to avoid

- **Suppressing differences as we focus on patterns.** To avoid this we find it useful to ask, "What are the similarities and the differences in these experiences?"
- **Trying to pursue everything in depth.** Instead, focus on one or two central ideas. We refer back to the objectives to decide what the focus should be; which means the objectives must be clear.
- **Putting someone on the spot.** Make sure that the lone woman is not asked to speak for all women, or the one person of colour is not asked to speak about racism.
- **Repeating the small-group discussion in plenary.** We have all been in deadly plenaries where nothing new is added. We need to think about how collectivizing the experience will move the discussion forward—raise a new point, expand on an important issue. For example, in a gender analysis of the economy, we might ask groups to discuss the impact on women of changes to jobs and social programs in only one of four areas—at home, in the community, at work, and in the union— giving each group a different area. In the plenary, each of the four groups explains and posts their cards, and we ask participants to look for patterns and connections across the different sites.

Mike Desautels, Karen Lior, Gord Johnson, Regina Labour Educators' Exchange, October 2002.

4. Adding and deepening information or theory and connecting it to participant knowledge

Why do it?

We want to expose participants to a range of information and thinking. This point in the spiral provides an opportunity to make links with other outside issues and struggles. Useful frameworks and theories help people organize and deepen understanding of both their own experience and that of others. In some cases, specialized knowledge can be important to the union jobs that people are being asked to do.

But often there's no connection made between the knowledge and experience that participants have shared at the beginning of the workshop and the new material. When we don't build from what they know and understand, participants

- don't learn that their own knowledge is important;
- continue to think that the real expert is always the teacher; and
- don't learn from each other.

And the educators

- don't learn anything from the participants;
- keep listening for the right answers; and
- can't gear what they know to the most primary concerns and feelings of the participants.

Learning from our successes—things to think about

- **When is the best time to add new information?** Consider the energy level of the participants and the time of day. For example, it is best not to make presentations (or show videos) immediately after lunch.

- **How can we link new information to what people already know?** Try to link new information back to the patterns in people's experiences that have just been identified. The weaving together of participant and educator knowledge is a subtle process. Facilitators have to truly listen to judge when to build on what participants have said; or when to omit something from a planned presentation because participants already know that piece; or when to confirm the importance of what participants already know. Moreover, we don't just add new information at one moment in a presentation. New information and analysis are also being presented through questions posed, task sheets that set up discussions, and summaries of key points.

- **How can we add new information in a creative way?** For example, in one workshop two union instructors used the bodies of participants to track the grievance process. One person (with a bad back, who needed to stand a lot anyway) wore the sign "complaint" and was shepherded by another member to the steward. The two of them took the complaint to the supervisor, and so on. You can put key points on balloons, use cartoons, present an instructor role play, show a video, or use songs.

- **How can we show the key points visually?** We often note key points on flip charts or cards, which we post one at a time as we're speaking. When you are making a presentation, visual props help participants retain the main points. They also help us remember the flow so we don't get lost in the detail.

- **How can we focus attention on one point at a time?** People tend to read ahead, so too much visual information at one time will be distracting. We often lift and tape up the bottom of the flip-chart page to cover the writing and then unveil the points one at a time, or use cards that we can post one at a time. Overheads and computer slides are often helpful for this purpose.

- **How can we make a presentation interactive—get the participants involved?** For example, as part of a presentation on active listening, we began with a set of questions on a flip chart and asked what kind of response each question invited before we presented material on open and closed questions. We then asked participants to turn a set of closed questions into open-ended questions.[4]

- **What questions might help a facilitator's presentation?** Some examples:

  What did your reading tell you about this?

  How does this theory connect to your own experience?

  What does this new information mean in light of your own story?

  How does this connect to or challenge what we said or did before?

- **Are there examples or visuals that will help people remember?** The Maquila Solidarity Network (MSN) uses a huge papier-mâché model of a Nike shoe in their presentations on sweatshops. The Nike shoe becomes the focal point for a discussion of what the worker is getting paid; how the worker is being treated; what the consumer pays for the product; and who is benefiting from this situation. Participants will remember that discussion every time they see a Nike shoe.

- **Is there a way that participants could make the presentation or be part of it?** For example, in a workshop on free trade, the facilitators gave groups background materials and a set of questions on different trade agreements, with time to research the answers. The participants became the experts on that agreement, presenting their findings to the whole group. You might also have participants play roles in a story you're telling. For example, people might become bankers, International Monetary Fund functionaries, the World Bank, a debtor nation, and so on, to illustrate how international debt works to the benefit of the rich.

- **How do you deepen what participants have already developed at this stage?** It is often more effective to use an exercise or a set of good questions rather than a presentation to have participants delve more deeply into an issue or topic. Some of the exercises in chapter 6 and the appendix relate to this point on the spiral; see also CHAPTER 7, "Asking Good Questions."

- **Does the method of presentation fit the context?** If you are making a presentation in a course, you have different options than you do on the shop floor. For example, the papier-mâché model of a Nike shoe is portable and easily adapted for either the shop floor or a workshop setting.

---

4. See the APPENDIX for a detailed description of this presentation.

Learning from our mistakes—things to avoid

- **Giving people too much information.** We now try to identify two to four key points, which is about all people can absorb at one time, and structure material around them.
- **Reading from notes.** Use small cue cards if you need to, but if possible use visual props that will also help participants retain the information.
- **Arguing with people during a presentation.** In most presentations a facilitator is not called on to make decisions or offer definitive opinions, and everyone does not have to agree on the ins and outs of an issue. The purpose is to get people to think and be able to ask questions, as well as respond to challenges.
- **Paper storm**—handing out so much material that people feel overwhelmed and less confident than before the session started. You may want to consider giving out documents in small doses, as they are needed.
- **Long complicated sentences with big words and no headings; closely spaced text with no visuals.** See the Canadian Labour Congress (CLC), *Making it Clear*, a publication on "clear language and design," for suggestions and tools that can help us avoid this mistake.

Deb Barndt

5. Practise skills; strategize and plan for action

Why do it?

Union education is also about building the skills and confidence of our members. In addition to nurturing or supporting activists we also want to build the organization by strategizing and planning for action.

Learning from our successes—things to think about

- **What actions are doable and which ones will people support?** How can everyone participate in the action in a way that is comfortable?

- **What are the obstacles to participation in the action?** What do people need to be able to participate? For example, is day care available for women or men with children?

- **Where is the energy?** You allocate fifteen minutes to a discussion, but when the time is up people are really into it and there is clearly a lot of learning going on. Or, after five minutes, it feels like pulling teeth to keep any discussion going. When we have a choice, we go with the energy in the room—we keep the discussion going, perhaps longer than planned, or we close it down early, as need be. Usually, the only ones with a detailed schedule are the facilitators, so use the scope!

- **What questions will we ask?** Some examples:
  What changes can we influence?
  Who are our allies?
  How can we apply what we've learned?

Deb Barndt

- **How can people have fun with the action?** Making collective banners, doing popular theatre, producing buttons with slogans or developing chants, songwriting, making puppets—the list of "fun actions" is endless. In the area of popular theatre, for instance, one group came up with the idea of doing guerrilla leafleting around the issue of free trade. Group members dress up as waiters and carry leaflets on trays. They go up to people in a government building, on the floor of a conference, or on the street, and ask, "Excuse me, did you order free trade?" Then they offer the leaflet and say, "because you are paying for it!" (This is a variation on an action done during the U.S. intervention in Central America in the 1980s.)

- **How will we make sure that everyone feels safe practising new skills?** There is always a risk in performing before your peers, and participants will feel some anxiety. Building in adequate preparation time helps to reduce anxiety levels. Group presentations take more preparation time but are less stressful than solo performances.

Quebec City, 2001.

Learning from our mistakes—things to avoid

- **Trying to plan something in too short a time.** It is better to set up a process (another meeting, perhaps) to plan the action. Trying to do detailed planning in a limited time frame can cause frustration.
- **Insufficient time to practise new skills and reflect on learnings.** People need time both to present their thoughts and findings and then to discuss the experience afterwards. If a sessions leaves no time for reflection, the learning is minimized.
- **Correcting participant presentations.** Often, as facilitators, we step in too early and too often to correct participants in practice sessions. In their presentations participants rarely make serious errors that remain unchallenged by others in the group. Our interventions as facilitators inevitably carry more force than do the statements or suggestions of other participants. We need to think about how we can intervene in a way that helps people develop more, not less, confidence. We often develop with participants a set of guidelines for giving and getting feedback.[5]

6. Evaluation

It is crucial to learn from past work. As a result, we dedicate all of CHAPTER 9 to this important issue.

(Right) Denise Gagnon,
Toronto Labour Educators' Exchange, August 2002.
(Below) A protest at Organization of American States
meeting, Windsor, June 2000.

Deb Barndt

Barb Thomas

5. For sample guidelines, see Arnold et al., *Educating for a Change.*

THINKING EQUITY

WE BRING OUR EXPERIENCE OF INEQUITY OR PRIVILEGE "out there" in the world into our program design and into the classroom or wherever learning takes place. Inequities and our biases are reflected in the examples we use or avoid, the materials we use or avoid, and the discussions we take up or avoid. They are reflected in who teaches and in who gets to courses. In our work we have come up with a few tools that help us apply an equity lens to our spiral design work—something that we are still learning how to do.

Barriers to equitable participation

In training courses for worker educators we have used the "circle diagram" which follows, as a tool for helping along a discussion of the barriers to equitable participation in union education—barriers that we need to anticipate and deal with in a course design. Our goal, in the central circle, is to achieve "equitable participation" in the classroom, union hall, or wherever learning is taking place. The middle circle represents individual barriers that participants may face—whether it is a back problem, being new to the union, or shyness, among others. The outer circle represents systemic barriers in society that are reflected in both the union and the classroom: racism, sexism, and homophobia, for instance.

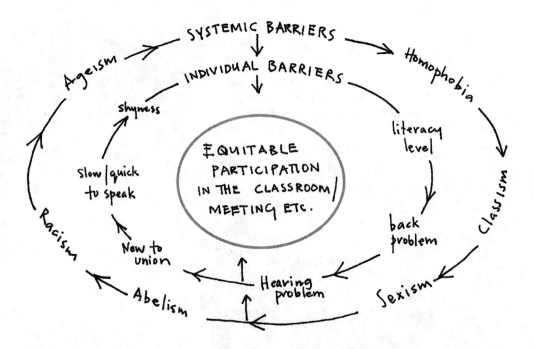

As educators we need to anticipate these barriers in our program design and keep our focus on challenging unequal power relations. We have found a number of general questions helpful in doing this:

■ What approach will help us ensure that everyone has a voice?
■ How will we illuminate power relations in the questions we ask and the materials and activities we use?
■ What processes will help build a sense of community, of solidarity?

Taking equity into account on the spiral

A number of specific issues at each point on the spiral can help us "think equity" as we develop our design.

Practise skills/strategize and plan for action:

- Have people practise dealing with relations of power in different sites: workplace, home, union, community.

- Know about services in the community helpful to members (for example, English as a second language classes, sexual assault centre).

Start with the experience and knowledge of participants:

- Anticipate that inequities in the world will be present in the classroom.

- Don't assume that everyone is comfortable talking in a large group.

Find patterns:

- Recognize differences as well as similarities.

- Make sure that everyone's voice is heard.

Add new knowledge/analysis:

- Theorize differences in power that people have in society.

- Ensure that different voices present new information (that not all speakers in the film are white men, for instance).
- Take different literacy levels into account.

Tips for equalizing participation through preparation and design

♱ Check out the site ahead of time to make sure there is natural light, wall space for flip charts, space for flexible seating, proximity to washrooms, accessibility, no distracting noises.

♱ Make sure the facility is wheel-chair accessible, and that people with mobility problems can move around the room.

♱ Check dietary needs ahead of time.

♱ Try to encourage a mix of participants through work with political leadership.

♱ Survey people ahead of time, whenever possible, about learning goals and the conditions they need to participate effectively. E-mail is great for this.

♱ Examine your materials for reading levels and visuals.

♱ Think about the examples you'll be using to explain things; make sure they don't exclude anyone and that through the course they will refer to everyone's situations.

♱ Think about your language ahead of time. Assume that men, women, gay, straight, and bisexual people will be in the room. For example, don't assume that families are headed by heterosexual couples.

♱ Use small-group activities and mix the groups.

♱ Ensure that course flyers mention equity; that visuals portray a variety of people.

♱ Plan to use a variety of methods to introduce the course (visuals, printed words, verbal descriptions).

♱ Design an icebreaker so that people can quickly feel comfortable with each other.

♱ Set up the classroom flexibly so that people with hearing and visual impairments can position themselves for maximum participation.

♱ Plan to start and end on time. People may have arranged to call children or family members or do other tasks during scheduled breaks.

♱ Seek a mix of facilitators—with regard to gender, race, disability, age—and meet ahead of time.

As we continue "thinking equity" when we are on our feet facilitating, other questions and tips will come to mind (see CHAPTER 7).

An important skill in a facilitator's craft is the ability to design a program or adapt a design to meet the needs of participants. The more wrinkles we can anticipate in the design, the fewer problems we will have working "on our feet" during the program.

The spiral design model helps to ensure that we begin with the experience of the workers in our programs. It helps us to link new information and analysis to what people already know, and it provides an opportunity to practise new skills and strategize for action. The equity lens applied to the spiral helps to ensure equitable participation in our union education programs. The building blocks in the design, though, are the activities, which form the subject matter of the next two chapters.

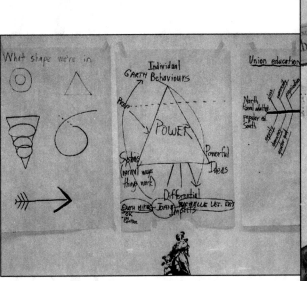

Barb Thomas

(Above) Facilitator training, Saskatchewan Federation of Labour, January 2002.
(Right) Regina Labour Educators' Exchange, October 2002.

Dorothy Wigmore

Making Activities Work

CONTENTS

STEPS IN AN ACTIVITY....79

CHOOSING ACTIVITIES
    Considerations in making activities work....79
    Dealing woth discomfort....80
    Getting the work done....81
    When the source of the activity is management....81
    Taking our own bias into account....81
    Where you are on the spiral....82

USING ACTIVITIES
    Including everyone in the room....83
    Power relations and roleplaying....83
    The politics of furniture....84

FACILITATING ACTIVITIES: SOME TIPS
    Dividing people into groups....85
    Introducing the activity....86
    Getting reports from small groups....87
    Doing a synthesis....88

CHOOSING WHICH ACTIVITIES TO USE in a course or workshop is not always easy. Sometimes we know roughly what we want to do. Sometimes we have a favourite activity, or something new we want to try, and we look for a way to squeeze it into a course or workshop. This chapter outlines our current thinking about how to decide whether, when, and how to choose an activity, and it explores some of the issues that have emerged for us in using certain activities. Throughout the chapter are examples of "when we mess up"—to alert you to how we continue to struggle with these questions ourselves.

If you are an old hand at union education and this chapter seems like "covered ground," or if you are just anxious to get to some new activity ideas, feel free to move directly on to CHAPTER 6.

STEPS IN AN ACTIVITY

To facilitate or develop an activity, we have found it helpful to think about how an activity is structured. *Educating for a Change* outlines in detail the different parts of an activity. Here is a reminder:

1. Introducing the activity

- Divide people into groups.
- Explain the task and the time. What do they have to do? How much time do they have to do it? Where will they do it?
- Give some background to the activity, if appropriate.
- Explain the objective. Why are you asking people to do this?
- Hand out materials needed to complete the task.

2. Preparing the activity

- Participants work at the task (prepare the role play, discuss in small groups).
- The facilitator acts as a resource person to the groups: clarifies the task, helps a group with problems, monitors the time.

3. Presenting and discussing the activity

- Small groups report back to the larger group in a variety of ways.
- The facilitator helps the group clarify the experience and look for patterns.
- The facilitator adds new information if appropriate.
- With the help of the group, the facilitator synthesizes the discussion.

CHOOSING ACTIVITIES

Again, our six threads—collectivity and community, democracy, solidarity and equity, class-consciousness, strengthened organizational capacity, and union action linked to the common good—inform the activities we choose.

For example, activities that promote participation and an opportunity for people to hear from each other can help build a sense of collectivity, of being part of the union movement. Activities that give participants an opportunity to take leadership and practise skills can help strengthen organizational capacity. Opportunities to learn how to talk back to management in a workshop activity help build class-consciousness. Ensuring that activities are equally accessible to everyone helps build classroom democracy and equity.

For us, the work of choosing an activity boils down to two moments: whether to use it; and how to use it.

Considerations for making activities work

Here are some considerations we take into acount in choosing an activity:

- The objective: what are you trying to do?
- Who are the participants (cultural background, age, race, gender, traditions, physical limitations)?
- Clear language and literacy.
- The spiral: where are you in the design (drawing out participant experience, finding patterns, analysng a topic, adding new information, moving to action)?

- Participants' comfort level. At this stage of the course, will participants feel comfortable doing this activity?
- Your nightmares about leading the activity.
- Potential resistance by participants to the activity.
- The mix of activities you already have (to take into account different learning styles).
- Time: how much time you have; time of day.
- Logistics (furniture, size of room, wall space, access to resources/equipment).
- Number of participants.
- Source of the activity (if it's management, look for built-in biases).

Dealing with discomfort

Your level of comfort is a consideration in choosing an activity. Like you, we feel more comfortable doing some activities than others. But discomfort is information. For example, you might feel uncomfortable because you had a bad experience with the activity once as a participant. Or maybe you didn't run the activity well the first time you tried it. Perhaps it just isn't your style of learning. So what conditions help to make you more comfortable doing an activity? Our suggestions:

- observe someone else facilitate the activity to gain more confidence in running it yourself;
- work with a co-facilitator who likes to run the kinds of activities that make you feel uncomfortable;
- adapt the activity to make it more comfortable for you to use.

Your participants' comfort level with the activity may also influence your choice. For example, if the group is new to participatory activities, you may want to begin with small-group and paired discussions, rather than with drawing or drama.

Chelsea Looysen, Sharon Hurd, Jacques Théoret, Linda Delp, Regina Labour Educators' Exchange, October 2002.

Barb Thomas

Getting the work done

Will the activity meet your objective? For example, if the specific objective is to identify supports and obstacles to member participation, the activity we choose might be different than if the objective is to develop strategies for involving more members in an upcoming campaign. Will you have time to do the activity? If not, can it be adapted successfully to a shorter time period? The range of activities possible in a longer program is much greater than those possible in a one-day course.

When the source of the activity is management

Corporate training programs have introduced many innovative approaches. As a result, some of the activities used in union education in areas such as communications, public speaking, strategic planning, and team building come from management training manuals.

Barb Thomas

The problem is that management thinking is embedded in these activities, and it becomes part of the unintended learning that results from using these materials. For example, in management materials on team-building, the underlying objectives or interests of management and workers are fudged to appear the same. In reality, the main management objective is to increase productivity (profit) while the union is seeking to improve working conditions for its members and to build pride/solidarity among workers. We suggest using management materials with a critical eye to make their biases visible— or you could rewrite the activity from a union perspective.

Taking our own bias into account

We may have used our equity lens in choosing the activity, but because of the limitations of who we are (our own social identities), we may not see how certain biases are embedded in the tool itself.

For example, we have used a visual tool we call the "learning heads" as a way of pointing out that people retain more of what they learn if they use more senses and have a chance to discuss and apply what they are learning. A participant in one of our workshops pointed out that this tool is biased towards people who can fully see and hear.

Looking at racism in the media, Barb Byers, Nicole Bluteau, Danielle Legault, Regina Labour Educators' Exchange, October 2002.

Making Activities Work

For a deaf or blind person, the learning heads would look different. An indigenous participant told us that when he first looked at the heads, he couldn't relate to it because in his culture learning is mainly oral, through story-telling. So the visual also has a built in cultural bias. We may still want to use this tool and make visible these built-in biases as we introduce it, or develop a new tool that is more inclusive.

Learning Heads

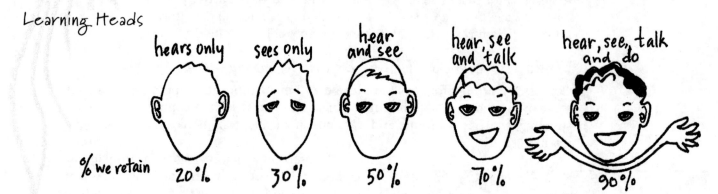

hears only — 20%
sees only — 30%
hear and see — 50%
hear, see and talk — 70%
hear, see, talk and do — 90%

% we retain

Where you are on the spiral

Drawing out the participants' experience suggests a different kind of activity than adding new information. There are certain activities used for doing critical analysis, and others for developing planning skills. Some activities can take you right around the spiral. A key, then, involves considering where an activity fits on the spiral.

Dorothy Wigmore

Working energizer, Labour Educators' Exchange, Toronto, August 2002.

USING
ACTIVITIES

Including everyone in the room

Just as we consider the issue of equity in deciding whether to use an activity, we also use our equity lens in thinking about how to use it. Ensuring that everyone's voice gets heard in the discussion is a major challenge for facilitators. One step in meeting this goal is to design activities that make it easy for everyone to participate. Would the cultural background of some people make them uncomfortable doing the activity? How can you take different language levels/literacy into account? How will the activity permit equitable participation for those with difficulty moving, or problems hearing? Taking equity into account may involve reshaping the activity.

Power relations and role-playing

We most often use role plays to give people a chance to practise what they have learned or to practise dealing with a difficult situation. For example, in our role plays in training workshops for grievance procedure and arbitration, some participants take the role of management, which means that others get a chance to practise dealing with management. Some educators report that this experience can lead to a lingering identification with the management role; people find it difficult sometimes to step back and look at management issues from a union perspective.

To address this difficulty we take time to discuss the role play during the exercise itself—while people are still in their roles—to clarify the different interests that are coming through. We always refer to "so-and-so's" character, making it clear that the participant is simply playing a role. Jim or Juanita are not managers; they are playing roles. Then we do something physical to "shake out" their roles. Finally, after leaving the role plays behind, we focus on union strategy.

Sometimes we use role plays at other points on the spiral to deepen understanding of issues or to discuss strategies from different viewpoints. We ask participants to take on a set of predefined roles. For example, in a workshop on free trade, a facilitator outlines a fictional scenario: a plant is going to close down in the community and move to Mexico. Participants divide up into groups representing different elements: community and church organizations, the union, the company, Mexican workers, the town council. Each group has to decide how to respond to the company decision and consider how to form alliances and with whom.

Stereotypes can readily emerge in this kind of role play, especially when people take on the role of someone from another country or social identity (in this case, perhaps, the Mexican workers). Educators often debate whether this kind of role play should even be used; some say it is useful just because it helps to name and confront the various stereotypes that arise in discussions of the issues.

When you use this kind of activity, you can warn people up front to try to avoid stereotyping, to remember the complexities of all human beings. But when a stereotype does emerge, be sure to probe it. Help participants name it, and deal with it when you take time out to discuss the role play. All of us are capable of communicating stereotypes; this is not an exercise in catching someone out. It is a process of learning for everyone, and of working together to create a strong and inclusive movement.

Barb Thomas

Chelsea Looysen and Barb Byers, Regina Labour Educators' Exchange, October 2002.

The politics of furniture

How you set up the room tells participants how much you want them to participate. The traditional classroom set-up, with the teacher at the front and the students in rows, delivers a clear message: the teacher will talk and the students will listen. Room set-ups also need to accommodate a range of activities.

Our favourite arrangement is to place round tables in a semicircle, which makes it easy to move from small-discussion groups to the large group. The arrangement also leaves an open space in the centre when needed for an activity. At other moments it provides the option of setting up the chairs in a circle. In our experience, hotels and other workshop locations tend to use a square arrangement or the traditional classroom set-up—so be prepared for some resistance if you ask for round tables.

FACILITATING ACTIVITIES: SOME TIPS

Each of the steps in an activity—from introducing the activity to preparing the activity to presenting and discussing the activity—involves a number of tasks. We have organized these tasks into the following "tip sheets" (which we hope you will be able to photocopy for use as handouts).

Tips on dividing people into groups

† Think about who should work together and why. For example, bringing together people with diverse experience (time in the union, gender, worksite, different regions, public/private sectors) can enrich a discussion. Diverse groupings can help draw out and build a sense of experience—new members "tell us what it's like" or participants from the north tell us about their particular challenges.

† Break up cliques.

† Separate disrupters.

† Take mobility factors and possible disabilities into account.

† Avoid confusion. For example, tell people whether or not they need to take their belongings with them when they go off to the activity.

† Don't single out or target participants or create situations where certain people feel uncomfortable or threatened.

† Consider how much time is needed for people to move into groups. (You don't want people to spend all of their discussion time getting into the discussion groups.)

† Create occasions for participants to meet new people.

† If possible, use a method for dividing into groups that ties into the activity's objectives. For example, if the theme of the session is free trade, you might have cartoons about free trade cut up into puzzle pieces and groups form by putting the pieces of the puzzles together.

Some methods

1. For an activity after a break: ask each participant to put their name card (or one of their belongings with their name on it) on one table. During break, put the name cards or belongings on different tables, ensuring a good mix among participants. When people return, ask them to find what belongs to them and to sit at that table.

2. Have participants line up according to seniority in the union. Then count off to ensure that newcomers and veterans are mixed in the small groups.

3. Ask experienced people to come to the front of the room. Ask everyone else (newcomers) to vote with their feet for the theme they want to discuss. Then assign the veterans among the groups.

4. Explain that you need four groups and that you want them mixed by gender, seniority, and worksite. Ask people to stand and form groups by talking with other participants to ensure the appropriate mix.

5. Have people pair up with someone they don't know.

When we mess up

"I always forget and ask people to pair up with the person on their left. Of course, everyone turns to their left—and no one knows who to work with!"

Tips on introducing the activity

- † Have people form into their groups first.
- † Prepare, in advance, visual props that reinforce what you are saying (flip charts, overheads, pictures, task sheets). Use colours consistently as another clue.
- † Distribute any materials or written instructions before you begin the explanations.
- † Tell people why they are doing the activity.
- † Situate where they are in the course and where they are going.
- † State the question or task in plain language.

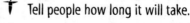

- † Tell people how long it will take.
- † Don't assume people will "get it" the first time.
- † Ask for feedback. Is everything clear? Any questions? And give people time to think about it and respond.
- † Make sure your voice is clear, unhurried.
- † Give people the overview and then move to the details.
- † Follow up with pairs or groups as they begin work to make sure instructions are clear.

When we mess up

"While my co-facilitator was reviewing the task, I thought I would help out by handing out the materials (pens and cards) the groups would need to do the task. Afterwards my co-facilitator gently told me that my handing out the materials distracted people from what she was saying—so that she had to repeat all of the instructions again."

Natasha Goudar, Regina Labour Educators' Exchange, October 2002.

Barb Thomas

Tips on getting reports from small groups

† Don't repeat all the small-group work, but do leave space for people to have their say.

† Advance the conversation from the small groups.

† Make the report-back an opportunity to build speaking skills and confidence among newer people.

† Ask people to face the whole group when they are talking.

† Limit the amount of reporting back by each group. (For example, groups report on only one question; each group reports on a different question.)

† If the same people are doing all the reporting, encourage new participation.

† Avoid putting people on the spot. (Reporting in pairs helps shy people.)

† Circulate the reports: get one point from each group, then a second point from each group. In other words, don't let one group dominate.

† Sometimes, encourage participation from each person—cards and stickies can help.

† Think about where people will place their cards. How can the reports-back create a new, collective picture?

† Encourage movement. For example, ask people to move to the wall to place their card.

† Help people see connections between their experiences—the similarities and differences in the room.

Some methods

† Participants, in pairs, report back key points on cards or stickies, which are posted and clustered according to similarities.

† Small groups each call out one point, in rotation, and a facilitator records the points under agreed-upon headings.

† Spokespeople for each group report; with the spokesperson changing if there is more than one round.

† Skits depict either a problem or an approach.

† Ads emphasize the key points the group thinks are important.

† Posters, buttons, visuals, group collages.

† Coloured paper T-shirts used in place of cards or stickies for reporting back. These are hung on a line made of string and clustered according to themes or similarities.

† A song; agree on a tune, and each group prepares a verse incorporating their key points.

When we mess up

"Participants were reporting back with cards, which we had asked them to post on the wall. We had not limited the number of points or questions for each group to report on, so that each group had a lot of cards. When the reports were finished, the wall displayed a mass of material. We just started to laugh."

Bev Burke, facilitating at the Asia-Pacific Regional Womens' Workshop, Seoul, Korea, 2001.

Tips on doing a synthesis

✝ Use the synthesis to wrap up the session and make a bridge to the next.

✝ Build common ground by pulling out common themes in the reports or the discussion.

✝ Acknowledge significant points of divergence, if any (for example, nearly all the reports said workload was an issue for their members, but one report stated otherwise).

✝ Don't simply list what was already said.

✝ Relate the synthesis to the objective of the session or the goal of the course.

✝ Use the words and images of the participants and refer to any cards or objects used in the reports.

✝ Now and then, name the source of the ideas (which group/individual said what), but do this without appearing to be "grading" the reports.

✝ Raise your own questions, fill in gaps of information, or clarify key concepts as you go along in a way that ties together the different threads of the conversation.

✝ Sometimes the group reports themselves will determine how you synthesize.

✝ In the end, acknowledge and celebrate the newly created collective knowledge.

Some methods

- Clustering: use the cards/stickies from the reports/discussion and group them together based on cards with similar ideas or themes. Once the clusters are formed, give each a tentative heading or label. Use creative labels that fit the ideas. For example, from reports on the usual employer responses during negotiations, headings might be "Blah!" "Grrrr," "ZZZZ," "Yes, but ...."

- Listing: list similar ideas under one heading or category. This method implies that you already have a few categories you want to use or suggest before you can start listing, unlike "clustering," where the clusters emerge from the process. Ideally, limit the number of lists to three to five. In practice, listing involves consolidating and collapsing several ideas (with the support of the group), rather than a mere physical listing of what was said.

- Mapping consensus: make one list for points common among all reports; another for points representing a divergence of opinion; and possibly a third list for "not sure," "not clear," or "needing further clarification." Try not to make any list too long.

- A matrix: list the locals (or other groupings) involved on a horizontal column; and the "report items" on a vertical column; then check off the locals that mentioned any of the "report items." Pull out the items with the highest and lowest number of check marks, and make your synthesis around those key items. This method is best done when the items on the vertical column were actually the focus of the reports.

- Linking: draw a line between related ideas from the reports (perhaps using different colour-coded markers). This can be difficult to do unless you have all the flip charts right in front of you in a way that allows you to draw the lines.

- Check marks: move from one flip-chart report to another, checking off similar points or key issues. Then summarize the major issues you have checked into a list. If there are several categories of issues, you can use colour-coded check marks.

- Metaphors: for example, use a "tree" to summarize a discussion on the different forces involved in bargaining. The task of the small groups was to name these forces, as specifically as possible. The synthesis then introduced the concepts of social, economic, and political forces, using the examples from the reports; and a discussion on the relationship among forces capped the synthesis. In this example, the roots were "economic," the trunk was "political," and the branches were "social."[1]

- Diagrams and drawings: use concentric or overlapping circles, arrows, and boxes to depict relationships, contrasts, tension points, different phases, and so on.

When we mess up

"It was only a two and one-half hour session, but felt like one long day. Each group did a year-end 'program evaluation,' then reported back on their three top items for 'accomplishments' and three top items for 'gaps and omissions.' Reports ranged from broad generalities to the 'nitty-gritty,' mixing discussion of results with justification for non-results. My head was whirling with the participants' elaborate explanations and points-counterpoints. I realized then that there was no way I could pull it all together. Now I do this kind of report-back before a break so that I can pull some of the key points together and then feed them back to the group for further discussion."

---

1. The source of this metaphor is Barndt, *Naming the Moment*.

Our Favourite Union Education Activities

6.

CONTENTS

OPENINGS AND CLOSINGS
    Solidarity bingo....92
    Lineups....95
    Head, heart, feet....96

ANALYSING OUR EXPERIENCE
    Mapping the membership....97
    Historical timeline....100
    Identity cells....103

LINKING NEW INFORMATION TO WHAT PARTICIPANTS ALREADY
  KNOW
    Questionnaire research: a way to avoid boring lectures....107
    The triangle tool—take 2....111
    Ten chairs: visualizing poverty statistics....114

PRACTISING NEW SKILLS AND STRATEGIC PLANNING FOR ACTION
    Skits: talking union to the member from hell....116
    Open space technology....119
    Triads: practise listening skills for difficult conversations....121

ENERGIZERS LINKED TO COURSE CONTENT
    Group juggling....124
    Rainstorm....126
    Rosa Parks....127

EVALUATION
    Sticker evaluation....129
    Card game reconstruction....131

As educators we are constantly on the lookout for new ways of making our work more creative and effective. Here we offer some of our favourite ideas for approaching different kinds of learning. (For even more, see the APPENDIX.)

Between ideas for "Openings and Closings" and "Evaluation," the activities are grouped, roughly, to follow the spiral design model—though we have also added in a section on "Energizers Linked to Course Content." Symbols placed beside the title indicate whether an activity can be used for several purposes.

We hope you will feel free to have fun with any or all of the activities, both here and in the APPENDIX. Pull them apart and reshape them—and be sure to share your new ideas with us.

Dorothy Wigmore

Janice Gairey, Toronto Labour Educators' Exchange, August 2002.

Tips for building equity into our activities

† When there is a short text, read it aloud.

† Ask small groups to have a volunteer read text to the group.

† Encourage a range of people to be involved in reports-back.

† Whenever appropriate, ask questions that encourage people to think about equity.

† Think about who will play different roles and how groups will be divided.

† When an exercise requires standing or movement, think of how it can be adapted to include chairs or be done from a sitting position.

OPENINGS AND CLOSINGS

SPENDING TIME ON OPENINGS AND CLOSINGS is always important—but it is even more crucial when you are trying to build a social movement. To build solidarity, people need to get to know and trust each other. You need to allow for time at the beginning to give this a chance to happen. Then, at the other end of a session, a closing activity offers people a chance to talk about what they have learned and to express their solidarity with each other and the union.

Some unions and federations have begun to draw on the rich spiritual traditions of their Aboriginal members. Among our most beautiful learning experiences were the times when a conference opened with a sweetgrass ceremony and an educational event closed with an Aboriginal healing circle. The sweetgrass ceremony must always be conducted by an Aboriginal elder. It is a powerful expression of solidarity: with each other, with the earth, and with those who have gone before us.

SOLIDARITY BINGO

Why use it?
- as an icebreaker—to have participants meet each other
- to introduce the theme of the program or course

Time it takes
- 10-15 minutes

What you need
- "solidarity" bingo cards for each person

How it's done

1. Explain the purpose of the exercise (see "Why use it?") and hand out the bingo cards.

2. Review the rules of the game:
   (a) the object is to seek out other participants and get signatures on as many squares as you can.
   (b) Each player signs another player's card once only.
   (c) Don't feel that you have to disclose personal information, and don't pressure anyone else to do that either.
   (d) Introduce yourself as you go around collecting signatures.
   (e) The game is over when the instructor calls "time."

3. Play the game for about ten minutes. Then ask who has more than eight boxes filled, who has more than ten, and so on until you have a winner.

4. Choose one of the "content" boxes and ask someone who signed that box to say a bit about it. You might also ask for a show of hands on several of the boxes, to see how many people matched the content.

5. Some possible final comments or questions:
   (a) The differences among us—and only some of them are on the card—are a resource for the union. We all win when we value and respect our differences.
   (b) Who is not here? Whose perspectives do we need to think about in the course?

Variations
- Have participants play to get one line covered (as in regular bingo) and distribute prizes to the winners.
- Put different characteristics in the boxes, depending on the theme.

Challenges
- If you make it into too much of a contest, people don't take the time to talk to each other.
- If you have boxes that might contain information that is new to the participants (such as the box on "Zapatistas" in this example), be sure to take those examples up in the full class after the game. If there are more than one or two such boxes, provide an "answer sheet" as a handout.

Building in equity

- Keep the language simple in the boxes. If you are aware of language difficulties, you might have the exercise done in pairs, with two people getting signatures on one card. This does require some movement around the room, although it is minimal.

Source

- Many variations of this exercise exist, which makes the original source difficult to identify.

Note

In the sample bingo card: Zapatistas are members of the EZLN (Spanish for the National Zapatista Liberation Army) in Chiapas, Mexico. The largely indigenous Zapatistas are fighting for land and other rights that have been denied them for decades.

Deb Barndt

Protest at Organization of American States meeting, Windsor, 2000.

SOLIDARITY BINGO

Rules of the Game
- The object is to fill as many squares as possible with a signature in the time you have available.
- Each participant can only sign your card once.
- You can sign your own card once.

B	I	N	G	O
Knows what it's like to be laid off	Born and raised on a farm	Knows who Zapatistas are and where they live	Has taken a union course in another union	Experience in union organizing in another country
Has travelled to a country other than the United States	Lived in more than one Canadian province	Lived in more than one country	Born in a different decade from you	Filed a grievance him/herself
Experience as a union officer	Born in a country other than Canada	A union member	Walked a picket line for another union	Wears glasses
Attended a labour council meeting	Has taken more than one union education course	Can sing the chorus and one verse of Solidarity Forever	Has been unemployed in the last 5 years	Writes with a different hand (left/right) than you
Has been to arbitration	Experienced workplace harassment	Protested against free trade in Quebec City in 2001	Lost time from work due to injury	Speaks a language other than English

LINEUPS

Why use it?
- as an energizer and a way of sharing experience

Time it takes
- 5-10 minutes

What you need
- dates written on cards (before 1970, 1970–1980, 1980–1990, 1990–now) posted on the wall at intervals
- a large open space
- one chair to begin each line

How it's done
1. Indicate the time periods posted on the wall and explain that you will be asking the participants to line up according to the time that is related to the question.

2. Lineup questions should relate to your course. Sample lineup questions for a stewards course might be:
   (a) when they joined the union
   (b) when they got active in the union
   (c) when they became a steward.

3. After each question, you might ask clusters of people to briefly tell the others in their group why they put themselves at that point on the timeline. You can also ask for a few comments to share with the full group.

Variations
- You can ask participants to line up in many other ways. For example: line up by how you are feeling about an issue, with HOT on one side of the room and COLD on the other.
- The facilitator can make a graph of, or add up the years of, experience in the room on each question.

Challenges
- Keep the pace moving. If you leave people on their feet for too long, you will lose them.

Building in equity
- Have a chair available in each line so that anyone with difficulty standing can have a seat.

Source
- the authors

HEAD, HEART, FEET

Why use it?
- to evaluate a session at its conclusion
- as a closing activity

Time it takes
- 30 minutes (but depends on number of participants)

What you need
- the image of a person, drawn on a flip chart or sketched life-size on a large sheet of paper
- small strips of paper (three for each participant)
- flip chart, markers, tape

How it's done

1. Post the flip chart drawing on a wall or place the paper person in the middle of the floor.

2. Distribute three strips of paper to each participant.

3. Ask participants to identify three things (one on each strip of paper) they learned in the workshop or course: a new idea, a feeling, and an action idea or skill (something they can use back home). Invite contributions in words, headline form, or drawings.

4. Ask participants, one at a time, to select one of their three strips of papers to share with the group by reading it and placing it on the corresponding part of the paper person: (idea) head, (feeling) heart, (action) feet. Time permitting, you may invite them to share all three.

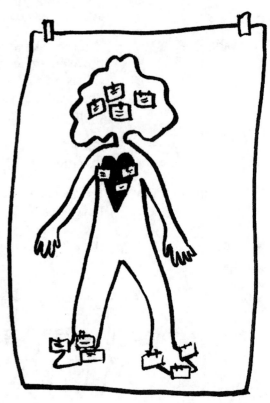

Variations
- Ask participants to draw their head, heart, feet on a paper, using markers. Ask them to record new ideas they learned on the head, new feelings on the heart, and new action ideas or skills they can use on the feet. You can also ask people to tell the group about one of these things they have learned; they can hand in their drawings/evaluations.

Challenges
- None that we have encountered

Building in equity
- Give participants a choice of using words or visuals to describe their learnings.

Source
- the authors, with Marsha Sfeir

Education for Changing Unions

TOOLS FOR ANALYSING OUR EXPERIENCE

IN ALL OF THESE ACTIVITIES, the emphasis is on learning the skills necessary for doing an analysis. The process of doing the analysis, then, becomes as important as the outcome.

MAPPING THE MEMBERSHIP

Why use it?

- to analyse the social composition of the membership
- to identify differences between locals in membership profile and implications for mobilizing
- to apply equity concepts to practical union business

Time it takes

- 30–45 minutes

What you need

- social mapping chart
- collective profile sheets, posted on the wall

How to do it

1. Explain the purpose of the exercise. Note that it is not important to have statistical accuracy. We just need a "rough cut" to identify "who's here" and "who's not here."

2. Have participants work in teams based on unit/local/union affiliation. Locals can join together if necessary.

3. Ask the teams to fill in the social mapping chart, using estimates or rough ratios to indicate membership breakdown. Ask them to start with four categories only (for instance, function, length of service, family status, and language). Then, if time allows, they can proceed to the other categories.

4. Post four "collective profile sheets" on the wall, one for each of the four selected categories. Each group enters their data on the collective profile sheets, which then become a summary of data.

5. Invite the group to look at each of the profile sheets, one at a time. For each profile, explore a number of questions, such as: Is there a pattern in membership composition? Is there an exception? Why? Is the pattern recent or long established? If recent, what would explain the change?

6. Explore the implications of the data by asking, "What does this information mean for bargaining? For organizing? And so on.

7. To summarize, ask: Are there any insights, surprises, from this profile of the membership? How confident are we of these numbers? (Do we need to do further research?)

Variations
- The categories on the map may need to be changed for different unions.

Challenges
- Initially some participants may not understand why this exercise is important to do.
- Some participants may focus on the "statistical accuracy" of the exercise rather than on the analysis.

Building in Equity
- This activity can help activists understand the importance of knowing their membership if they want to mobilize the union or local around bargaining issues.
- You can use this exercise to begin a discussion of equity not so much as a question of human rights (which it is) but more as a matter of strategy: equity as a means of achieving a stronger contract.

Source
- adapted by the authors

A SOCIAL MAPPING OF MY LOCAL

STATUS Categories	Number of people who are full-time	Number of people who are part-time
Function: Technical, administrative, clerical		
Length of Service 0–2, 3–5, 6–10, 10+		
Family Status with dependants, without dependants		
First Language English, French, other		
Race Aboriginal, People of Colour, White		
Requiring accommodation or not		
Age Below 30, 31–45, above 45		
Gender Male, Female		
Sexual orientation Heterosexual, gays/lesbians, bisexual or transgendered		

HISTORICAL TIMELINE

Why use it?

- to examine the tensions that occur in our struggles (for instance, political campaign, organizing, or strike mobilization)
- to learn about union/local history in a way that validates participants' knowledge
- to situate discussion of an issue or event in a historical perspective
- to link local issues/events to broader union movements and global forces

Time it takes

- For a group of twenty people, about 1.5 hours, including the synthesis portion

What you need

- historical "timeline" placed on wall
- large sticky notes or one-quarter pieces of coloured paper
- markers, tape, or glue stick
- activity sheet

How it's done

1. Introduce the activity (objectives and steps) and the activity sheet.

2. Divide participants into groups, with people from the same local/area working together.

3. Have the groups work for about 20 minutes, using the activity sheet.

4. Prepare a large historical timeline and place it on the wall, to be used in group reporting.

5. Have subgroups report back. Using the sticky notes, each local/participant places their "key moments" on a section of the timeline, naming the event, when it happened, and why it is important to them. Go quickly from group to group, without a lot of group discussion in between.

6. After all the sub groups have reported back, lead a large-group discussion on the significance of events, connections between events or issues, any contradictions between forces, any noticeable trends, and so on. Resist the temptation to give a "history lecture."

7. During the discussion, the facilitator and the large group may continue to add key moments to the timeline.

8. At the end, with the help of the group, do a synthesis of the key themes, highlighting the common threads among the stories, such as common issues, key forces (economic, social, political, ideological, environmental), major trends over the last five to ten years, or major gains or losses.

9. Connect the synthesis to the objectives of your session or program. Your wrap-up can be something like "celebrate our victories, reclaim our history."

HISTORICAL TIMELINE

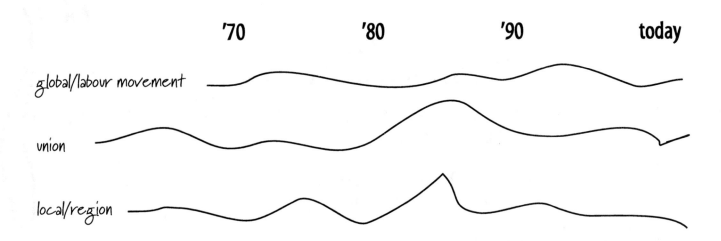

'70   **'80**   **'90**   **today**

global/labour movement

union

local/region

Variations
- You can be more specific with the exercise. Instead of the history of the local/union, you can focus on the history of organizing, on events related to a round of bargaining, or on a grievance, for example.
- You can simply ask people to talk about their experiences related to your workshop theme and then line up their key moments chronologically. For example, "Tell us about one inspiring experience you have had in union education that made you want to take action, and when it happened."

Challenges
- People might get stuck around determining the accuracy of dates.
- The exercise becomes simply a "narration of war stories," without analysis.
- The more veteran members of the group might dominate the story-telling; the greater the diversity, the richer the story-telling and the analysis.
- Facilitator gets caught trying to do an exhaustive listing of events.

Building in Equity
- Equity-seeking groups can form one discussion group and tell their story from their perspective.
- Step back from the exercise and ask, "Whose stories are being told? Whose voices are not being heard? Where are the gaps in our collective memory?" Then explore the implications of the situation.
- The exercise highlights the importance of "voice" as being critical to analysis, reflection, and action.

Source
- adapted by the authors from the Naming the Moment process, developed by Deborah Barndt and the Jesuit Centre for Social Faith and Justice, Toronto

ACTIVITY SHEET

HISTORICAL TIMELINE

1. Working in small groups, select 3–5 key moments or events that you know of either at the local and/or regional level.

2. Then select another set of 3–5 key moments that happened in your union or in the Canadian labour movement as a whole.

Guidelines
- Write each "moment" on a large sticky note: choose two or three words to describe the moment.
- Make sure you enter one moment on one sticky note.
- Use the marker, and write big and bold for everybody to see.
- A "moment" is an event that took place at a given time and place. (That is, don't say "recession," but rather name a specific event, like "Wall Street crash" or "closure of a factory.")
- Do what you can in the time available: 20 minutes.
- When you're done, place your stickies on the giant timeline on the wall, in the appropriate row and decade.

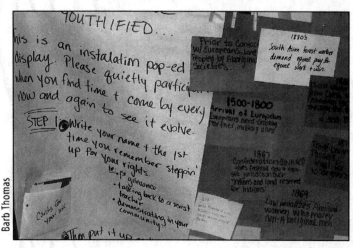

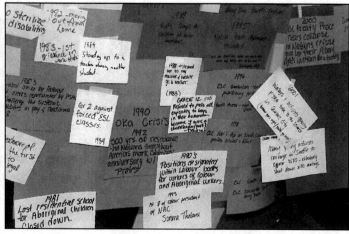

Examples of historical timelines

Barb Thomas

IDENTITY CELLS

Why use it?
- to explore the complexity of all of our experiences with oppression and privilege
- to explore how our identities influence our participation in our unions
- to develop a firm basis for coalition/organizational work together

Time it takes
- 2.5 to 3 hours

What you need
- a room where people can move around, with wall space for posting headings and flip-chart paper
- 8–12 headings, each written on a different piece of coloured paper—the "identity cells"
- for each heading, flip-chart pages with statements
- Magic Markers with each flip-chart page

How it's done

1. Post the "identity cells" around the room, each with a heading: sexuality, age, disability, language and culture; class; race/colour; place of origin; gender; HIV status; spirituality/religion; blank.

2. Introduce the exercise by saying that all of us carry multiple social identities; some of them are dominant and some of them are the targets of discrimination and oppression in this society. We want to look at the complexity of these identities and what it all means for working in the union. This activity will help us identify:
   - our experience of discrimination in society
   - where we have privilege in society
   - our experience of discrimination in the union
   - where we have privilege in the union.

3. Review the identity cells to make sure that everyone understands what they mean, and to see if there are other identities that should be included (body size, for example).

4. Place, at each cell, a sheet of flip-chart paper with two statements:

   - I know I'm experiencing this form of discrimination **in society**

     when I see, hear, feel_____.

   - I know I'm experiencing this form of discrimination **in the union**

     when I see, hear, feel _____.

5. Participants choose an identity cell for "discrimination" and record key comments (15 minutes). Facilitators note the numbers of entries at each cell.

6. Take reports from cells (30 minutes, depending on numbers).

7. Summarize the differences and common ground among the experiences of different forms of oppression (15 minutes).

8. Repeat the process, this time for the experience of privilege. Add a second flip-chart page at each cell with the statements for "privilege."

    •   I know I have privilege in society based on this identity when I (can)

        _____.

    •   I know I have privilege in the union based on this identity when I

    (can)_____.

    Because privilege is much harder to recognize, appearing to be "normal" when we have it, facilitators should provide a couple of examples of invisible privilege (such as being able to talk to a bank teller over a counter designed for a certain standing height).

9. Participants choose an identity cell for "privilege in society" and record key comments (15 minutes). Facilitators note the number of entries.

10. Take reports from cells (30 minutes, depending on numbers).

11. Summarize the differences and common ground among the experiences of different forms of privilege (15 minutes) emphasizing the role of "ally" (see INTRODUCTION).

12. Have small-group discussions of what these findings mean for union work (15 minutes), using these questions to guide discussion:

    •   Which forms of discrimination in our unions, as identified in this exercise, could we do something about?

    •   How can we use our privilege to work towards more justice within our unions?

13. Facilitate a brief sharing of strategies in large group.

Variations

- You can stretch this activity to a whole day, particularly if you are using it as the basis for coalition-building with a group that will be working together for a longer period of time.
- You can add a census to look at who's present in the group, and who's missing; and how multiple our identities are. Prepare a grid with a list of the identity cells down the left, and two other columns, "Participating" and "Could have participated." When each cell reports, note the number of people in the group under "participating" and ask who else could have gone to that cell. Jot that number down under "could have participated." This recognizes that people had to make a choice when they went to an identity cell.

IDENTITY	PARTICIPATING	COULD HAVE PARTICIPATED
GENDER	6	3
RACE	3	1
AGE	2	4
HIV+	1	1

Challenges

- People will be anxious about exposing themselves. This includes both people who are worried that they will be retargeted by the exercise of talking about their experience of discrimination, and people worried about being accused of having too much privilege. Take time at the front end to review the identity cells, and to add others if necessary. Stress that most of us carry the simultaneous experiences of oppression and privilege, and that we rarely have a supportive environment to explore them. This activity is about using the experience of both discrimination and privilege as a basis of action.
- People may want to choose several identity cells, but ask them to choose only one at a time. Acknowledge that many people could spend time at several of the identity cells.
- The identity groups will vary in size; there may be one person at "racism" and six people at "class." People can be on their own at a cell if that is the most important place for them to be.
- Ask people to be specific when they write on the flip-chart paper. For example: "I know I'm experiencing sexism when a man gets the credit for something I just said."
- Keep the small-group reports moving, so people don't get worn out.

Building in equity

- Equity issues are the major focus of this activity.

Source

- the authors, with Tina Lopes

TOOLS FOR LINKING NEW INFORMATION TO WHAT PARTICIPANTS ALREADY KNOW

IN TRADE UNION EDUCATION we tend to add new information by making a presentation. As a result, we have been experimenting with ways of making presentations more creative and interactive. (Among the activities described in the APPENDIX is an interactive facilitator presentation on listening and questioning.) As workshop tools we have tended to use the flip chart or the video rather than overhead projectors or power point presentations, which tend to be widely used by management to dominate our thinking. Even when used in union education programs, these presentations tend to be "management style," offering little opportunity for participation. But all of these are legitimate tools, if we can shape them for our purposes.

Tips for making the presentation interactive

The verbal presentation

† Ask the participants questions at various points.

† Have your main points visible on a flip chart or on cards. Add these points to any lists generated by participants.

† Ask participants to signal their relation to the points you're making. (For example, "How many of you learn best by reading a manual? By watching others? By talking with a co-worker?")

† Ask participants to post or organize information that you are presenting. (They might do this on a timeline, for example.)

Overheads or power point presentation

† Put any equipment off to one side. Don't let the technology control the class.

† Pause the presentation and ask participants questions.

† Use images with little text—and ask people for their reactions.

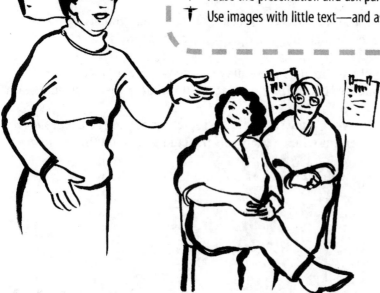

QUESTIONNAIRE RESEARCH:
A WAY OF AVOIDING BORING LECTURES

Why use it?

- to practise finding technical or legal information
- to clarify rights of and restrictions on management and union (in an organizing drive)
- to build member confidence to learn and understand technical information
- to avoid boring lectures

Time it takes

- 1.5 to 2 hours

What you need

- Activity sheet: for example (in the case we use here), "Researching the Law"
- Questionnaire: Labour Relations Act (or a sheet adapted for some other issue)
- *Labour Relations Act* (or other document you want to use)

How it's done

1. Divide into four groups.
2. Review the Activity sheet and the main issues raised by the *Labour Relations Act*. Stress that each group will be "teaching" the rest of us what they learn. It's okay not to be sure of the answer; simply mark it as a question and identify what is causing the confusion for your group.

3. Assign each group an equal number of questions related to the issues. If one group finishes answering their questions before the other groups do, they can continue on to do other questions.

4. Small groups work on their part of the research, recording their responses on flip-chart paper for presentation to the rest of the group (about 20 minutes).

5. Groups report in the order of the questions assigned to them (group one, questions 1–5, group two, questions 6–10, etc.). Ask the reporting group to cite the provision(s) in the act where they found the answer. Record questions arising, trying to answer these as you go. Often there is a contradiction between what the law says and what employers do. This calls, then, for a discussion of strategy.

6. Distribute any response sheets you have prepared in advance, and review any comments there that have not come up in the discussion.

Variations

- In member-organizing courses, we have designed a similar Questionnaire using four separate pieces of legislation: *Labour Relations Act; Employment Standards Act; Hospital Disputes Resolution Act; Human Rights Code*. We had four or five basic questions on each Act, with some directions on where to find answers, and each group was assigned a separate Act. This was not meant to provide an in-depth knowledge of these acts, but to break down the fear that many workers experience in trying to read legal documents; and to give an overview of what is covered under each Act.
- We've used a variation of this activity in anti-harassment courses, so that workers know what the human rights legislation says.

Challenges

- Keep the task manageable for each group (about four or five questions each).
- Review the instructions carefully, so that each group is clear on its task.
- Ensure that each group has something different to research so that its members feel responsible for teaching each other.
- True and false questionnaires are easy to follow, but they tend to simplify things. That's why, for each question, we ask participants to cite the exact provision of the law, and the questions that it raises.

Building in equity

- This task requires reading, but it does not require each person to be able to read. You can ask each group to put their members in pairs to divide up tasks.
- Encourage each group to find a way to use all of its members in the reports-back.

Source

- the authors

Quebec Economic Summit, Quebec City, April 2001.

Education for Changing Unions

ACTIVITY SHEET

RESEARCHING THE LAW

1. Leaf through the parts of the Act assigned to your group, marking sections you think might come up in an organizing situation.

2. Along the way, check whether you think the statements assigned to your group (see work sheet) are true or false, based on the text you have in front of you. Underline the "True" or "False" if the answer is clear. Underline the "Don't Know" if there is not sufficient information to be sure. Be careful not to answer based on what you think the Act *should* say.

3. For each statement you answer, enter the relevant section and subsection of the Act, and in the comment section indicate any issue you want discussed in the full group, such as the reason you are saying you "don't know."

4. Prepare to teach the other groups about the part of the Act you have reviewed:

    (a) the sections they should be aware of

    (b) your responses to the statements assigned to your group.

5. If you are finished early, continue with the rest of the questions.

Paul Keighley, CEP

QUESTIONNAIRE

Note: These are just examples. The questions should draw from the labour relations act that the union has to deal with.

"Employees who work in confidential labour relations matters can't join the union."

True ☐   False ☐   Don't know ☐
Relevant section of the Act:
Comment:

"Domestic workers employed in private homes can belong to a union."

True ☐   False ☐   Don't know ☐
Relevant section of the Act:
Comment:

"Where a union has been certified but still has no collective agreement, another union can apply at any time to represent those workers."

True ☐   False ☐   Don't know ☐
Relevant section of the Act:
Comment:

"The union needs to show that 40% of the proposed bargaining unit are members of the union before the Board will call for a representation vote."

True ☐   False ☐   Don't know ☐
Relevant section of the Act:
Comment:

"The representation vote is held any time after the union files for certification."

True ☐   False ☐   Don't know ☐
Relevant section of the Act:
Comment:

"An employer can legally threaten or dismiss an employee suspected of union activity."

True ☐   False ☐   Don't know ☐
Relevant section of the Act:
Comment:

"The union has the right to organize during working hours."

True ☐   False ☐   Don't know ☐
Relevant section of the Act:
Comment:

"The employer can use work time to persuade workers not to join the union."

True ☐   False ☐   Don't know ☐
Relevant section of the Act:
Comment:

THE TRIANGLE TOOL . . . TAKE TWO

Why use it?
- as a way of seeing connections between individual behaviours, and the invisible systems and assumptions that support them
- as a tool for talking about how power works
- as a tool for making a presentation in a way that's visual and participatory

Time it Takes
- 10 minutes to introduce it by itself; 30–60 minutes if you are using it inside another activity such as the puzzles exercise ("Puzzles as a way of introducing equity"— see the APPENDIX)

What you need
- two large sheets of flip-chart paper taped together and posted on the wall

How it's done

Note: We have altered this tool since we first described it in *Educating for a Change*. We put individual behaviours on the top as the tip of the iceberg, or what you can see above the table. We draw a dotted line between that point and the foundations beneath—the systems and the assumptions/powerful ideas. We have added "impact" because the impact of this triangle is different, depending on whether you're part of the dominant group or of the communities targeted by discrimination.

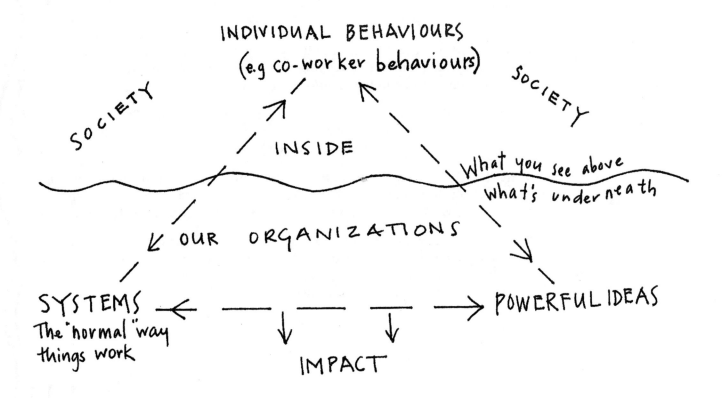

1. Write "INDIVIDUAL BEHAVIOURS" near the top of the flip-chart paper, in the middle. Say that most often when we talk about inequity or discrimination, we think about the offensive behaviours of an individual towards another person.

2. Write "ASSUMPTIONS/POWERFUL IDEAS" about two-thirds of the way down your sheet to the right. Say that our society is full of very powerful ideas about which groups are competent, which communities are smart, dishonest, lazy, business-like, civilized, and so on. We rarely speak out loud about this, but these notions turn up in jokes, in the assumptions of journalists who report news, in who we think of as heroes. Individuals are not born with these ideas. They learn them from living in our society.

3. Write "SYSTEMS/THE 'NORMAL' WAY THINGS WORK" to the left of assumptions/powerful ideas. Say that the "normal way things work" is difficult to identify—just because it's so normal. But inequitable systems are those ways of doing things that might look okay, but which keep producing the same inequities. For example, the employer may routinely give managers large raises and incentive pay. It may be "normal" to pay managers ten to twenty-five times the average salary of a worker, while a union has to fight just for a 2 per cent increase in pay. That is a "normal" part of the system of compensation for labour. The system is based on powerful ideas that even workers may begin to believe—that managers' work is worth more than workers' work; that managers need large salaries to live but workers don't; that being in charge of someone else makes you more worthwhile than a person who isn't. These understandings—all below the surface—often mean that managers think they have the right to behave disrespectfully to individual workers.

4. Draw lines between each of these points on the triangle, with arrows joining the three sides, pointing in both directions. The three points on the triangle are obviously connected, and they reinforce each other.

5. Write the word "IMPACT" just below the triangle, in the centre. The impact on different groups of people is different depending on whether you are exercising power (as in the case of the managers) or you are the target of that power (the workers).

6. Write "Society" outside the triangle, and the words "inside our organizations" in the middle of the triangle. Say that what happens in our society also happens inside our workplaces and unions, unless we consciously try to challenge it.

7. Take an example of an incident raised by one of the participants, or a case study you have provided, or the Christopher Columbus image used in the puzzles exercise, and help participants map it on the triangle. (See the instructions for "Puzzles as a way of introducing equity," in the APPENDIX.)

8. Summarize the main points:

- Discrimination and inequity are more than just individual behaviours.
- You can also see evidence of inequity by looking at the unequal impact—women get paid less than men for work of relatively equal value; there are few Aboriginal people or people of colour in the workplace, despite their presence in the community; all the union officers are white men.
- This does not mean that anyone *intended* to discriminate. But the normal ways of doing things and the hidden powerful ideas keep producing the same old inequities.
- What exists "out there," in our society, will exist in our workplaces and unions until we actively challenge it.

9. Give participants a chance to practise applying the triangle model to a case study, or to one of the puzzles in the puzzles activity. (see APPENDIX)

Variations

- This activity can be used to do an analysis of gender, race, (dis)ability, class, heterosexism, and other forms of power relations.
- We have found it most effective as analysis mid-way through a case study or the puzzle exercise.

Challenges

- This tool requires practice to use well; and it sometimes takes participants a while to be able to use it.
- It requires active listening to help participants locate what they're talking about on the triangle.
- It requires some flexibility to use it as a way of framing what participants have already been saying (see "Puzzles as a way of introducing equity" in the APPENDIX).

Building in equity

- This tool encourages people to examine the relations between elements that keep changing. It's a challenging way of thinking for all of us. Make sure people don't feel stupid because they can't figure out where something goes on the triangle. The point is not to rigidly pin things down, but to use the triangle as a tool for a good discussion of how inequity works.

Source

- the authors, adapted from *Educating for a Change*

TEN CHAIRS: VISUALIZING POVERTY STATISTICS

Why use it?
- to illustrate the inequitable distribution of wealth in Canada and in the world

Time it takes
- 15 – 30 minutes

What you need
- ten chairs lined up at the front of the room
- the latest statistics on wealth distribution

How it's done

1. Explain that this is an exercise to look at how wealth is distributed among people in Canada and in the world. Explain that by wealth we mean what you own minus what you owe. What you own includes what you have in the bank and any property you own. Wealthy people also own stocks and bonds and businesses as well as property. It is also possible to have negative wealth—you owe more than you own.

2. Ask for ten volunteers to come up and stand in front of (or sit on) one of the chairs lined up in front of the room. Explain that each person represents one-tenth of all households and each chair represents one-tenth of all of the private material wealth. If wealth were evenly distributed, this is what it would look like—one person, one chair.

3. Note that in 1993, according to World Bank statistics, the top 10 per cent of people in the world owned half of the private wealth and the bottom 90 per cent owned the other half. Ask the volunteer representing the top (wealthiest) 10 per cent to take possession of five of the chairs. The remaining nine people—representing 90 per cent of the entire world population—need to scrunch into the remaining five chairs.

4. Explain that the situation is similar when we look at the distribution of wealth in Canada. According to 1999 Statistics Canada figures, the top 10 per cent of households own 53 per cent of the country's wealth, while the remaining 90 per cent own 47 per cent. (So have the participants stay where they are.) However, the top 50 per cent own 94 per cent of the wealth. (Four of the nine people take up an additional four and one-half chairs, leaving the remaining five people with only half of one chair.)

5. But the distribution is better in Canada than it is in the richest country of the world. In the United States in 1997, the top 10 per cent owned 70 per cent of the wealth, while the other 90 per cent owned only 30 per cent. (One person moves to take seven chairs, with everyone else taking up the other three chairs.) If we broke this 90 per cent down, we would have a lot of people on the floor.

6. Ask: "To make this a more fair distribution of wealth, what should happen? What usually happens?"

7. The facilitator should emphasize (if participants don't make this point) that often those at the top remain invisible, while the rest of us battle it out with others based on race, gender, sexual orientation, age, and class for more space on the remaining few chairs. And the gap between rich and poor is getting bigger, not smaller. In Canada the top 20 per cent has gained 39 per cent more wealth since 1984 while the wealth of the bottom 20 per cent has shrunk.

Variations

- A group of CUPW worker educators created a long wall drawing—a parade of the distribution of income in Canada (described in Linda McQuaig's *Behind Closed Doors*, pp.35-37). This drawing could be adapted to illustrate wealth as well as income.
- Instead of chairs, you can make ten squares of one foot square each on the floor with masking tape. You can involve the whole group this way. We've run this excersise with floor squares with over eighty people.

Challenges

- You need to find the most up-to-date stats you can. This is not always easy for those of us who are not researchers. Try the research departments in the larger unions, or call on groups such as the Centre for Social Justice in Toronto or United for a Fair Economy in the United States (see the BIBLIOGRAPHY).

Building in Equity

- Offer the option of sitting on a chair to do the exercise.
- Focus on how our differences are used to divide us to the benefit of the wealthy.

Source

- adapted by the authors from *United for a Fair Economy*

PRACTISING NEW SKILLS AND STRATEGIC PLANNING FOR ACTION

SKITS: talking union to the member from hell

Why use it?
- to practise listening when it's not convenient
- to practise dealing effectively with common issues and questions raised by the members
- to deepen understanding of "members from hell" and their concerns

Time it takes
- 45–60 minutes

What you need
- "research sheets" on the issues you want participants to practise
- instructions on a flip chart or small-group activity sheet
- space for three or four groups to work separately

How it's done
1. Divide the participants into three or four groups. If you've got lots of people, divide into more groups, but give the same assignment to more than one group.

2. Assign a question to each group, and point group members to the research sheet, or collective agreement, or information on that question, and explain how the activity will work. If you don't have research sheets, ask the group to pool what they know on the topic and prepare to work with that.

3. Give groups fifteen minutes to prepare their responses to the question and to choose two people from their group who will play the fearless steward facing the "concerned worker." Their group will sit behind the steward(s) to support and provide advice. The "concerned worker" (the "member from hell") will be played by the course facilitator, or someone from one of the other groups.

4. You will probably have no difficulty identifying common concerns of members from your group of participants. Here are a sample few that always seem to have some juice:

Sample concerns
(one assigned to each group for research)

- Unions have outlived their usefulness in the global economy.

- What am I getting for my dues?

- I have an okay relationship with my manager, and I can get things done, but the union acts like a third party and screws things up.

- What's the point of having a union when they can't even guarantee your job?

- Unions are getting in the way of the financial viability of this organization so we won't have a job, let alone a union.

- The secretarial staff here aren't unionized and they got a raise just the same as we did. Why do we need a union?

5. Give each group a maximum of about five minutes to stage their "conversation." After each presentation, the facilitator pulls out tips for dealing with that issue with members.

6. After all presentations, ask:
   - Why is it important to "listen" to these members?
   - What can we learn about what the union is doing/not doing from what these members are saying?
   - What emotional impact do such members have on you? How can you limit their negative impact on you and other members?

Variations
- Each group can stage the whole skit using one of their own members as the "member from hell."
- We've used a version of this as the "nightmares" exercise (see *Educating for a Change*) in training worker educators/facilitators.

Challenges
- Keep things moving, and keep it light.
- Encourage activists not to dismiss all member questions and complaints as griping.

Building in Equity
- Read aloud any instruction sheets to everyone. If groups are working from "research sheets," suggest that a couple of people volunteer to read the content aloud to their group.
- Encourage the groups to choose "fearless stewards" who haven't done much talking yet.

Source
- the authors

ACTIVITY SHEET

TALKING UNION

Small Group

Each group has been assigned one common question or statement that members raise to stewards.

Group 1:   Unions have outlived their usefulness in the global economy.

Group 2:   I'd be better off without the union. I have an okay relationship with my manager, and I can get things done, but the union acts like a third party and screws things up.

Group 3:   "Where do our dues go?"

Group 4:   What's the point of having a union when they can't even guarantee your job?

In your group, you have fifteen minutes to:

1. Review any materials that may be useful in preparing a response. Share what your group knows on this question.

2. Make a note of the key points you want to make.

3. Select two people from your group to role-play the steward responding to a member who will make this statement to you, and who may argue with your response.

4. Prepare for a three- to five-minute real conversation with the member.

OPEN SPACE TECHNOLOGY

Why use it?
- to help a diversity of participants find common ground on contentious issues
- to provide a structured environment for new leadership to emerge
- to reassert the value of passion and responsibility as guiding practices for working together

Time it takes
- Preferably a full day

What you need
- a confident and experienced facilitator, who has carefully read the short book by Harrison Owen, *Open Space Technology*
- a minimum of ten people, a large meeting room with two blank walls, and plenty of blank paper and masking tape
- two additional meeting (or breakout) areas (or more if the group is larger than twenty people)
- flexible, buffet-style food available throughout the day
- access to three or four computers, with one person designated to pull the reports together into a single document

How it's done
1. Have people sit in a circle ("who ever heard of a square of friends"), with the facilitator in the middle along with some markers and blank cards on the floor. Briefly explain why you decided to use open space technology and how it works. Introduce the basic question for the day (for example, "What do we need to do collectively to better represent the members?").

2. Tell the participants that by the end of the day they will have a written report on issues raised and discussed, and don't let many questions bog you down.

3. Invite people to take a card and to jot down a sub-theme related to the overall topic—something about which they feel passionately and are prepared to lead a discussion (not make a speech). For example: "bargaing process," "training stewards." Have them sign their card, step into the middle of the circle and read it out, and then stick it on the wall.

4. Wait until plenty of topics are posted. If there are too many topics, participants can draw similar ones together into a common category, if they want to. If there are too few, wait until there are enough (which takes nerve). Open the "village market": people sign their names on the cards that interest them most. Sort the cards into the times and meeting spaces available.

5. Remind people that each group will have a facilitator as well as a recorder who, immediately after the session, will type the summary of key ideas and specific suggestions from the subgroup.

6. Get out of the way; and offer coffee, typing, and other supports to the subgroups.

7. Help pull together the subgroup reports; and write a short introduction. Complete compiling the reports within two hours of the end of the last workshop, and make enough copies for everyone to receive one (either at supper or early the next morning). Mark clearly on the cover page that this is a discussion document, and a collective production, which aims to bring new ideas into the internal discussions of the union movement.

Variations

- The activity can be done in a half-day, but loses a good deal of richness.
- It is well-suited to meetings with community and political allies, but should be used very cautiously with management given the power differences and risks of subsequent manipulation.

Challenges

- It requires firmness in shaping the process, and in holding the space for leadership to emerge.
- The facilitator must have absolutely no investment in the conclusions to be reached. Indeed, if the facilitator knows that the leadership has already made a decision on how to move on the basic question being addressed, the activity will backfire.
- It works best if followed by reflection or a probing of ideas on the following day, before the group moves too quickly into action-planning.
- Note-taking is often difficult with union representatives, both for technical reasons (such as inexperience in typing) and for social reasons (such as gender tensions, when the men articulate the direction and the women write it up).
- The final text needs to be vetted to ensure that individuals can't subsequently be singled out, with the possibility of political reprisals.

Building in equity

- Shy people can retreat and hide out at first. They need to be supported to step forward, and you need to allow time for them to recognize that maybe nobody else will take leadership on the issue that most concerns them.

Source

- Harrison Owen, *Open Space Technology: A User's Guide*; and the authors' experience in using this technique

TRIADS: practise listening skills in difficult conversations

Why use it?
- to get everyone practising active listening skills
- to strengthen skills in difficult conversations, such as first-contact discussions in organizing, challenging discrimination, talking with hostile union members
- to practise giving good feedback to each other

Time it takes
- 45-90 minutes

What you need
- short conversation starters, either typed with copies handed out to each person, or written on a flip chart and initially covered
- a diagram to help clarify instructions

How it's done

1. Organize participants into groups of three, preferably of people who haven't worked together before or who don't know each other very well. (If there's an odd number, you will have a group or two with four people.)

2. Explain how the activity works, outlining the following steps 3 to 6. After that you will come back into the large group before taking up other "conversations."

3. In each of the triads, the participants will carry on three consecutive conversations, with each person taking a turn as a listener, a worker, and an observer. Each of the three conversations will begin with a short conversation starter.

4. Each triad selects who will go first into the roles of the worker, the listener/organizer, and the observer.

5. Introduce the first conversation starter, reading it aloud.

6. The course facilitator keeps time as the "worker" leads off, and will stop the conversation sharp on three minutes, giving time in each group for feedback:
   - the listener to say how s/he felt it went;
   - the worker to say how s/he felt it went;
   - the observer to report what they observed.

7. In the large group, have a brief discussion in the large group of insights emerging from the first round. You might record these under the heading "Tips on active listening"or "Tips on a first-contact conversation" or whatever you are using this exercise to do.

8. Repeat twice more, using the other conversation starters.

9. Summarize key insights from the three rounds of listening exercises. Triads report a couple of insights each.

10. Introduce any points you want to raise that have not been raised by the participants.

Sample conversation starters
(for a potential member and a union organizer)

Conversation Starter 1

"I know there are some people who are really interested in this union thing, but I've been pretty happy here."

Conversation Starter 2

"My employer just told us that we'll be getting a raise, and they are looking into getting us benefits. I don't want to rock the boat right now."

Conversation Starter 3

"Since there's been talk in my workplace about a union coming in, it's already divided us. I like the idea of us all getting together and everything, but I think a union will do the opposite."

Variations	• We've used this exercise to practise dealing with a harasser, talking with management, member-organizing training, talking to hostile members. Often we do a little work on active listening skills first; other times we introduce this exercise after presenting an analysis of why some conversations are so difficult, and offering some ideas for different conversational strategies.
	• Sometimes we write more complex scenarios based on stories people have told us, and we use an observer's checklist to emphasize key points that we want to get across.
Challenges	• Take time to ensure that instructions for the whole activity are really clear.
	• Keep the activity moving.
Building in equity	• Include equity issues as subjects for the conversations—dealing with harassment, for example.
	• The activity is structured to ensure everyone plays each of the three roles.
Source	• the authors

ENERGIZERS LINKED TO COURSE CONTENT

An effective energizer . . .

- ❏ is easy to do
- ❏ is short
- ❏ deals with sluggishness
- ❏ is fun
- ❏ is appropriate for all of the participants
- ❏ allows people the option not to participate
- ❏ builds co-operation, not competition
- ❏ makes people more, not less comfortable

Barb Thomas

Stephanie Arellano leading an energizer, Montreal Labour Educators' Exchange, April 2002.

GROUP JUGGLING

Why use it?
- to build group solidarity in a playful way, including remembering names
- to change pace in a very verbal environment
- to create occasions for a display of different talents in a group

Time it takes
- 10-15 minutes

What you need
- diverse small non-breakable objects (for example, tennis ball, rubber duck, small plush doll), enough for one per participant (best found in a dollar store or novelty/party store)
- a bag you can use to transport and conceal the objects

How it's done

1. Have people stand in a circle; provide a very brief verbal introduction (for example, "The only rule in this exercise is not to throw hard").

2. Start by pulling a fairly conventional object out of the bag (a tennis ball, for example); call out a person's name, and toss the object to that person.

3. Ask that person to call someone else's name, and throw the object to that person. At the same time, tell people that they will need to remember who throws the object to them and who they throw to.

4. The person who now has the object repeats the action—but throwing only to someone who hasn't yet caught anything.

5. Monitor the activity to make sure that nobody catches the ball more than once in the initial pattern, and that the last person throws it back to you. Run the activity through a second round to be sure that everyone gets the pattern.

6. Halfway through the third round, pull a second object from the bag, and put it into play.

7. As the fourth round starts, add a third object, and keep adding until you feel the system is overloading (for example, one person is being loaded down, or several people are dropping objects). Encourage people to keep going, and begin withdrawing objects from play until you are back to the initial one.

8. While people are still standing in the circle, ask a couple of questions, such as:
   - how they felt when everything moved in sync
   - how they felt when they dropped something
   - if they noticed anything about the person from whom they received or to whom they threw
   - if they noticed how people were treated when they dropped something
   - how they felt about the laughter (which normally happens a lot)
   - how they thought the group dealt with overload (that's a powerful question, perhaps to be used a second or third time you run the activity with the same group).

Variations
- This activity is most effective when it is kept relatively short and repeated several times during a course (for example, at the start of each day, to set a tone or "get in sync").
- After the first time, have someone else start, guide, and end the activity. Ask the person and the group how they felt about that (that is, about distributed leadership in the group).

Challenges
- Physical and perceptual limitations can inhibit or embarrass some participants.
- It demands dexterity and playfulness on the part of the facilitator.
- It is most effective in groups of ten to fifteen people.

Building in equity
- If you see a person likely to have difficulty, brief them in advance and even practise with them. Then make your first throw to them.

Source
- Marjorie Beaucage and Natasha Goudar

RAINSTORM

Why use it?
- it works well as a closing exercise for the day or for the course
- it can also be used as an energizer during the course

Time it takes
- 5 minutes

What you need
- a large space
- a rainstorm text, if you plan to use one

How it's done

1. Ask the group to stand in a circle, with their hands free. Tell them that when you begin a motion the person on your left should follow when you make eye contact with them, then the next person, then the next person, until everyone around the circle is doing the same motion.

2. Then begin a second motion that will go around the circle in the same way. Again, everyone follows the person to their right. Repeat with other motions.

3. If you are co-facilitating, one person leads the motion and the other can read the text.

4. A final motion we use is the stomping of feet. When everyone is stomping you can end with a slogan, appropriate to the course or to the group.

A Sample Rainstorm Activity

Action	Sample text
Rub hands together	One person decides to organize.
Begin to snap fingers	More people get involved.
Begin to clap	We organize a union to make us stronger.
Begin to slap thighs	We work with the unorganized to make all our voices heard.
Begin to stomp	We join with thousands of others in the social movement.

Variation
- You can just do the actions, without the words. Introduce the activity by saying that we are going to feel how we are stronger when we work together.
- As a closing activity, continue the exercise by working backwards through all the actions until everyone is just rubbing their hands together again. This sequence leads to a calm sound and is a good way to end a workshop.

Challenges
- None that we have encountered

Building in equity
- The exercise requires no reading, and the movements are stationary.
- If there are mobility problems for any participants, do the exercise sitting down.

Source
- Suzanne Doerge and Denise Nadeau

ROSA PARKS

Why use it?	• to recognize activists in struggles for justice that have gone before us • to raise energy levels—useful as an after lunch activity
Time it takes	• 5–10 minutes
What you need	• a chair for everyone in the group • a copy of the story as a handout
How it's done	1. Introduce the exercise: this is the story of how one person can spark a movement for change. 2. Ask people to do the actions called for in this true story. 3. Read the Rosa Parks story.
Variations	• You can use the story of any activist who has been engaged in this kind of direct way in the struggle for social justice.
Challenges	• If some participants resist doing the actions to the story, it might help to explain that doing the actions both helps us move the blood from our stomachs to our brains after lunch and helps us listen more carefully to Rosa's story.
Building in equity	• The story we've used here focuses on the fight against racism and honours one of its heroines. • The activity can be done from a sitting position, and the actions can be adjusted so that everyone in your group can do them.
Source	• Canadian Union of Postal Workers Pacific region

Rosa Parks

It was late one evening in Montgomery, Alabama, when a seamstress named Rosa Parks stood at the bus stop. She looked to her left and saw a bus coming, so she waved her right hand and the bus stopped. Rosa climbed up the three steps of the bus, paid her fare, and proceeded to walk down the aisle. She shaded her eyes and first looked to the left for a seat at the back of the bus. There was no seat. She turned to the right and looked for a seat in the back. There was no seat. She looked straight ahead and still there was no seat in the back of the bus. But right beside her there was a seat. It was vacant. It was also in the white section of the bus.

You see, it was 1955 and there was racial segregation in Alabama.

Rosa had recently completed a course at the Highlander Center, sponsored by a union.

Rosa tapped her chin while she decided what to do. She sat down in the seat. She crossed her arms in front of her and sat staring straight ahead. The bus driver told her to move to the back and to give her seat to a white passenger. Rosa just shook her head and refused to move. Passengers started shouting racial slurs. Rosa covered her ears and refused to move. Finally they were approaching her stop, where she would get off the bus. She reached up and rang the bell. She stood up and walked to the front of the bus. She walked down the three steps to the ground. She sat down on the bench at the bus stop and waited. The police came. They made her stand with her hands on the top of her head. They arrested her and jailed her. She sat on a chair in a cold cell.

This brave action sparked the civil rights movement.

Rosa Parks, Dr. Martin Luther King, and others called for the Montgomery bus boycott. This resulted in African Americans like Rosa Parks walking great distances back and forth to work each day. For Rosa it was a long walk, so sometimes she walked very slowly. Sometimes she put out her thumb and hitched a ride.

Rosa Parks was fired from her job for her actions. She stood up for her rights that day. She stood proud and tall for an end to racism and for dignity and equality. Her actions were the catalyst for a new movement.

Rosa Parks continued the struggle. She marched in demonstrations for freedom. She sat at numerous lunch counters that refused to serve African Americans. She reached for the sky.

Sometimes Rosa felt that being in the movement was like walking in circles. Other times she felt it was like writing new rules on a huge blackboard. Sometimes it was like swimming with sharks. But all the while, Rosa felt that she was linking with people in an unbreakable chain for freedom.

By sitting in the white section of that bus, Rosa Parks made a better world for all of us.

Let's applaud Rosa Parks!

EVALUATION   CHAPTER 9, "Evaluation for Impact," lists tools for evaluation. Here are two additional ones that are among our favourites:

STICKER EVALUATION

Why use it?
- to provide a lively, playful assessment of what worked and what didn't in a course or conference
- to help participants recognize that different parts of the course are aimed at meeting different needs
- to provide facilitators with specific feedback on what participants want changed in future similar events
- to make a good complement to conventional individual written evaluation sheets, and form a good prelude to a more serious "go around" for closing a course or conference

Time it takes
- 20 minutes for a two-day course, 40 minutes for a five-day course (not suitable for less than a two-day course)

What you need
- Post on the wall a single prepared flip chart for each session (minimum six sessions), with the title and the name of the invited resource person if appropriate.
- Gather a set of differently coloured stickers (from a party store or dollar store) and, using a flip chart, prepare a "code sheet" indicating the significance of each sticker.

How it's done
1. Starting with the flip chart for the first session, walk around and point to each sheet in turn as a way of reminding people of each session, its content and process, reviewing and summarizing the course. Tell participants that this is your turn to talk, and they will have theirs; but keep it short (maximum five minutes).

2. Reveal the code sheet, with some flourish, and display the stickers, which will be used to evaluate the sessions. For example, gold stars might mean valuable; blue dots difficult; birds easy; hearts emotionally engaging; lemons irritating; dogs exciting (or boring, depending on your own views); or whatever. Have some fun in explaining them, but also clarify that this session will demand serious thought.

3. Divide people into groups, with each group exclusively responsible for one type of sticker; and set the groups loose to place stickers on the flip charts in whatever order they like. They can also write a couple of words about the session on the flip chart if they like, but that's not the focus of the activity. Let the noise rise, and chaos reign.

4. When people have finished, walk around the room again, starting with the sheet for the first session, and summarize what you see, asking people to correct you if you misunderstand.

Variations

- You could give each person two or three of each sticker, and ask them to place them where they want. This can initially work more rapidly, but is much less rich in results and can lead to lengthy explanations in the plenary at the end.

Challenges

- If someone present was responsible for a particular part of the program that upset the participants, warn that person to maintain a thick skin for this activity.
- If the objective of the leadership or the facilitators was to shake participants up, this activity risks crystallizing their resistance.
- Give people another opportunity to express their individual views on a written sheet, preferably with numerical scores on it and some room for people to write comments. This will reassure those for whom the activity seems frivolous.

Building in equity

- People with bad eyesight will have trouble with this activity, particularly in the closing summary. You may want to get large and brightly coloured stickers.

Source

- Collège FTQ-Fonds and the authors

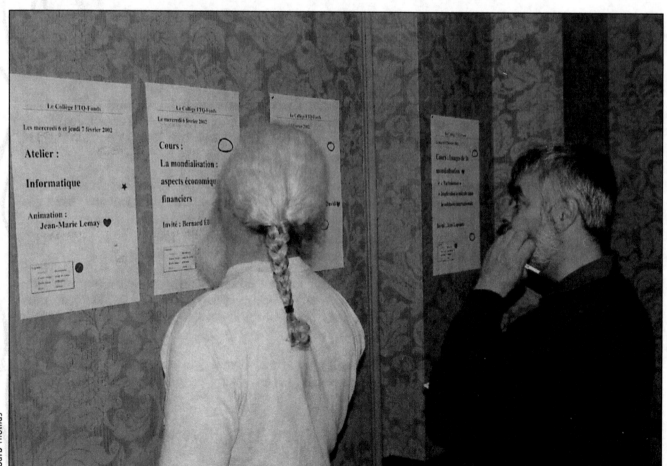

Evaluating the course, Collège FTQ–Fonds, April 2002.

CARD GAME RECONSTRUCTION

Why use it?
- to remember an activity or a session (in this example, it is used to reconstruct the day)

Time it takes
- 15 minutes

What you need
- a specially prepared deck of cards, one for each activity used, for each team
- wall space or a table for each team
- masking tape at each space

How it's done

1. Before the session, prepare a deck of cards—one card for each activity done during the day; or a number of cards to represent longer activities. Copy the cards so that each team can have a deck.

2. Shuffle the decks of cards so they are out of the order in which the activities occurred.

3. Number off to form three or four teams, depending on the number of participants.

4. Give each group a deck of cards and assign wall space or a table for each group. The groups' task is to stick their cards to the wall or table in the order in which the activities took place during the day.

5. The facilitator notes when the first team is finished. When all the teams are finished, the first team finished outlines its results, which are checked by the other teams; the other teams then follow in turn with their results, which are similarly checked.

6. The facilitator reveals the flip-chart list of the order of activities.

Variation
- Reconstruct one activity in particular. (For example, the game could be helpful after presenting the steps in the grievance procedure to be sure that people "got it.")

Challenges
- Make sure that one or two people in a group don't take over the task

Building in equity
- If there are several dominating participants in the group, try to ensure that they are in the same subgroup for this activity.

Source
- the authors

7.

Facilitation

CONTENTS

THE FACILITATOR'S ROLE
    Facilitation skills map....134
    Tips for equalizing participation through facilitation....135

CHALLENGING MOMENTS: USING MIND, HEART, AND SPIRIT
    Listening....136
    Asking good questions....139
    Developing "right answers" through dialogue....143
    Challenging uninformed opinions respectfully....145
    Political baggage handling....147
    Inviting without intimidating....150
    Interrupting power plays with compassion....153
    Exposing yourself as a learner....156

BRINGING PEOPLE (AND SKILLS) TOGETHER....158

Facilitate: to make easy, promote, help forward (action or result). *Oxford Dictionary*

WE THINK OF FACILITATION as what you do with a group of people, *in the moment*, to help achieve the objectives of the education session and move social change work forward. If you are about to facilitate in a meeting, workshop, or course, we hope—though this is not always the case—that you've had some time to prepare for it (see CHAPTER 4). Even if you are fully prepared, effective social change facilitation requires a readiness to work with the energies and conditions of the moment.

What we put forward here is a framework for thinking about the facilitation roles of the union educator; and we explore some of the more challenging demands of those roles by providing a case situation, a few questions to think about, and some tips—all of it aimed, as we conclude, at "bringing people (and skills) together."

THE FACILITATOR'S ROLES

Within the larger purpose of working for social justice, the facilitator navigates the tension between:

The TASK (getting the work done)—which might include sharing information, timing, clarifying concepts, summarizing, making decisions, learning particular content together in a course, and so on; and

The PEOPLE (supporting individuals and building the group)—which means both individual people who are learning and committed, and a collective of people ready to do something together. The work requires pulling together and building a group of individuals—people with different identities, unequal organizational power, different agendas and experiences—who can disagree but stay together.

Some people think of this as the tension between content and process—"content" referring to task, and "process" to people. Indeed, these terms are loaded with values and judgements: with "content" being perceived as "real," "purposeful" work; and "process" as being more fluffy, soft, "touchy-feely."

What we are proposing here is that there is "content" both in getting the task done and in effectively dealing with people and building groups. Both elements are necessary, real work in building a social movement. Therefore, good "process" is how the facilitator and group get the work done.

Public Service International

Asia-Pacific Regional Womens' Workshop, Seoul, Korea, 2001.

FACILITATION SKILLS "MAP"

PROCESS

THE TASK—getting the work done

- clarify/negotiate an agenda
- give clear instructions
- **listen** for problems, confusion
- **ask good questions** that draw out people's knowledge/experience
- help name whose perspective is being heard, whose is missing
- connect individual and group experiences to global issues
- focus discussion
- name/clarify the issues
- **develop "right answers" through dialogue**
- pose familiar problems to analyse and develop strategy
- make sure that reports-back move plenary discussion forward
- connect what you know to what participants know
- encourage visual and other ways of generating knowledge
- summarize key points/themes, and help identify what's missing
- encourage far-out ideas, concrete debate, creative solutions
- **challenge uninformed opinions respectfully**
- time/pace/schedule—keep things moving
- assess strategies by asking who's affected, and how, and who benefits
- be on the lookout for learning moments as they unfold, and acknowledge tension points
- solidify, synthesize, and celebrate new knowledge
- evaluate and keep revising the work; revise agenda as needed

- **listen**—to hear content, to catch feelings, to discern best intentions
- **ask questions** to clarify, to offer space, to encourage critique
- equalize participation; acknowledge all contributions
- **invite** people, **without intimidating,** to try something new
- challenge oppressive behaviour, supporting people to treat each other respectfully
- **interrupt power plays with compassion**
- work with resistance
- **handle political baggage**
- use humour that includes everyone, to build spirit
- **expose yourself as a learner**—make it safe for others to learn
- give and take feedback
- clarify different and common agendas in the room
- work the corridors—follow up in the breaks
- change a process that isn't working; take help from the group
- acknowledge/deal with different tensions

THE PEOPLE—supporting individuals and building the group

Tips for equalizing participation through facilitation

✝ Encourage a variety of people to report back from groups, and to take different kinds of responsibilities in the group.

✝ Try for a balance in who gets to speak, to avoid domination by certain voices.

✝ If only a few predictable people talk, break into pairs, triads, or small groups for some of the work.

✝ Vary the seating arrangements.

✝ Refer to comments made by some of the quieter people to encourage them to contribute again.

✝ Vary the work in a co-facilitation, to make sure that neither facilitator is stuck in a particular role.

✝ At the beginning, stress that all input has value and deserves respect.

✝ Develop guidelines for respect and participation and refer back to them if things get out of hand.

✝ Read the anti-harassment policy and identify at least two people to go to with problems.

✝ Use humour and stories to keep making it fun and attractive to participate.

✝ Ensure that participants can take on a variety of roles in the process—for example, as support people, observers, leaders of energizers, or sources of knowledge on different issues

✝ Pay attention to logistics, breaks, and the comfort of participants.

✝ Challenge disrespectful and/or discriminatory behaviours or comments, without attacking the person.

✝ Watch for power imbalances between individuals and groups of participants—for example, many men, few women, and the women not talking. Raise it as an issue for the group to address.

✝ Be prepared to stop the program and deal with the situation head on.

✝ Remember that the most important communication comes through your eyes, face, body gestures, and openness. You can say welcoming things, and your body can give people the opposite message.

✝ Be prepared to change the pace, the activity, the set-up if it isn't working for participants. There are hundreds of ways of reaching the same goal.

✝ Check to make sure that everyone can hear and see well. If someone has a hearing difficulty, make it everyone's responsibility to speak loud enough to be heard.

CHALLENGING MOMENTS: USING MIND, HEART, AND SPIRIT

Listening

> *Those who want to understand injustice, or be in solidarity with the silenced, must learn to listen carefully to the language of silence. Silent resistance needs to be transformed into stories of resistance.*
>
> —dian marino, *Wild Garden*

Why it's important

Most of us think of ourselves as good listeners, and yet most of us spend more time talking than listening. Western culture rewards good talkers more than it applauds good listening. And we get more perks for smart talking than careful listening in our social movements. Listening is difficult for social activists with points to make, elections to win, demonstrations to mobilize.

And yet listening is a critical skill for communicating with members, understanding what management is really saying, and grasping what is going on in group process. Good listening communicates to people that

- we care about what is happening to them
- what they have to say is important
- we have something to learn from them
- we aren't going to shove a solution down their throats
- they are part of developing a strategy.

Good listening also gives us insight and information about

- what the real problems are, not just what we think they are, or ought to be
- what really hurts, angers, moves, mobilizes this person
- what is blocking or enabling this person right now.

And good listening

- calms a person
- connects the different worlds/perspectives of listener and speaker
- builds consensus
- leads to better decisions
- is the essential ingredient to beginning new conversations.

AN EXAMPLE

It was the fourth day in a five-day union instructor/facilitator training course. Tensions had been building between a few of the men and women. The day before, in the brief practice sessions, Mauritza, a member instructor, had been upset by a couple of comments made by Jim, who had referred to women as "girls" a few times, and had done a couple of "wink/wink, nudge/nudges" with his buddy when the facilitator had taken up this point.

One of the facilitators had seen Mauritza when she was leaving for home, and she was visibly upset. When the facilitator asked her what was wrong, she had said, "Oh, nothing—just the usual. There's nothing we can do about it. We just have to live with it."

In the "hangovers" section beginning the day, the facilitator asked if there was anything hanging over from the day before that needed to be taken up. There was a long pause. Then Mauritza said she felt unsafe to practise facilitation that day. She referred vaguely to big tensions in the group.

The facilitator pressed her gently to be more specific, if she could. She took a small step and gave a small example. The facilitator encouraged her to say more if she had any more examples, explaining that the more specific she could be, the more recognizable the behaviour, and the more likely that people could learn. Mauritza then described the impact of the "nudge/nudge, wink/wink" on her, and why she hated being called a girl.

Then Jim, with arms crossed and red in the face, spoke. He said that he'd been bending over backwards not to offend anyone, and that he was tired of smothering everything he wanted to say. He was beginning to feel he didn't belong here and he wanted to get up and leave. The tension in the room ratcheted up several notches.

The facilitator spoke directly to Jim. She said she could hear he was angry but she hoped he wouldn't leave. She said it would be a real loss to the group, and she acknowledged important contributions he had made that week. But, she said, "You're getting feedback that some of your other actions are affecting people negatively, even if that's not your intent. This is a real chance to clear the air—if we can all stay in the room and really listen to each other and have a different kind of conversation."

Jim sat back, unfolded his arms, and the conversation continued until people had agreed that they would try to treat each other with respect; and agreed to stop the snide references to women and the indirect sniping. Mauritza said she thought her issues had been named and dealt with, which created the necessary conditions for her to continue to participate actively in the workshop.

What do you think?

- Where is the facilitator on the skills map: "Getting the task done" and/or "dealing with the people"?
- Why was it important to deal with Mauritza's issue?
- How did the facilitator demonstrate good listening skills in dealing with the issue?
- What else could she have done?

Tips for active listening—helping the other person talk

- **Listen for what is *not* being said.** Non-verbal cues such as tone of voice and body language are often more important to "hear" than the words. Most of us have had the experience of asking someone (such as Mauritza, in our example) how they are feeling about a situation or an apparent problem. The person says "fine" but the sound of the voice says something else—and so too do the arms, wrapped around the body, and the flushed face.

- **Invite information.** There are many ways to encourage participants to speak. We can provide an encouraging place for people to talk. Building in "hangovers" at the beginning of the day, for example, can provide a space in the program to deal with issues that might otherwise be left to simmer. There are many ways to show participants that we want to hear what they have to say: moving closer to where they are sitting in the room, making direct eye contact (when it is culturally appropriate to do so), and asking open-ended questions, for example.

- **Ask clarifying questions.** Good questions can help participants more clearly explain what they want to say. We try to avoid questions that begin with "Did you?" or "Were you?" They usually only get a yes or no answer—and may suggest that we know what the person should have done or should say.

- **Summarize key points.** Summarizing shows we are listening—and is a check to make sure we have correctly interpreted what the person is trying to say. In our example the facilitator might have said to Jim, "So you called the women in the group 'girls' and they told you they didn't want to be called that."

- **Reflect the feelings that you "hear."** When you pick up on the non-verbal communications, make sure that you then show you understand how the person feels. Hearing their own feelings named by someone else can help people clarify their thoughts. For example, the facilitator might have said to Jim, "You're upset because you feel misunderstood by the women in the group. Is that right?" Or to Mauritza, "You're angry about something. Do you want to talk about it?"

- **Speak to the best in people.** Acknowledge good intentions and values. As a matter of course, facilitators need to show respect for people without necessarily agreeing with what they have said. Acknowledging the speaker's good intentions may help pave the way for a self-critical look at a behaviour that is causing a problem. For example, "Are you saying you'd like the group to know that you respect women and that you didn't intend to offend?"

- **Highlight points of agreement.** This is especially important in union education, where we are trying to build unity and solidarity. While we need to address our points of disagreement, we need to connect similar ideas and try to establish common ground. In our example of Mauritza and Jim, the participants were all able to agree on guidelines for their behaviour over the rest of the course.

- **Listen at three levels: to key points/ideas, feelings, intentions/values.** When we listen we are trying to hear and understand the speaker's key points or ideas. But we need to do more than that to fully understand the situation. We need to listen and watch for other information as well; to grasp feelings (anxiety, fear, excitement, whatever), and intentions, values, or what's important to the speaker.

Asking Good Questions

It's not a matter of answering all the questions, but a matter of questioning the answers.
—Jojo Geronimo, in a paraphrase of Paulo Freire

Why it's important

Good questioning is a critical skill for social activists and facilitators. Good questions are exploratory. They open up possibilities instead of shutting them down. And, as we've seen, good questions are closely connected to good listening.

Asking the wrong question can shut people down. It can make people feel defensive, cross-examined, or suspicious. Careful questions can help us to:

- encourage information-sharing
- explore common ground
- clarify facts, fiction, stereotypes
- communicate that we're really listening
- communicate that we are also learners
- communicate that others have something to teach
- invite new or different perspectives or points of view
- challenge assumptions on the part of participants and ourselves
- demonstrate critical thinking skills.

An Example

The education staff members of a large union were having a four-day retreat. About one-half of the staff had worked in their jobs for over fifteen years. The other half were relative newcomers who tended to dread these occasions in which everyone seemed to assume they knew what their colleagues were going to say before they said it. One of the newer staff members argued persuasively for an outside popular educator to provide a one-day working session to strengthen facilitation skills. Two staff members gave mild resistance to the idea. They were worried that the time was already "too short to get the business done."

They brought in the facilitator, who worked with the group to identify instances in their work that called for better facilitation. One of the scenarios became the focus of an extended role play involving everyone present.

In this situation an education staff character (Carlo) was trying to work more effectively with a staff rep character (Sam) to implement union policy on providing local education around issues of harassment. An actual education staff person took on Carlo's role, and a staff rep in real life took on Sam's role. In the role play, Sam was resisting the overtures for education made by Carlos. Things got bogged down, and the facilitator kept intervening to inquire what was going on with each character and to find out what, from their points of view, might help move things forward. Sam, the staff rep character, kept saying, "He doesn't understand my situation." Carlo, the education staff character, kept trying new arguments, with similar results. Finally, in a time-out, the facilitator asked Carlo why he didn't ask Sam some questions about his position on education. Carlo said he knew this guy, and knew why he was resisting. The facilitator encouraged Carlo to experiment with a simple question, like "Why aren't you carrying out the policy on local education?" Finally Carlo said, "Sam, I don't understand. Why aren't you promoting education in the local?"

Sam sighed and said, "I know you don't like me, Carlo, and you think I don't believe in this harassment stuff. But you don't know my members here. You come in here with all your grand ideas, and you never ask me what the hell it's like to work here. Lots of members want more education, but with one or two exceptions I can't get any of the local presidents to take it seriously. And quite frankly, I've got so much else on my plate, that it's gone down my list."

Carlo looked at Sam in amazement.

What do you think?

- Where is the facilitator on the skills map: "Getting the task done" and/or "supporting individuals and building the group"?
- Is either Sam or Carlo trying to sabotage the meeting?
- How did the facilitator use good questioning to help Carlo and Sam work more effectively together?

Barb Thomas

Naomi Frankel and Martha Tracey, Regina Labour Educators' Exchange, October 2002.

Tips for good questioning

† **Don't assume you know.** (Ass/u/me makes an ass of you and me.) In our example, Carlo's incorrect assumptions about why Sam was resisting meant that he was unable to move union policy forward in that local.

† **Try not to prejudge what a person will say.** We also make assumptions as facilitators about the participants in our courses. For example, someone might make several rambling, not very help-ful interventions early in a course. We might be tempted to tune those kinds of people out rather than help them put their ideas together.

† **Don't ask questions that are really statements with the answers built in.** For example, "Don't you think that your members need more education?"

† **Start with easy questions.** It is better not to make someone state a view or take a risk right at first. Later you can work towards more demanding communications. A beginning, for example, might be, "What were you doing when that happened?"

† **Practise using more open-ended questions.** They can draw out more information and help the speaker to be concrete and specific. Open-ended questions start, for example, with "What," "How," and "Can you say/describe, give an example ..." The question the facilitator suggested to Carlo—"Why aren't you carrying out the policy on local education?"—gave Sam the oppor-tunity to talk about his situation.

† **Don't put individuals on the spot.** A nightmare for many participants is being asked a question by the "teacher" that they can't answer— a flashback to our days in school. Open-ended ques-tions are usually best thrown out to the whole group—not to an individual who is then put on the spot.

† Keep in mind those different points on the spiral model (see CHAPTER 4).

EXAMPLES OF QUESTIONS ON DIFFERENT POINTS OF THE SPIRAL

Practise/
strategize/plan for action

- How can you apply what you've learned from this experience?

- What changes can you influence?

- Who are your allies?

- What can you do individually/as a group?

- How will you work strategically from your social identities?

    - What

5.

4.

Start
with experience and knowledge

- What happened (who, when, where, how, to whom)?

    - How did you feel about that?

    - How did that affect you?

        - What did you do?

1.

Add
new information and theory
linked to what people know

- What does this new information mean in light of your own story?

- How does this framework connect these different experiences?

- What key concepts and ideas underlie these experiences?

- How does this analysis/information reshape your understanding of the issue?

3.

2.

Identify
patterns and themes

- Who else had the situation?

- Who reacted differently?

- What patterns/themes do you see/hear? What's the same/different?

- How does race, gender, class, age, language, sexuality or disability shape your experience?

    - Whose perspective is missing?

Education for Changing Unions

Developing "right answers" through dialogue

Why it's important

Fishing for the "right answer" is one of the most common temptations in education programs— and we still fall into the trap ourselves from time to time. While it's not easy to overcome, it is an important pitfall to avoid, for at least a couple of reasons.

- The facilitator could be wrong—or only partially right. Sometimes we think we have the "right answer," when there are actually several "right answers." We have had the experience many times of being surprised by participants who come up with other dimensions or points we had not thought about.

- Our goal as union educators is to build a movement, and to build the individuals within that movement. Asking questions that call for "right answers" can leave participants feeling stupid when they don't come up with the correct responses. We need to ask ourselves which matters more: that the participants conclude that the instructor is brilliant, or conclude that they themselves are brilliant ? Our work is meant to lead people to discover inner strengths and capabilities that sometimes they have not as yet recognized in themselves.

An Example

A union educator is training some worker instructors in how to teach union courses. It is the last day of the course, and the purpose of the first exercise is to identify ways in which learning was assessed during the course. To prepare for the activity, the facilitator has written the tools used during the week for assessing learning on cards in large letters (for example, "process stewards reports," "feedback on presentations," "parking lot").

The facilitator holds the cards and asks his question: "How did we assess learning this week?" A participant replies, "By talking with the facilitator." The facilitator asks, "Are there any other ways we assessed learning?" Another participant mentions the process steward reports (see CHAPTER 9). "Right," says the facilitator, and he posts the card "process steward report." The process is repeated, and the participants begin to try to look at what is on the cards to identify the "right answers." As they do so, the facilitator pulls the cards closer to his chest. The activity finally turns into laughter as participants crane their necks to see what is on the cards, and the facilitator becomes aware of what's happening.

What do you think?

- Where is the facilitator on the skills map: "Getting the task done" and/or "supporting individuals and building the group"?
- How does the facilitator tell participants non-verbally that there are "right answers" to his questions?
- How could the facilitator have handled the situation differently?

Tips for developing "right answers" through dialogue

† **Don't fish for "right answers."** If you want participants to understand a particular point, say it. Don't engage in a game of having participants guess the answers that you want people to give: for example, "I meant to highlight two points in the case study. What would you say those two points are?" In our example, the facilitator might have posted his points and asked for additions to those points. Or he might have brainstormed a list with the group, writing down the listed points on a flip chart and then using his cards to add any points not covered by the participants. The latter method has the advantage of showing people how much they know, because the group would probably have come up with most of the points on the facilitator's prepared cards.

† **Ask real questions and expect real answers.** Open-ended questions invite reflection, diverse opinions, and discussion. If the discussion turns up views that are factually wrong or potentially damaging, correct those points gently at the end. If the discussion turns up opinions that differ from your own, think twice before making that known.

† **Don't just write down the answers you like.** Recording points on a flip chart sends the message that what people have to say is important. When you don't write down someone's contribution you are giving out the reverse message. Even if you don't agree with the response, write it down. You can always come back to the point later if you think you need to pose some critical questions around it.

† **Be aware of how you signal "the right answer" or "useful comments"** by nodding, eye contact, or tone of voice. If you do that you can end up treating some people's knowledge or experience as more valid than that of others.

† **Be ready for participants to come up with new points you haven't thought of.** In our example, the facilitator had not thought about talking with the participants as a means of assessing learning. To be prepared for additional points from participants, facilitators could have some blank cards at hand; they can enter any new points on the blank cards and add them to the list.

Challenging uninformed opinions respectfully

Why it's important

Sometimes the views of participants in a course or session simply echo the dominant perspective, and effective union education does not allow these views to go unchallenged. Indeed, an important part of our education work is to challenge popular misconceptions. Opinions shaped by the mass media, for instance, often serve to divide us as workers and pit us against other possible allies. Sometimes only one person in a class may be brave enough to voice an opinion like "People would rather collect welfare than work." But it is highly likely that others in the class will have also picked up this message from the mass media.

How we choose to challenge misinformation can either help build the movement or alienate the people we want to reach. As educators, one of our first tasks is to protect the targets of the remark. We need to act as though some of those targeted by the voiced opinion are in the room. We also need to help people learn. If our response to an uninformed opinion makes a person feel stupid or marginalized, their original views will most likely become more, not less, entrenched. And we have to deal with stereotypes in a way that challenges them, not confirms them.

If there is no climate to allow misinformation to surface, it goes unchallenged.

AN EXAMPLE

In a discussion of current social policy a union member remarked that at least cracking down on welfare abuse was saving taxpayers some money. The facilitator asked the participant to say more about "welfare abuse." The participant began to vent about all those people who would rather collect welfare than work. The facilitator intervened gently to ask if anyone else had thoughts on this statement. Other people disagreed with the participant and said why.

The facilitator kept the conversation moving with questions like "What are our main sources of information about welfare abuse?" When people began to talk about the press and how it wasn't saying anything about "corporate abuse," the facilitator asked, "Does anyone have any information about this?" The discussion gradually moved to an examination of comparative statistics on the costs of corporate tax evasion and welfare fraud. The original participant was an active participant throughout and had shifted his opinion by the end of the course.

What do you think?

- Where is the facilitator on the skills map: "Getting the task done" and/or "supporting individuals and building the group"?
- How did the facilitator respond to the misinformed opinion of the participant?
- What were the key elements in the response that helped shift his opinion?

Tips for challenging uninformed opinions respectfully

† **You don't have to agree with or like an opinion to respect participants' experience.** In our example, the participant is repeating the assertions of right-wing politicians and think tanks—assertions that get a lot of play in the media. The facilitator's role is to help participants question what they "know" and deepen their understanding.

† **Whenever possible, involve other participants in the discussion.** In our example, the facilitator asked what other participants thought about the statement. This allowed the facilitator to challenge the misinformation without using the power of her position as "instructor."

† **Present an alternative, more critical perspective.** There may be situations when you judge that the class response would not challenge the uninformed response. In such a situation, you might then invite them to look at the issue from a different and more critical perspective. Although you might not get them to "agree" with you (and you don't want to engage in a "who's right" kind of debate), the more important thing is that they begin to question their "answers." Our goal is to at least subvert the complacent and uncritical acceptance of ideas that maintain a power imbalance.

† **Use questions, not statements.** This is one method to engage participants in critical thinking. In situations like our example, it can be tempting to launch into a short presentation (rant) to set the participant straight. The result is unlikely to shift the opinion of the participant and may shut people down. It is better to use questions as a way of adding new dimensions to the discussion. In our example this approach kept the participant and others in the conversation.

† **Avoid having someone who appears to fit the stereotype answer the question.** There might be someone in the room who has been, or is, a welfare recipient, or has family members on welfare. Here—as in the situations in which racist or sexist remarks are made—the role of the facilitator is to make sure that this person is not targeted or singled out in the discussion.

Political baggage-handling

Why it's important

Most of our progress in unions comes through conflict—in collective bargaining or on the picket line when talks fail. Many union activists have faced police and other forms of repression in fighting for their rights. Inside the union, activist leaders are involved in leadership contests that pit them against each other in tough elections; or they stand on opposite sides of key policy debates. So they come into the union education program with a lot of political history in varied sorts of baggage.[1]

In the union education program, this historical baggage (personal and/or political differences) can:

- create false fights;
- prevent listening;
- perpetuate old power relations; and
- make the classroom unsafe for learning.

Our goal in union education is to validate the experience of all, not just some, of the participants. This requires that participants learn to be "bilingual." The competitive, fighting reflex that they need in many parts of union life is not very useful in the education program. It prevents the openness needed to learn new ideas and ways of doing things. The facilitator's job is to create an environment that will encourage and support taking risks—making it okay to show what you don't know, as well as what you do know, or to express feelings of insecurity rather than pretending confidence.

But why not just ask people to leave their political baggage at the door? Because it is like asking people to leave their purses or wallets at the door before entering. Ignoring the baggage doesn't work in a passionate environment like the labour movement; and as educators we want to validate the right to dissent, to think critically. People have real disagreements on issues. The liberal conflict resolution model, which tries to avoid the conflict, is not helpful in these situations. Once the conversation starts, we as educators are interested in unpacking the baggage and critically examining its contents in light of the values and goals of labour education for social change.

AN EXAMPLE

At a two-day union staff retreat people were taking the usual positions. Up until recently, they had worked independently, and almost in competition with each other, united only in their criticism of the central office.

On the first afternoon of the retreat, the group was trying to agree on goals and an outline for a new basic stewards course that would reflect popular education principles. They had already agreed on the political agendas that would need to be addressed in the course, as well as what they wanted stewards to get out of it. They were in remarkable agreement.

Just before lunch that same day, one of the education officers had made a pas-

---

1. With thanks to the IAMAW (International Association of Machinists and Allied Workers), in whose jurisdiction baggage handling usually falls.

sionate speech about the need to emphasize the mobilization of the members. Three of his usual opponents then made speeches about how stewards had to have the basic tools to do the job, and that educators couldn't shove "the mobilizing thing" down people's throats. The group broke for lunch in apparent disagreement about a number of issues.

After lunch the facilitators started the session by asking people to line up according to the degree to which they thought the course should be a "tool course" (at one end of the room) or "provide skills to mobilize the organized" (at the other end). The usual suspects arrayed themselves at opposite ends of the line, with most people in between.

As people spoke on the issue from their positions in the line, the facilitators pressed each of them to say whether the goals and principles already agreed to were different from what they were now talking about. One person after another along the line expressed strong agreement on the established principles and goals.

Barb Thomas

Indeed, it became apparent as the last couple of people talked from the line that the entire group agreed on the key goals of the new course. It turned out that a few people had reacted unduly to the person who had made the passionate speech before lunch; they had not heard that what he was saying was simply a different way of saying what they themselves had previously said. They recognized that their responses had been triggered by each other's rhetoric. Despite the labelling of "progressive" and "reactionary," they had remarkable agreement on some new directions for union courses.

What do you think?

- Where is the facilitator on the skills map: "Getting the task done" and/or "supporting individuals and building the group"?
- How did the political baggage among participants show up in the course?
- What did the facilitators do to help people move past the baggage to look at real differences on the issues at

Jacques Théoret, Regina Labour Educators' Exchange, October 2002.

hand? What else could they have done?

Tips on political baggage-handling

† **Unpack the political baggage if it gets in the way.** Participants will often check their political baggage so that it doesn't interfere with the course. But when it does surface, it needs to be identified. In our example, the facilitator used the lineup as a way of helping participants visualize their apparent differences on the major goals of the stewards course.

† **Work from common ground.** To help build a movement, we want wherever possible to focus on our areas of agreement. In our example, the facilitator used questions in the lineup to help people recognize that their historical baggage had obscured fundamental agreement on the goals for the course.

† **Anticipate political baggage in your design.** Perhaps, early in the program, you can divide people into groups so that cliques get separated. You might have participants break into a wide variety of groups during the first day so they will work with a cross-section of other participants.

† **Have the group as a whole set ground rules.** Give participants a chance at the beginning of the session to say how they would like to be treated during the course. Later, if problems come up, you can return to the ground rules and ask people to assess how they are doing.

† **Challenge underhanded or coded comments or jokes as they happen.** Ask, for instance, "Is that something you want us to talk about in the class?" Or you might refer to the group's ground rules about being fair to everyone, showing respect, or not having side conversations, for instance.

† **Ask people to explain in-jokes.** You can say that maybe everyone didn't get the joke, so to make sure no one is excluded, "perhaps you might explain it."

† **Validate important fights.** If there is a significant disagreement about a strategy issue, you might want to get the agreement of the class to make room in the program to give the issue the time it needs. Your role is to help people have a constructive (rather than a destructive) debate, following the ground rules they have set for themselves.

† Help the group stick to the issue at hand. As a union educator, you may even have brought your own personal baggage along with you. It would be helpful to anticipate any problems along these lines, and if possible ask your co-facilitator to help out—possibly to take over in situations in which you have strong feelings that could impinge on your ability to carry out your facilitator roles effectively.

† **Be clear about your own position.** Although ordinarily you won't want to take a position that unduly or prematurely influences the result of a discussion, you still need to know where you stand on an issue or dispute. Self-awareness is an important tool in navigating the sometimes

treacherous waters of a political debate.

Inviting without intimidating

I celebrate teaching that enables transgressions—a movement against and beyond boundaries.
It is that movement which makes education the practice of freedom.
—bell hooks, *Teaching to Transgress*

Why it's important

Workers already know about the pressures to conform. That's one of the reasons they form unions. They quickly recognize the energy that suggests "We know what's best for you," "You're not one of us," "You're stupid," "You're not good enough," or "You'll be punished if you don't follow along," even if nobody's saying those words.

In the continuous work of building support to fight oppression and promote an alternative social vision, we often change the content, but not the strategies, used to mobilize people. The "troublemakers"—the potential leaders of our movements—can smell when they're being tyrannized to think a certain way: to adopt popular education as their new mantra, for example. They resist the tyranny, as good troublemakers should.

AN EXAMPLE

The group was a mixture of experienced union instructors—mostly staff reps—in their late forties and fifties, dubious about "new methods," and young, impatient women—mostly members—who welcomed the chance to get popular education training. The generation gap was apparent to everyone when the facilitators did a lineup by decade of birth, and then asked people to sit at a table, in a circle of tables, with people from their same decade. The veterans, both men and women, and the "newcomers"—all young women—gazed across the room at each other. One of the veterans said, "God, I can't escape my age here!"

Bob, a veteran staff rep, sat a bit apart at his table. He had refused to play the opening icebreaker aimed at getting people talking with each other and claiming the space in the room. The facilitators hadn't pushed him. When they were examining factors that helped and blocked people's learning, Bob had refused to get up with his teammate to post their points on the wall. He watched, he would occasionally comment, and he kept himself a bit apart. When the facilitators spoke to him at the break, Bob said he'd been teaching union members for years, that this "new stuff" didn't have much relevance for him, and would make his members uncomfortable. The facilitators encouraged him to keep participating in whatever ways he found comfortable; and he was clearly more relaxed when a facilitator was introducing a framework, or some new information, rather than when participants were talking. It was a full morning; everyone took the chance to speak; the energy was high at lunch time.

The focus after lunch was on "Bringing the Body to Union Education." The point was to examine where stress from different kinds of work lodges in the body, and how union educators can acknowledge and address this condition. The open-

Barb Thomas

Deborah Rosenstein,
Regina Labour Educators' Exchange,
October 2002.

ing energizer required people to stand in a circle, facing each other, and one by one say their names and do a common gesture from their workplaces. At each point the group would repeat the person's name and gesture before moving on to the next.

Bob was in the circle, which surprised a few people. When it came to be his turn, he said his name and then fell to his knees in a prayerful position addressed to the president of his local, who was standing beside him. The group convulsed with laughter at the playful way this staff rep portrayed his relations with the local's president.

What do you think?

* Where is the facilitator on the skills map: "Getting the task done" and/or "supporting individuals and building the group"?
* Was Bob trying to sabotage the workshop?

• How did the facilitators deal with his resistance?

Tips for inviting without intimidating

† **Keep connections open with a person who is resisting.** You might seek the person out during breaks.

† **Don't engage in bad-talking the resister.** In our example, the facilitator declined to express impatience with Bob or to develop a notion of good and bad participants.

† **Leave the option open to pass on an activity.** People have various reasons for resisting an activity. They may be unable to do it because of a physical problem you are not aware of. They may be shy, or they may want to send a message that this "new stuff" isn't for them. Providing the option of participation or not according to comfort level sends a message to all of the participants that they are in control of their learning.

† **Give people the time and space to pause and think critically.** Just as we encourage workers to think critically when confronted with management manoeuvring, we should also not expect them to turn off their critical thinking when they converse with us. Often people need time to assess and reflect, in the light of their own experience, what they are being exposed to, especially when it is for the first time.

† **Validate different forms of participation.** People may come in at different times in a course or in an activity. Some people are more verbal than others. Non-verbal clues can show you whether a person is present or not in the course. In our example, the facilitators encouraged Bob to participate in ways that were comfortable for him.

† **Don't let one person demobilize or sabotage the activity.** Focusing attention on a resister will inevitably sabotage an activity. In a group of twenty participants, one person who resists participation is not going to disrupt the activity and the learning process for the nineteen others, particularly if you communicate that it is okay with you if the person sits this one out.

† **Don't create unnecessary divisions in the room.** If facilitators use their power to pressure a person to participate in something that person feels uncomfortable doing, others in the class may well decide that it is necessary to protect the rights of the resister. Continual efforts to encourage everyone to participate in a way that is comfortable to them will avoid unnecessary divisions.

Interrupting power plays with compassion

Hatred is the fury of those who do not share our goals, and its object is death and destruction.
Anger is a grief of distortions between peers and its object is change.
　　　—Audre Lorde, "The Uses of Anger: Women Responding to Racism," in *Sister Outsider*

Why it's important

Repeated interventions, a loud voice, or continued mocking: sometimes a person tries to dominate the group, and the facilitator has the responsibility of intervening. The purpose of intervention is not to smash the power player, but to protect the target from harm and maintain a sense of safety in the room. It is important to stop the behaviour of the power player before that person gets too much invested in the power play and can't back down; and to keep others from getting scared of speaking for fear of being attacked. Facilitators have to find ways of interrupting power plays so that participants themselves can imagine doing so in other situations.

Effective union education strives to be democratic, but it is not neutral. Indeed, democracy requires an anticipation and interruption of power plays that would (re)produce relations of domination. One of the goals of the education—as well as an important part of the process—is to expose unequal power for critical reflection and action. This goal applies not only in the meeting or classroom, but also in the union, workplace, and, for that matter, rest of the world. All of us have been the victims of dominating actions; all of us have tried to shut someone else down, or to get the best of them.

Maintaining a sense of compassion means communicating to the power player that theirs is human—not subhuman—behaviour, and that the intervention is a challenge, not a judgement.

An example

In a workshop of labour educators, small working groups were reporting back on their discussions to the full group. One of the two facilitators, a woman, asked if there were any additions to the group report. Hoi Yee, one of the women who were reporting, said she wanted to talk more about the impact of the class backgrounds of labour educators on their work. She said she felt very tentative, that this seemed to be very risky to be talking about, but she had read some recent data on the subject and believed that the group might be able to discuss the issue in a different way.

Michael, the convener of the workshop (as well as a participant), interrupted Hoi Yee, saying he had important information and needed to correct her. He started citing data on the subject. His tone was authoritative, aggressive, and definite. The room went stiffly quiet. Nobody understood what had prompted his reaction. Hoi Yee looked surprised, and said maybe she should not have raised the question.

The woman facilitator asked Michael what he had heard Hoi Yee say, because she herself had understood Hoi Yee to be suggesting a new line of inquiry for the group. Michael repeated that Hoi Yee was just wrong, and that he had the information to correct her. The facilitator tried again, this time asking whether Michael had heard Hoi Yee's point as an invitation to dialogue or a criticism of some kind. Michael started talking again before the facilitator's question was finished. The male co-facilitator moved in at that point. He called Michael's name several times and asked him to stop talking.

The woman facilitator then asked the group to say what, for them, had just happened. Three women immediately said more or less the same thing: "Michael shut Hoi Yee down." The facilitator asked how Michael had done this. Another woman said, "He started correcting when there was nothing to correct; he bullied her. It felt very patriarchal."

The woman facilitator asked Michael what he had been trying to do. Michael said that he thought this was a teaching moment, and he had only been trying to correct incorrect statements. The facilitator said she thought Michael might have misheard Hoi Yee. She thought that Hoi Yee's intent had been to invite thinking on a difficult and very important topic. As a facilitator, she saw it as being her job to ensure that Hoi Yee and anyone else had a safe space in which they could raise difficult issues, and that while Michael may not have intended to shut anyone down, his actions had that effect on some people.

What do you think?

- Where is the facilitator on the skills map: "Getting the task done" and/or "supporting individuals and building the group"?
- How did the facilitators try to interrupt the power play?
- How did the different social identities of the facilitators influence this situation?

Tips for interrupting power plays with compassion

† **Don't corner people.** In a union education course everyone in the room is important to the movement. So we want to keep everyone in the room with their pride intact if we can. This means leaving space for people to back down with dignity, rather than having them feel backed into a corner where the only option is to take a stand (even when they can see it is the wrong one).

† **Don't allow abuse.** While we want to leave people with their dignity intact, we cannot tolerate abusive behaviour. As facilitators, we are responsible for ensuring that people in the room don't get hurt. Most unions have anti-harassment policies that you can refer to in these situations; but the bottom line is that we need courage to do the job well.

† **Don't step in too harshly too soon.** In the ideal situation, we want to support participants who have been hurt and we want to help the power player learn something. If we move too quickly to condemn, we may lose the opportunity to keep the power player in the room.

† **Be aware of your own feelings.** You need to be aware when your own anger or other feelings make it difficult for you to play your facilitator roles effectively. This may be a time to ask your co-facilitator to step in.

† **Call a break to lower tension.** As facilitators we also have emotions. Sometimes our own feelings about an issue or statement can be overwhelming. When we see that happening, it is an ideal time to call a break, allowing time for reflection by both the facilitators and the participants. This does not mean that you sweep the issue under the carpet. You may need to come back to the conversation to have closure.

† **Maintain a connection to the power player.** A break offers the opportunity to talk individually with the power player if you feel that would be helpful. If the violation of ground rules has been subtle, try to find the source of any discomfort and reaffirm the person's commitment to the ground rules and the value of the course.

† **Use your co-facilitator.** In our example, the male facilitator stepped in and used his social identity to help deal with Michael. But this approach has its pitfalls too (for more on co-facilitation, see CHAPTER 8.)

† **Use tension as an opportunity to learn.**

Exposing Yourself as a Learner

I believe quite firmly that we cannot not learn. In the sense that teaching always involves learning from the point of view of [the teacher], even if it is unacknowledged learning. . . . I also don't think we can teach our students to be challenging and self-critical, socially critical, if we aren't struggling to get better at doing that ourselves.

—dian marino, *Wild Garden*

Why it's important

Union educators have limited expertise in many areas. We might not, for instance, be familiar with all of the technical content of the course we are teaching; we might be outsiders to the region or union local where we are asked to teach; or the social identities of some of the participants may be different from our own.

An acknowledgement of our lack of expertise or a mistake can create a climate in which it is okay to make mistakes and a person doesn't have to know everything to participate. This is the kind of climate that can help build the confidence of participants. Asking participants to contribute some of that missing expertise also helps shift the traditional power balance between teacher and student towards a more democratic relationship. Allowing yourself to be vulnerable in front of the group can only happen if you have a strong sense of self and a truly respectful regard for others.

An example

In the third day of a training workshop for union educators, the facilitators were working with case situations to give participants practice in dealing with racist and sexist remarks on their feet, in front of the class. In the evaluation of the exercise, Sue, a talented worker-educator, said she was concerned that homophobia was not being raised in the course. Sue noted that none of the cases had people deal with homophobic remarks—and that she had experienced those kinds of remarks many times in union courses. She also said that the book used in the training, *Educating for a Change* did not deal with homophobia at all.

The two women facilitators looked at each other in dismay. They immediately confirmed that what Sue noted was true, and they thanked her for bringing it to their attention. They asked participants to contribute cases that could be incorporated into the exercise and asked for suggestions to add to the readings. They closed the discussion by reflecting on the importance of learning from those with social identities different from your own.

What do you think?

- Where is the facilitator on the skills map: "Getting the task done" and/or "supporting individuals and building the group"?
- What kind of impact would this situation have on the facilitators' credibility?
- What would others in the class learn from this incident?

Tips for exposing yourself as a learner

- **Don't be afraid to say you don't know.** In our example, the facilitators were not threatened by Sue's critique. There are many situations in which we as facilitators will encounter gaps in our expertise or experience—or in which we don't have the information requested by the participants. It is okay to say we don't know. We can suggest ways of finding the missing information or leave that up to the participants to discover themselves.

- **Invite participants to bring in new materials and ideas.** In our example, the facilitators recognized that some of the participants had more expertise and experience in working on issues of homophobia than they did. So they asked for their help.

- **Follow up the workshop with additional resources** identified by participants and/or yourself after the workshop. In our example, the facilitators decided it was important to ensure that the additional resources found their way into the next training program.

- **Make your learning from the participants visible.** When someone in the course brings up a point, example, idea, or analysis that is new to you, say so. It is a way of empowering people in the room, of communicating that they know things and that what they know is important.

- **Establish your credibility with the group.** How and when you expose yourself as a learner is also a judgement call. It's easier to be vulnerable once you've established a rapport and credibility with the group.

- **Acknowledge that struggle is part of the journey.** When the situation is confusing, it is only natural to be confused.

BRINGING PEOPLE (AND SKILLS) TOGETHER

AT THE BEGINNING OF THIS CHAPTER we introduced the tension between the task and the people. Most of the examples we've given involve "the people" side of the skills map—supporting individuals and building the group. This is not to say that "the task" side—getting the work done—isn't important. The challenge is to balance the two. But most of the "thorny moments" we have as facilitators are about people. How we deal with these situations will determine whether our work helps to build a movement or further erodes the confidence of workers.

In many respects, all of us are control freaks wanting to have everything ready, organized, and flowing smoothly—taking care of the "tasks." Balancing this quite legitimate concern with the people aspect of facilitation will always be a challenge. But sometimes we just need to let go, as in opting to "work the corridors"—taking time to talk to people at breaks and after class, getting into informal conversations even when we know we should be inside the classroom putting up the flip charts. We need to remind ourselves that ultimately it's not our "performance in the classroom" that is key, but the coming together of people, with all their messiness and richness, for a stronger labour movement.

As we try to balance the task and people requirements, let us not forget that we as educators are people too. We also need nourishment of body and spirit; we are vulnerable to enticements of power or threats of marginalization; we have our own thresholds of pain and fatigue. We all need to grow in our self-awareness and our positive regard of ourselves. We need to take time for self-care, if we are to offer care.

Because this work draws on all of our strengths and tests our limitations, we are almost always more successful when we work in teams—which leads to the subject (and the power) of co-facilitation.

Barb Thomas

Elise Bryant and Rodrigo Salazar,
Montreal Labour Educators' Exchange, April 2002.

The Power of Co-facilitation

CONTENTS

WHY AND WHEN TO CO-FACILITATE....159

TEN COMMON BLIPS AND SOME TIPS....160

Despite our best efforts we often reproduce the same patterns. For example, in our training programs, men are highly rated for clarity and passion in communicating the union message, whether or not they listen. The women are highly rated for having good rapport with participants.
—Johanne Deschamps, Director of Education,
FTQ (Fédération des travailleurs et travailleuses du Québec)

WHY AND WHEN TO CO-FACILITATE?

Why co-facilitate?

Why would a union use two facilitators when a lone facilitator is cheaper, easier to schedule, and can wing it without having to consult anyone? Lone facilitators don't have to deal with all the hassles involved in getting along with a co-facilitator who has different expectations and ways of operating from themselves.

Lone facilitation is still the most frequent practice in unions, for all the above reasons and because . . . well, it's always been done that way. Given limited internal resources, "doubling up" seems like a luxury. Sometimes the issue is one of power or insecurity. For some, the course is "their course" to design and implement, and nobody else can or should do the work. Old assumptions still hold sway about whose knowledge or expertise is valuable, and who can or can't facilitate.

Still, there are many pragmatic reasons to adopt co-facilitation in a union that is giving more emphasis to mobilizing. Co-facilitation leads to better education, and better results. It also provides a chance for:

- veterans to teach and coach new facilitators, and thus expand the pool of educators;
- new methods of learning to be introduced without having to convince veterans that they need training;
- members to begin facilitating with staff, in a period of shifting roles of staff and members;
- participants to learn from the skills and knowledge of two instead of one facilitator;

- mixed identity teams—men and women, white people and people of colour—to model ways of working together, and to blend their experience and knowledge;
- facilitators to model learning from each other; no one person has all the skills and knowledge;
- facilitators to stay fresh, and the participants to feel a sustained energy in a long course;
- new thinking to emerge about the course or conference through joint planning; co-facilitators can give each other feedback;
- new relations and capacity inside the union to emerge.

When to co-facilitate

We choose to co-facilitate whenever we can, for all the reasons we've already cited. But co-facilitation is particularly important in these situations:

- new or pilot courses (where you need to make revisions after the pilot)
- longer courses (several days)
- difficult or complex issues or themes to address
- high-risk situations or anticipated higher than usual tensions within the group
- the group is larger than usual
- the group is multisectoral or from different regions.

TEN COMMON BLIPS AND SOME TIPS

SMOOTH CO-FACILITATION BETWEEN TWO ACTIVISTS who have different levels of experience, different social identities, and different power and influence in the union does not just happen. Co-facilitation calls for careful planning and close attention to internal dynamics, difficult to ensure in a union stretched to respond to so many external pressures.

To begin with, we assume that you and your co-facilitator are "equal" in terms of your formal roles as facilitator, whether as staff or as a member, and regardless of differences in experience. When one person is formally designated a "mentor" and the other is assigned to a "developmental situation" within an organizational context, there would be different expectations.

Not all tensions between co-facilitators can be resolved. Sometimes people don't like each other, or they don't respect each other's methods. Sometimes they are political rivals or have a history they can't put behind them.

In most cases, though, people can work through tensions. As an aid to this work we outline, below, some common difficulties, and some tips we've found helpful. Please note that all of the ten scenarios are focused on our (or your) co-facilitator (who, for ease of writing, is alternately female and male). But in each case our own behaviour could well be contributing to the co-facilitator problems; or perhaps we ourselves might instead be the focus of some or all of the problems.

1. Your co-facilitator doesn't feel any preparation is necessary

What is going on?   Your co-facilitator may be overwhelmed with other work, or bored with the course after teaching it so many times; it may be a matter of asserting authority and veteran status, or a lack of familiarity with how to have a planning meeting, and a sense of unease about revealing this. There may be other dynamics going on, including gender and race politics. Whether your facilitator is mindful or unconscious of what she is doing, it will have an impact on you and the quality of the course.

Some tips   ✝ Start by giving the benefit of the doubt, by assuming there is a good reason for the lack of preparation, and ask for an explanation.

✝ Don't be defensive about wanting preparation time. Give specific reasons for why you want to prepare; given that you're working together, it's really important to co-ordinate things. For example:

- you've never taught together and need to divide up the work;
- there are changes needed, and you need to discuss them;
- problems occurred last time, and you want to avoid them this time;
- you need help in thinking through particular sections;
- the union is encouraging more prep time to improve the quality of courses.

✝ Try to accommodate the other person without erasing yourself. For example, if no other time is available, see if you can get her to arrive a few hours early before the course starts, perhaps to prepare flip charts and set up the room.

✝ Make a list of the preparation that you think is necessary, and e-mail or fax it to your co-facilitator, asking which parts she wants to do, while being careful not to impose.

✝ If you still have problems, say that you are going to be preparing for the course at certain times and encourage your co-facilitator to join you. Keep it as light as you can. You'll need to keep the relationship open in order to teach with her.

Public Service International

Asia-Pacific Regional Womens' Workshop, Seoul, Korea, 2001.

2. Your co-facilitator doesn't show up and you've only prepared your parts to teach

What is going on? It could be any one of a thousand things. (In one instance a co-facilitator had a horrible car accident on her way to the training site.) The main point is that you've got to do the course by yourself and you're only partially prepared.

Some tips

† Let participants know your co-facilitator couldn't attend, which means there will have to be some adjustments to the program.

† Turn your mind to the participants, and pay full attention to the opening session. If people have a good experience here, they'll help you out along the way. (See "Openings" in CHAPTER 6, "Our Favourite Union Education Activities.")

† Find out if there are participants with expertise in areas in which you feel weak, and enlist their help in selected sections.

† You'll be working late to review material. What else is new?

† Figure out ways to rejig the course so that participants benefit from the expertise you do bring. Work from the sections and activities that you feel most comfortable with. Be sure to try a couple that are new.

† In future—we'll just say it once—you need to be familiar with the whole course.

† As soon as possible, find out what happened to your co-facilitator.

3. Your co-facilitator keeps interrupting and taking over a piece you're facilitating

What is going on? Your co-facilitator might be trying to show off how much he knows. He might not have any confidence in your ability or might be completely unconscious of his own behaviour. He might think he is being supportive, or he might be trying to signal to you that something isn't working. Or he might be overwhelmingly passionate about the issue.

Some tips

† Stop and ask yourself how it's hurting you and your facilitation. What is it saying about your relationship with your co-facilitator?

† Don't let it fester. Deal with it as soon as there's a break.

† Try not to jump to the conclusion that he is a jerk right away, no matter how irritating his behaviour is.

† At the break, ask him if he knows that he is interrupting a lot. Explain that it's having an impact on you. If it's a signal that something needs to be changed, work it out together. If it's an unconscious habit, ask him to raise his hand before he says something, and that you will recognize him along with the other participants you're trying to get to speak.

✝ If the behaviour continues, talk to him again, on the side, about the impact it's having on you, and on your ability to ensure broad participation. Mention any other dynamics that may be at play here—competition, unconscious racism or sexism, or other forms of discrimination. Do it matter-of-factly, and stick to the behaviour, rather than attacking the person. Stay with the impact.

✝ If he still continues, stop his interruption when it begins, by saying that you know he has something to say, but you're going to ask him to hold it until some of the participants have had a chance to speak.

4. Your co-facilitator wants you to do all the facilitation, while she just writes on the flip chart

What is going on? Your co-facilitator might lack confidence, might think you're a better facilitator, might be afraid of making a mistake, or might be feeling intimidated by you. Does she feel that you have the "controls"? People who are the targets of discrimination may also anticipate harsher criticism and more risks in learning on their feet. Or your co-facilitator might just want to relax.

Some tips

✝ Let it be for the first session or two; then review the situation to see how you might change roles in another session.

✝ Find out whether there is something in the situation (or your relationship) that's making your facilitator less active, and try to deal with that.

✝ If the conditions and relationship are okay, find out what she feels safe trying, and encourage her to start with that.

✝ Talk through the risks she feels in facilitating. Find out specific ways you can support her—for example, not interrupting when she is facilitating; providing feedback and suggestions in break time; writing for her on the flip chart; agreeing to share the facilitation when she signals that she needs help.

✝ Make your own slips and mistakes transparent so that they become a source of learning not just for yourself but for your co-facilitator and participants. This creates a climate in which it's safer for everyone to try new things.

✝ Don't get stuck in your impatience at the extra effort. The development of people's capacity is the key purpose of union education, including both you and your co-facilitator.

5. Your co-facilitator appears to agree with a homophobic remark made by a participant

What is going on? Your co-facilitator might actually agree with the remark; he might not have recognized it as homophobic; he might not agree with the remark but doesn't know what to do; he might not agree but doesn't want to irritate the particular participant.

Some tips

† Remember that letting the remark go by without comment will hurt people who might be its targets; this could create a climate in which other such remarks seem acceptable; communicate that facilitators feel no responsibility for creating a safe climate; leave the person who made the remark free to do it again.

† Don't jump to conclusions about your co-facilitator; but quickly consider whether you can intervene in a way that:
- does not undermine either your co-facilitator or the participant;
- turns it into a moment in which everyone can learn;
- includes yourself as a learner;
- suggests a different way of talking.

† If possible, raise your hand, get recognized by your co-facilitator, and say something like: "I was uncomfortable with what you said, Sam. I know you didn't intend it, but it seemed to be putting down lesbians because . . . I would have heard it differently if you'd said . . . We're all learning about assumptions we've taken for granted all our lives. For example, I just learned last week that . . ." Say that none of us thinks of ourselves as a harasser, but whether intended or not, these behaviours have the impact of harassment. They are outlined as such in the union's harassment policy, and all of us have a responsibility to help each other avoid harassment. It's not just your opinion; it's union policy.

† If for some reason it's not possible to say something at the moment, talk to your facilitator at the break and signal that one or both of you need to come back to that remark and deal with it.

† After the break, return to the remark with some version of the suggestion above.

† If your co-facilitator agrees with the remark and is hostile to any intervention on your part, remind him of the harassment policy and make it clear that this is not a debate between you and him. It's union policy and you both have a responsibility to implement it.

† At the end of the session or day, do a quick review and include the incident.

6. Your co-facilitator thinks she can rest while you're facilitating, and she starts reading the newspaper, turning the pages loudly; or simply leaves the room

What is going on?

Your co-facilitator might feel irrelevant, bored, competitive, ticked off about something. She might be expressing confidence in your ability to facilitate, and/or have a very limited notion of co-facilitation.

Some tips

✝ Say quite loudly that you're going to "be drawing on Georgia's expertise in a moment," which should alert your co-facilitator. Then ask a question that requires her to respond.

✝ Talk it through at break, by asking why she is withdrawing from the process. You could learn something important: that you're taking too much responsibility, for instance, or that she feels left out. You will need to respond to the feedback and be prepared to change the ways things are working.

✝ If your co-facilitator is just wanting a break, explain the impact it has on you; for example, that it's distracting, that you feel abandoned by her, that you and the participants can't benefit from her eyes and ears on the topic, that if you flounder you can't count on her help. Work out a way that she can get a break and still remain available and helpful when you are facilitating.

Barb Thomas

Adriane Paavo and Dorothy Wigmore ,
Regina Labour Educators' Exchange, October 2002.

7. Participants are tuning out your co-facilitator, and he doesn't seem to notice

What is going on? It might be the time of day, or people might need a break. Your co-facilitator might be lecturing too much, or confusing people. There are any number of reasons as to why people might be tuning out. But there's a definite problem if your co-facilitator isn't doing anything about it. You can't be sure that he doesn't notice. He might just be trying to stick it out.

Some tips

✝ First, check to see if you're reading the group properly—how widespread is the problem?

✝ Get your co-facilitator's attention and say, "I'm noticing the low energy in the room. It could be the heat or the time of day. Are people needing an energizer or a break before we continue?" Participants will usually be grateful, and tell you what they need. And this step may fix the problem.

✝ If there is a larger problem, at break time check with your co-facilitator about whether he noticed the same problem. See if you can break up the session even more between the two of you; possibly the participants will be more energized by the variety. Check to see if the activity is just not working and needs to be changed. Agree whether you might ask participants for feedback and suggestions.

✝ Check informally with a couple of participants to see if there's anything you should know, such as unresolved issues from an earlier session.

✝ If your co-facilitator is reluctant to make substantial changes in the program or process, try to get agreement on having more frequent energizers or on doing a joint monitoring of the energy in the room.

Asia-Pacific Regional Womens' Workshop, Seoul, Korea, 2001.

Public Service International

8. Participants are getting restless and raising questions with your co-facilitator, and she is getting defensive, which only makes the situation worse

What is going on? The activity simply may not be working, or it may be inappropriate to the group. Or participants may be experiencing your co-facilitator as being too rigid or concerned with right and wrong answers. Political rivalries are also always a possibility.

Some tips

T Signal to your co-facilitator that you'd like to speak, and respond to one of the questions, taking the heat off your partner and showing solidarity with her.

T Suggest a break and talk to your co-facilitator about what she thinks is going on. Strategize.

T Interrupt the dynamic by saying that you're a little puzzled by the energy in the room. Is there something that's not working that *we* need to fix. Participants may offer concrete suggestions, or they may name what's going on, or they may chuckle a little and back off.

T See the tips for point no. 7, when participants are tuning out.

T Or do nothing. Maybe it's only a matter of time; your co-facilitator may be working through a process, and your intervention might be premature or disruptive.

9. You feel your co-facilitator knows much more than you do, and will judge you if you make a mistake

What is going on? It may be true—your partner does knows more than you do; and he may judge you, because he wants everything to be perfect. Still, it may be you who is afraid of making a mistake. We know of no facilitators who don't make mistakes.

Some tips

T Remember your strengths—what you can contribute. Acknowledge your co-facilitator's strengths, as well.

T Talk it over with your co-facilitator. Be frank with each other about strengths, vulnerabilities, and trouble spots.

T Decide how to support each other so that you get to work with your strengths and improve your weaknesses.

T Ask your partner for help when you need it. It's a measure of good partnership to ask, to give help, and to receive it.

T When you make a mistake, go easy on yourself, and ask your partner to do the same. Be playful about it.

T After a session, check in with each other about what you both thought about the co-facilitation.

10. Your co-facilitator is taking twice as long as anticipated to do her piece and doesn't seem to be aware of the time

What is going on?   The activity might be working so well that people are really engaged in learning from each other. In that case, the "overtime problem" is really a tribute to the design and the facilitation. It is also possible that loose ends from preceding sessions were being taken up in this section. Or the design might be flawed in the first place, with an unrealistic time frame. Then again, your co- facilitator may be ego-tripping and giving all her best speeches, eating into the next portion of the course, which you consider to be crucial. Perhaps your partner is floundering, and doesn't know how to get out of her activity.

Some tips   † Agree on some cues for timing and spotting trouble ahead of time.

† Assess the situation. If the activity is working well:

- signal to keep going, and perhaps reallocate roles at the break so that the facilitation can be shared more equitably;
- drop something from the middle of the session so that you can summarize and leave people feeling unrushed and satisfied with the work they've done.

† If your co-facilitator's ego is a problem:

- check whether the session's objectives are being met by your partner's behaviour, and whether participants are gaining from the overtime. If good things are happening, hold your fire;
- signal the time to your partner, and wait;
- talk to your partner at break, indicating the effect on you, and perhaps reallocate the facilitation;
- if the behaviour is chronic, or your signals are being ignored, you can raise your hand during the session, and do a time check by saying something like, "Joan, I'm just doing a bit of a time check. If we continue, we'll need to drop something. Perhaps we can check with the group, to see how people's needs will best be served."

Tips on co-facilitation: the "don'ts and the do's"

The "don'ts"

- ✘ Don't try to "save" your co-facilitator.
- ✘ Don't bail on your partner by:
    - taking a long break
    - not showing up
    - not being prepared
    - not helping out.
- ✘ Don't have a "hierarchy" (one of you being more important than the other).
- ✘ Don't re-teach the material your co-facilitator has already covered.
- ✘ Don't be afraid of silence and don't try to fill in the void, especially when your co-facilitator is the lead.
- ✘ Don't distract participants when you're not facilitating.
- ✘ Don't leave details to chance.
- ✘ Don't tune out from the conversation in the room.

"The do's"

Before the event

Above all, make sure you and your co-facilitator have a clear agreement on the design, methodology, scheduling, and materials; on your respective roles, and how you will work together. These agreements should be based on a process of negotiation and a "contract to co-facilitate." Aim to develop a common ground around key values of co-facilitation, paying attention to issues of power and differences in location (gender, race, education, experience). More specifically:

✔ Take time to plan, design, and prepare, together if possible.

✔ Know your own material and your partner's material.

✔ Decide in advance how you will divide the work.

✔ Agree on cues for when you get in trouble, when you blank out, when the time is up, or to let you know how you are doing.

✔ Agree in advance on how you will support each other in flip chart posting and writing.

✔ Be clear on how you will deal with disagreements between each other.

✔ Agree in advance about when and how to come in when the other person is "on."

✔ Be frank with each other about strengths, vulnerabilities, and different styles.

✔ Discuss your different styles and how to use them best.

✔ Agree on how to deal with sexism, racism, or other problems as they arise, taking into account your identities (race, gender, age, sexual orientation, staff or member).

At the event

✔ Decide on where you will sit so that you don't trip over each other.

✔ Set up equipment so that both facilitators are visible, but the focus is on one person.

✔ Ask your partner for help when you need it.

✔ The co-facilitator who is "off" should watch the room.

✔ Be diplomatic in your responses to a co-facilitator who gives incorrect information.

✔ Ask your partner whether she or he would like to add anything before leaving a theme.

✔ Reassure and support each other.

✔ Check in frequently with each other on how things are going.

After the event

✔ Do a check on how you both felt about the co-facilitation.

9. Evaluation for Impact

CONTENTS

A FRAMEWORK FOR ASSESSING LONG-TERM RESULTS....173

HAVING AN IMPACT? SOME SHORT-TERM INDICATORS....178

EVALUATING LEARNING AND GROUP DYNAMICS DURING A PROGRAM....179

EVALUATING AT THE END OF A PROGRAM....182

LEARNING FROM A DISASTER....185

FOLLOWING UP IN THE UNION....186

*The pitcher cries for water to carry
and a person for work that is real.*
—Marge Piercy, "To Be of Use"

IN MANY UNIONS, a course "evaluation" consists of having people check boxes on a form at the end of the event. Facilitators are relieved to finish without a big blowup, and when participants seem happy, why look for problems? Well, we do so because there's really useful information in evaluation, even when we're too tired to look at it. This chapter is about pushing ourselves to ask: what kind of impact do we want union education to have, and how will we know when we've had it?

Going back to our six threads, we ask ourselves how we find out whether the education we're providing is:

- democratizing the union
- building organizational capacity
- helping members face management more effectively
- helping the union link its efforts with the community
- advancing equity, and
- linking union mobilizing to the common good?

To answer those questions, we suggest taking up or building in:

- a framework and indicators for assessing long-term results in union-building
- short-term indicators of effectiveness
- tools for evaluating learning during a course or program
- tools for evaluating learning at the end of an education program
- some methods for learning from a disaster
- ideas for following up to maximize the impact of our education.

Public Service International

Asia-Pacific Regional Womens' Workshop, Seoul, Korea, 2001.

A FRAME-WORK FOR ASSESSING LONG-TERM RESULTS

E FFECTIVE UNION EDUCATION has to work consciously against the impacts of neo-liberal globalization (see CHAPTER 3) by providing something different. It also needs to work with the new forms of mobilization that are occurring inside and outside our workplaces. To help determine the long-term effects, we propose a number of indicators related to our six threads. These items represent our best thinking to date, which means feel free to add to or refine them. In any case, they provide a basic start to the conversation—something we hope you might be able to use as a tool for discussion in your own union.

On good days, this is the long-term lens we try to bring to the evaluation of our educational efforts. These indicators represent the spirit as well as the substance of union education work, which our methods should serve.

A checklist for long-term results

Indicators	Never	Sometimes	Often
1. Collectivity and community			
1.1 Activists call each other for help			
1.2 Education, research, organizing, communications working together			
1.3 Less backbiting and competitiveness in union and against other unions			
1.4 Effective conflict resolution instead of festering resentments			
1.5 People credit other people for good ideas and contributions			
1.6 More playfulness, less fear			
1.7 Other?			
2. Democracy (see also no. 3)			
2.1 More women, youth, and racialized members involved at a basic level[1] (vote for collective agreement; vote in union elections; read union publications; attend union courses)			
2.2 Increased attendance at union events, not just meetings			
2.3 Less preaching and more healthy debate, i.e., people get through meetings where they disagree feeling they've had a good experience			
2.4 Inclusive styles of leadership are supported, not undermined			
2.5 Members are knowledgeable about different parts of the union			
2.6 Uninvolved members are attending courses			
2.7 Increased demand to attend union courses			
2.8 Other ?			

1. We owe the distinction between basic, institutional, and activist involvement to the evaluation work of Michelle Kaminski, Michigan State University, Labor Education Program, and Helena Worthen, Labour Education Program, Institute of Labor and Industrial Relations, University of Illinois.

Education for Changing Unions

Indicators	Never	Sometimes	Often
3. Solidarity and equity			
3.1 Members support union actions of international solidarity			
3.2 More women, youth, and racialized members are involved institutionally (talk with their steward; file grievances; attend union meetings; member of a committee; steward or other position; involved in negotiations)			
3.3 Members matter-of-factly challenge discriminatory comments and behaviours			
3.4 Collective agreement language bargained for international exchanges			
3.5 Collective agreement language to remove other barriers			
3.6 Other?			
4. Class-consciousness			
4.1 Increased number of union cards signed			
4.2 More members take problems to the union rep rather than to the boss			
4.3 More members can explain the union and its actions to other members			
4.4 More members are knowledgeable about other unions and the union movement			
4.5 Activists routinely bring uninvolved members to union events			
4.6 Activists identify and support new leaders to come forward			
4.7 Campaigns are supported by a majority of members			
4.8 More women, youth, and racialized members are activists (involved in the organization of campaigns; participate in demonstrations for the union; participate in demonstrations in support of other unions and community organizations)			
4.9 Other?			

Indicators	Never	Sometimes	Often
5. Strengthened organizational capacity			
5.1 Provides funds for education and training and a structure to administer it, e.g., paid educational leave			
5.2 Contract language to meet new members on paid time			
5.3 Provides funds for child care and to reduce other barriers to participation			
5.4 Has mechanisms to track participation of women and other groups of bargaining unit members			
5.5 Co-facilitation of courses and other union events			
5.6 Core of trained worker educators teach existing courses and create new ones			
5.7 Union education supports strategic priorities of the union, e.g., better contracts, organizing, public education			
5.7 Union educators use research, communication, and other resources of the union			
5.8 Education committee connected to the membership in all its diversity			
5.9 Other?			
6. Union action linked to the common good			
6.1 Union activists can talk in their own words about how the union benefits them and the larger community			
6.2 Members serve as union reps in community organizations and coalitions			
6.3 The union has at least one joint project with another organization			
6.4 Campaign literature links union goals to the larger good			
6.5 Other?			

An example of an evaluation for impact

We don't often have the infrastructure to evaluate the long-term impacts of our program in any depth. In this regard we were inspired by the Chicago-based Regina V. Polk Fund for Labor Leadership, which has sponsored women's union leadership education programs for a decade or more. Recently the Fund undertook to examine the impact of union education on women's increased activity in the union. Its researchers wanted to find out whether labour education had influenced women to be more active in their union and/or community; to become more committed to the labour movement; and to seek elected or appointed positions in their unions. Here is one of their tools:

A Union Member Survey

Please indicate how often you do the following things:

	Twice a year or less	3-5 times a year	6-8 times a year	9-11 times a year	Once or more a month
1. Attend local union meetings					
2. Seek advice from a steward or other union officer if you have a problem at work					
3. File a grievance					
4. Read a union newsletter or other publication					
5. Wear union buttons, T-shirts, or insignia, or sign a union petition					
6. Participate in an external organizing drive					
7. Research issues related to your work					
8. Help your union prepare for bargaining					
9. Attend union rallies or events that focus on issues related specifically to your workplace (e.g., picket your employer, or rally to save jobs in your industry)					
10. Attend union rallies or events that focus on workplaces other than your own (e.g., picket line against another employer, or rally to save jobs in another industry)					

Source: Kaminski and Worthen, *Regina V. Polk Fund & Labor Union Activism*, February 2001, p.4.

We've established our vision, then, for how union education can contribute to the long term. We turn now to the more routine aspects of evaluating what's going on with people in our programs and some tools for doing that. It's our daily practice that will have the long-term impact.

HAVING AN IMPACT? SOME SHORT-TERM INDICATORS

WE WON'T LIE TO YOU: having an impact can be a mixed blessing. Consider the following short-term indicators of impact:

You'll have to work even harder

You will soon start getting calls from a rep with three members who want to take "that steward course." The phone will ring with a variety of problems people think that education might solve. Officers will start asking you to help with board development and with "a couple of little problems we've got down here."

All in all, the result of good work is not only more work and more responsibility—without necessarily adding on more authority, staff, and resources—but also, sometimes, envy and resentment.

Education becomes more linked to other functions

There will be increased connections to organizing, research, communications, and equality issues. (See the indicators for organizational capacity in the checklist, pages 174–176.) People with different functions will talk to each other more. People with different functions will ask each other for help. And education people (staff, committees, worker educators) will know what's going on with the women's, human rights, health and safety, and other committees.

Education activities become an incubator

People will want to come to courses. They will start to expect to talk about important union and social issues. And they will most likely express a desire to do something. (See the indicators for class-consciousness, equity, and democracy in the checklist.)

Members may express more frustration with the union's inconsistencies

Education may begin to raise members' expectations of the union—to put pressure on other functions of the organization. Democratic education encourages a speaking out—not just about injustice out there, but also about hurt in the union.

Leadership may start to control education more closely

In particular at the local level, worker educators may have to prove political loyalties. Their popularity with the membership may be viewed as threatening competition, rather than an asset.

Activists start initiating effective action in their workplaces

Members start feeling stronger, more confident, and better about themselves, their union, and their activism. Probably they make more trouble for the boss.

People feel smarter

As one of our co-authors puts it, there is a bottom line to our work: "If participants feel they are stupid and the educator is smart at the end of a course, then I've failed big time."

You'll find it trickier to keep humble and keep learning, as well as keep performing

The success is the union's, and yet your survival and that of the education program are influenced by people's respect for you, your motivation, and your skill.

EVALUATING LEARNING AND GROUP DYNAMICS

What people are learning is not necessarily what you're teaching

People's learning has always been a somewhat subversive activity. Often we've assumed that what people are learning is what we intended to teach. As a result, union instructors often express intense irritation when participants do not actually learn what is expected of them. You'll hear, "I told them that the first session. It's right in the manual." Surprise—even when we "tell them," even when we "show them," learners are making their own sense of what we're providing.

Part of the work is also watching the dynamics of a session and assessing whether you should shift the process. Only by engaging with people throughout can we continue to shape learning towards movement-building goals, and learn from participants how to do this better.

To assess what's going on, we use a number of approaches and tools.

■ **We make use of activities that demonstrate and advance learning.** Examples include case studies, role plays, individual and group presentations, and small-group reports. These activities provide opportunities for facilitators to gauge what people are learning and to support, intervene, shift, and shape ideas and concepts in an affirming manner. It is a matter of being flexible and going with what is working for the participants.

■ **We notice how well people are working together.** You are building a community inside the classroom, or on the picket line, or wherever you're doing education. Watch for people's ease in:
  - talking with people they don't know;
  - problem-solving in groups;
  - talking when they're usually quiet; listening when they're usually talking;
  - feeling comfortable enough to take a risk;
  - truly "hearing" another point of view, even if it conflicts with theirs;
  - listening for the "ouch" when something is said that is hurtful or untrue, and being able to respond in a constructive manner.

■ **We use energizers that assess interest and participation.** We have several ways of energizing people while assessing their interest and participation:

- **temperature check**—people mark, on a large flip-chart thermometer, their energy level at the moment, and say a couple of words;
- **flow chart**—on a prepared chart of activities for the day, people mark their highest and lowest energy points; a couple of minutes of discussion helps the facilitator interpret the results;
- **vote with your feet**—the goal of the day is marked on the floor; people place their bodies near or far from the spot and say a few words about why they placed themselves there;
- **put yourselves on the line**—an imaginary spot on one side of the room marks "ecstatic about the day" and another spot on the other side marks "totally turned off"; people place themselves accordingly, and the facilitator encourages comments from a few different locations on the line. If you're using this to draw out tension from something that's happened during the day, leave lots of time to really use this as a tool to move forward; if it's a quick check, use less inflammatory language like "disappointed."

■ **We rely on process stewards.** For longer courses, participants can act as process stewards who become the voices for participants on a variety of issues—logistics, participation levels, pacing, and so on. They can also gather data on the most important concepts that people are learning. We introduce the use of process stewards at the beginning of a course with an explanation of the objective. Then we ask for volunteers. The day usually begins with the process observer's short report. Asking for new volunteers for each session of a course is a way of giving more participants an opportunity to fill this role. The process steward is given a sheet to remind her or him of the specific role. Be sure the process stewards understand their role and are prepared to fulfil it in a sensitive way. Results are often more insightful when observers work in pairs.

■ **We trust our instincts: stop the process to find out what's going on.** Sometimes you know that things are not working. Perhaps the process you are using is getting in the way instead of helping; perhaps something is going on in the group. You can stop the process and ask for help. "This doesn't feel to me as though we're going where we want to go. Is anyone else feeling that way..." is one opening we've used.

■ **We build in structured feedback peer to peer.** When people are practising new skills—for example, facilitating, talking to members, interviewing a person alleging harassment—we often use a structured feedback process with peers. Many of us don't have much practice giving constructive, critical feedback to each other in the union movement. So we provide some guidelines and a process to help union activists develop feedback skills, and to ensure that participants get helpful assessments of what they've been practising. (See "Sample Structured Feedback Process" below.)

■ **At the end of sessions, we assess and think ahead.** As a way of closing a short session or day in a longer program, we do a quick round (encourage but don't force people to speak) asking for one insight gained from the day; this activity can bring out questions or issues that participants want to spend more time on in following sessions.

To create the best atmosphere for this exercise you might move the participants away from the spaces they have been working in throughout the workshop. Have participants take their chairs and form a circle to make their reflections, or use an energizer. This type of reflection brings closure to the group while things are still fresh.

All of these methods—and many more you might already be using—can provide the information necessary to decide whether to keep doing what you're doing, to shift the emphasis or the energy, or to do something entirely different.

Sample Structured Feedback Process

After a participant, a pair, or a group have facilitated, we use the following process to generate constructive peer feedback:

1. Agree on guidelines for feedback. We've found the following list helpful. You can either start from scratch and develop the guidelines in the group; or post these items as a starter and get the group's changes and additions.
   - Check to be sure the receiver wants feedback.
   - Talk for yourself only, not for other people.
   - Be specific.
   - Comment on the action or ideas, not the person.
   - Be sure to say what you liked or what worked.
   - Make suggestions for how to change or improve.

2. The facilitating team says what they liked about the work they just did, and what they want feedback on.

3. Each participant, in turn, gives a maximum of two minutes of feedback in direct response to what the team has asked for. If you feel people are not following their own feedback guidelines, interrupt gently to ask questions like "What did you like about it?" and "What suggestions do you have?"

4. The facilitator gives feedback in the same manner.

5. The presenting team gets to say how helpful feedback is and, if time permits, asks for any further suggestions about ... whatever.

When peers are giving feedback, the presenting team does not interrupt, defend, or explain. The facilitator challenges people who are not following their own rules for feedback.

EVALUATING AT THE END OF A PROGRAM

EVEN THOUGH IT IS OFTEN NOT TAKEN SERIOUSLY, a real evaluation process at the end of a course or event can:

- help people consolidate their learning;
- strengthen a sense of a group solidarity;
- put closure to a group experience;
- provide political ammunition to justify more education resources;
- provide helpful suggestions for improving a course;
- suggest appropriate follow-up to the course; and
- be instructive to the leadership about their membership's needs, desires, views, and political awareness.

Your purposes will shape the kind of evaluation you use at the end of a program. We often use two kinds—a written, more formal evaluation, which we read, synthesize, and send out after the workshop; and an oral, informal round with people usually sitting in a circle (without tables or desks if possible). As well as doing evaluations during or at the end of courses, sometimes it is appropriate to also do an activity for closure.

There is nothing wrong with traditional evaluations, either oral or written—if people participate in them actively and fully. However, in our experience this participation rarely happens, and we lose a golden opportunity to help people integrate their learning and strengthen their social and union commitment. That is why we try to use metaphors and other creative approaches, to engage the right side of the brain. This helps people bring their whole selves to closing out events that we hope have been emotionally and practically significant to them. Closing the personal and political loop requires as much care and imagination as any other part of the process—even though sometimes we're worn right out and just want to get it over with.

Bringing closure

AN EXAMPLE

At the end of one class the facilitator was afraid to open up the evaluation. So much emotion had come out during the course. During breaks one person said she felt recognized and fully seen for the first time in years of union activism. Over a beer another participant had spoken of the climate of respect in the course, which seemed magical to him after the bitter battles within his local union. The facilitator also received a heartfelt note expressing a participant's appreciation for validating his contribution to fellow workers in the positions he had held. As a result the facilitator was afraid that an oral evaluation would get out of hand, with people crying and being embarrassed, and thus she was inclined to keep the end of the session quick and factual.

Sometimes we feel like we are losing family when a good course ends. As participants, we know how abandoned and lonely we sometimes feel when an intense collective learning experience wraps up and we go out of the building to face the outside world again. We want participants to take this collective experience and apply it in their union work. That's why we try, whenever possible, to bring closure to an educational process, and to follow up as much as the organization and our own time allow. Our concern with evaluation and follow-up isn't technical; it's personal and political.

To do this work we have used a number of approaches.

■ **Head, heart, feet.** This is one of our favourites, because it both does some evaluation and provides closure. (See CHAPTER 6.)

■ **Choose an object.** The facilitator brings a series of objects and asks each participant to choose one that best represents how they feel about the course. (Or the facilitator could ask participants to find or draw an object that best associates with the way they feel about the course.) Each person gets a chance to say a couple of words about the object and why they chose it.

■ **Playdough shapes.** We have placed some playdough in the middle of the room and ask people to choose a piece or pieces and fashion whatever shape they want to represent how they feel about the program and why they feel that way. (Dry comment from one of our readers of the draft manuscript on this one: "Risky, but I bet it was great!" We decided to leave this in and let you decide for yourselves.)

■ **Write a group song.** At the end of a weeklong facilitator-training program, participants agreed on a tune for a group song, and we divided into four groups. Within twenty minutes, each group had written a verse on flip-chart paper. We taught each other the verses and ended the program with the song.

■ **Write yourself a letter.** At the end of the workshop, the participants each write a letter to themselves about actions they will take and seal the letter in a self- addressed envelope. The facilitators collect the letters and have them mailed back to participants within an agreed-to time frame (perhaps three months). The participants thus receive a documentation of their own analysis and intentions, and the conversation with themselves can continue. The questions now are:
  • Did I take the action? If so, was it successful? If not, why not?
  • If I didn't take the action, why not? What barriers (if any) prevented me from taking the action? Or did the circumstances change?
  • If there were barriers, how can I overcome those barriers?
  • What support do I need?

■ **Written evaluations.** A written evaluation is important for detail, for follow-up ideas, and for building political support for education in the union.

SAMPLE EVALUATION SHEET

WHAT BENEFIT DID YOU GET OUT OF TODAY?

_____

_____

_____

_____

YOUR ASSESSMENT:

You felt able to participate.	No	1	2	3	4	5	6	7	8	9	10
You learned from other participants.	No	1	2	3	4	5	6	7	8	9	10
You're taking away ideas for action.	None	1	2	3	4	5	6	7	8	9	10

What parts of the day did you find most helpful?

_____

_____

_____

SUGGESTIONS FOR IMPROVEMENT

_____

_____

_____

FOLLOW-UP

_____

_____

_____

Course title and date _____

Name (optional)_____ Date:_____

THANKS FOR THE THOUGHT AND THE TIME.

LEARNING FROM A DISASTER

ALL OF US HAVE FACILITATED COURSES in which a couple of people with negative energy took over; or the participants didn't want to be there; or people got scared at the end and didn't really want to do anything, so they turned on the facilitators. Other times we got nervous, rigid, and bossy with people, and they mutinied. Perhaps we weren't well prepared and everything went wrong. And so on... it's all happened many times.

Even in these cases—perhaps most especially when it wasn't great—it's important to have closure so that people can go home feeling at ease with each other and with you; and so you can learn something.

Some tips for learning from disaster

† Acknowledge before people fill out written evaluations that you've learned a lot during the course, and you feel they could make suggestions that would really improve it next time. Actively encourage people to make practical suggestions to improve the course, as well as to say what did work.

† In the oral checkout at the end, ask people for one thing they learned and one thing they think could be improved. Ask people to stick to one point for each.

† Make sure that the more negative people speak early. If they start heaping criticism, remind them that everyone needs to speak; and ask for the main suggestion for improvement. When you move to someone who you know has something positive to say, be sure to remind them that you've asked for a suggestion and an insight. Usually that shifts the energy to help others remember the good moments along with the bad.

Ilda Januario

Darashani Joachim and Guillermo Perez, Montreal Labour Educators' Exchange, April 2002.

FOLLOWING UP IN THE UNION

FOLLOWING UP A COURSE OR SESSION is the hardest part. As union educators, we're usually rushing from one educational event to another, with paper bulging from briefcases and boxes ready for the next workshop in the trunk of the car. Follow-up requires some time in the office, and some conviction that this, too, is real educational work. Of course, it doesn't hurt to have sufficient support staff working with the program, but most of us aren't in that situation.

Put the infrastructure in place

We don't know anyone who's really good at maintaining the necessary infrastructure. We're conscious of how much time we waste trying to find things and of follow-up we can never do because we have limited systems. In the spirit of increasing our odds, we suggest the following tasks.

Keep up-to-date lists of...
- worker educators (phones, addresses, e-mail)
- locals and key players in them
- other unions and educators in them
- possible speakers, musicians, theatre groups, audio-visuals, academics, and community activists who could be brought into a course.

Develop the capacity for regular mailings
- letters to worker educators
- updates to activists
- new info, courses, conferences, materials helpful in their teaching
- education schedule, course description, location, time.

Demand or if necessary nag for good computer set-ups
- e-mail
- computer conference
- worker educators and other activists trained to use computers, e-mail, the internet.

Develop connection and credibility with officers
- Communicate programs well in advance.
- Send a summary of evaluations with a few of your own comments.
- Use any meetings you have with them to get their suggestions and to communicate the ways in which education is advancing union priorities.
- See other ideas in CHAPTER 10, "Worker Educator Programs."

Develop and maintain connections with community organizations

- Subscribe to community newsletters—and at least look them over to stay current.
- Communicate your interest in community connections to bargaining unit and union members who may be active in community organizations, and could help you establish contacts.
- Maintain connections with union committees—Women's Committee, Human Rights, Health Care Coalition, etc. Get names of effective resource people in these community groups.
- Draw on community resource people to educate workers and worker educators.
- Send union publications of interest to your community contacts.
- Explore possible partnerships and build on-going relationships.

Understand and use the strengths of the union's infrastructure

- Make friends with the support staff; they know things that can help you.
- Draw on the skills of other staff and activists.
- Draw on the resources of other unions close to your own.

Solidarity event organized by the Neighbourhood Assembly in support of a successful worker-takeover of a factory and private health care clinic, Buenos Aires, April 2002.

Communicate with participants after the event

A workshop, meeting, or conference is only one moment in the job of building the union. Even with little time, you can do one or more of a number of other tasks.

Send out the write yourself a letter

- See "Evaluating at the End of a Program," just a few pages back.

Summarize the evaluations, and requests for follow-up

- Make sure these go out to participants and officers within two weeks of the course.

Make sure participants have a class list

- This should include names, phone numbers, and e-mail and street addresses of the participants who have given permission for their information to be circulated; you are building a community of activists.

Provide access to follow-up materials

- Send participants a copy of progressive labour magazines such as *Briarpatch* and *Our Times*; put participants on the mailing lists of the union, and central labour bodies.

Bring participants back together after a course

- Applying what we've learned to our unions sometimes provokes resistance and requires support. Following is an example of a course that anticipated that resistance and used the group as a continuing resource.

AN EXAMPLE

A "Bargaining for Women's Equality" course built in follow-up to its planning from the beginning. The participants, at the end of the course, developed a six-month plan for themselves. The follow-up session took one evening (social) and one day (what's happening; what's working; obstacles encountered; ideas to address the obstacles).

The outcome of the follow-up was positive; the participants were able to share how their six-month plans were going. The stories were powerful, and women offered each other support and encouragement. One woman wanted to set up an area with resources—videos, books, pamphlets—for the other women in her local, and she asked for some money for bookshelves and an area in the local office. Her request was denied. She did have an ally in the local who built her bookshelves in his spare time and she set them up in the women's washroom. Even then she was questioned about where she got the money for the resources and bookshelves.

Keep developing allies and connections inside the union

Working effectively with other officers, staff, and structures within the union—knowing and respecting the political culture of the union—is bridging work. It is important and often difficult. One thing you can do is use the union structures to keep important issues on the agenda.

AN EXAMPLE

During a series of workshops to prioritize the union's issues, participants put all the policy issues and the obstacles to their implementation on the wall. Equity was an issue for many people, but it was not actually "named" on the policy wall, so there was no guarantee it would get considered.

The workshop report was to go to the steering committee, which would be prioritizing issues to be dealt with. The facilitators asked the steering committee to seek advice from the human rights and women's committees and, based on that advice, review the draft workshop report and comment on what was helpful and what was missing.

Another bridging action is to work with the officers, even when it's difficult to do so.

AN EXAMPLE

A vice-president of a local called a union educator to a meeting in his local, where there had been a lot of harassment, a member had called in the police, and both union and management were respondents to human rights complaints. The union educator went to talk with the stewards and later reported the results of that meeting to the vice-president. The educator made some practical suggestions to the V.P. to get him out of immediate trouble, and then suggested training for the stewards, giving examples of how that kind of work had been done in other places. The V.P. took the union educator's suggestions and got management to agree to pay for training for management and the stewards.

The union educator thought things were back on track and that they had an agreed plan of action. In fact, the V.P. told her they would be doing training only for the stewards. When the union educators arrived, much to their surprise all of the members of management were also present. They managed to get through it; the stewards were thrilled; the union looked good; and the vice-president became an unlikely champion of anti-harassment training.

Put new wine into old bottles

Another approach is to do the tried and true stuff in a new way. If there's political or budgetary resistance to new initiatives—for example, to anti-harassment training or a course on communicating with the members—work it into the programs that already have support.

AN EXAMPLE

One union used a case of sexual and racial harassment as the case study for investigating, writing up, and facing management with a grievance in the stewards course. The case was discussed as matter-of-factly as any grievance, with support materials on harassment. A few worker educators, who were being trained to teach the course, felt that harassment should not be in a steward's course, but acknowledged that it was common in their workplaces and that nobody knew what to do about it. Many worker educators and stewards began asking for some follow-up training on harassment, because they still felt uncomfortable dealing with it. The union educators took these requests to the education committee, the human rights committee, and the locals, where harassment was seen, even by the officers, as a problem. Support grew to develop an anti-harassment course.

This chapter offered a framework, some indicators, and some tools for evaluating our education programs. The next chapter explores another strategy for maximizing the impact of education in our unions, through worker educators.

Paul Keighley, CEP

Judy Darcy and Fred Pomeroy, Pay Equity rally, Ottawa, November 1996.

10. Worker Educator Programs

CONTENTS

APPROACHES TO WORKER EDUCATION PROGRAMS....191

ASSESSING YOUR UNION'S APPROACH....193

WHY USE WORKER EDUCATOR PROGRAMS?....197

STARTING A NEW PROGRAM
Some conditions for starting....199
Anticipating tensions....199
Examples from different unions....201
Selecting worker educators....205
Assessing your success....205

DEVELOPING AND SUPPORTING NEW WORKER EDUCATORS
Political planning....206
On the length of training....207
Objectives and content....207
Methodology....208

SUSTAINING THE PROGRAM
Coaching and support....209
Worker education program: sustainability checklist....210

WORKER EDUCATOR PROGRAMS AS PART OF A NEW
VISION OF UNIONISM....214

APPROACHES TO WORKER EDUCATION

By "WORKER EDUCATOR" PROGRAMS, we refer to the systematic use of members as facilitators and teachers of union learning, in courses and other union events. This practice is widespread in some unions and rare in others. Most unions in Canada involve members as well as staff in some aspect of educational work.

Worker educator programs are an important expression of one of our guiding threads, democracy. They also have potential to advance the other five threads of this book: class-consciousness, equity, organizational capacity, community, and the common good.

The task of increasing member participation in union education carries its built-in tensions. But for us and many others it is an integral part of a vision of member involvement and capacity. In this vision member educators are not just an add-on program; they are part of a larger plan to democratize the union, mobilize the members, and build broad union leadership. Member educators are considered in all organizational functions: in the overall budget, the administrative help required, and general union strategy.

To our knowledge, outside of Quebec there has been little assessment, or even description, of current worker educator programs. Part of the difficulty of looking at applications of worker educator programs is that every union has its own history and culture. Any worker educator program that functions effectively must emerge from, and be able to work well within, its own union's culture. With that in mind, we are going to describe four broad imaginary approaches to, or models of, worker educators in unions. We invite you to use these models to assess specific worker educator programs and to consider where, how, and why we might use worker educators in our own unions.

Model 1: on the margins

In this approach, the union recognizes that it needs to expand its teaching capacity and use the talents of some of its activists. Members occasionally co-teach or assist staff to teach. The union understands "teaching" as the passing on of information and knowledge, and the worker educators usually teach topics such as grievances and health and safety or offer basic stewards courses. Beyond an initial course here and there, the union provides little training for either staff or worker educators to become better teachers. On an irregular basis, people who teach may be sent to a course on a particular topic, but rarely to one that deals with being an effective adult educator.

In this model, staff conduct the education programs and members are seen primarily as assistants to staff. The main goal of education is to ensure that the elected union reps in the workplace can effectively handle grievances and health and safety problems.

Model 2: on the move

Here the union wants to expand training to more members. It may also want to expand mobilization in worksites and inspire new forms of union leadership. Education tends to be more varied, often looking to popular education for inspiration. Worker educators are a key part of the education program and occasionally have input into course development. Co-instruction usually pairs worker educators together; staff members are used as resources or have prime responsibility for developing or revising courses. If they want it, staff are offered training to be effective instructors. All worker educators get some training in good adult education techniques. The education department works with local officers to build support for worker educators at the local level.

Model 3: in the program

This approach builds on some of the aspects of the "on the move" model. But here the union is explicit in its agenda: it wants to mobilize members, mobilize workplaces, build member leadership, and maximize effectiveness in campaigns and lobbying. It sees education and the use of worker educators as a key strategy in doing this. Therefore the union tries to involve members in a variety of courses—on globalization, bargaining for equality, stress, facing management, for example—to draw on the interests and energies of members. The union places a high value on participatory education, and all education is based on popular education principles and methods.

The union supports worker educators in the development and revision of courses, and offers regular training and upgrading to develop teaching skills and keep them current. All courses are co-facilitated in recognition of the greater benefit to participants and to help build equity into union courses. Indeed, the union makes consistent efforts to have a cadre of educators who are diverse in gender, race, worksite, age, region, job, and (dis)ability. It brings worker educators together regularly (usually annually) to build skills, connection, and strategy, and to provide an additional forum for worker educators to influence the education program. Worker educators are a line item in a budget that includes money for education staff, replacement time, and administration.

The union also sees that its staff reps are trained to be effective union educators, but uses them only in courses in which worker educators may not yet have experience—for example, labour law and arbitration. It frees up education staff to provide more worksite support to activist/educators, write up mobilizing efforts, and co-ordinate links between worker educators.

These programs result in an increased excitement about education and member power. The union begins to enjoy the fruits of a better-distributed competence and increased activism from a wider variety of members.

Model 4: part of a wider change

This model seeks not only to achieve all the advantages of the "in the program" model, but also to transform other ways in which the union does its business. Members have influence in all aspects of union life, which is part of a union-wide strategy to democratize the union. The organization draws upon education to strengthen processes of discussion and decision-making and to connect all departments in joint work. The union sees education as vital to building and strengthening its links with various sectors in the community. Worker educators throughout the union have strong connections: all courses are co-facilitated. Indeed, worker educators co-facilitate conferences, conventions, and meetings.

The union takes leadership in advancing social justice both inside and outside. Effective, broad-based education in the workplace and elsewhere is essential both to reflect and reinforce this process. Staff reps support the skill development of members, including worker educators, and are active in building solidarity with the community.

ASSESSING YOUR UNION'S APPROACH

OUR FOUR IMAGINED APPROACHES to worker educators are closely connected to each other; but different in their goals and vision; roles of education in the union; philosophies of education and learning; roles of staff and members; and the tensions they raise. We hope the models will stimulate thinking about the possibilities and limitations of current worker educator programs. You might add points, or even think of a fifth approach, based on your own union experience.

What we want to do now is offer tools that could help you to assess your own situation, to identify where you and your union are in the use of worker educators. We offer these outlines not as a judgement, but as a stimulus to discussion in your own union about the pros and cons of a worker education strategy. The first one is a chart with blanks you can fill in as a way of beginning to ask questions in your own union.

Issues	Model	1. On the margins	2. On the move	3. In the program	4. Part of a wider change
Pressures for change; goals, vision					
Education that's top down ...bottom up? Think about whether workers' knowledge is used, workers teach each other, education mobilizes members to act, etc.					
Roles of staff and worker educators Who does what?					
Desired results What impact are you looking for, and how would you know if you were successful?					

The second tool uses the same four issues: 1) pressures for change; 2) education that's top/down or bottom/up; 3) roles of staff; 4) desired results. For each section, write in the number from one to ten that best describes where your union is on the particular issue. The number one puts you in the "On the margins" model; number ten is "Part of a wider change" model. Most of us have something going on in each of the models. You may be "wider change" on one issue, "on the move" in another, "in the program" on another aspect, and "on the margins" in yet another. The point is to think about worker educators and what roles they currently play, and could play, in our unions.

Issues	Model	1. On the margins	2. On the move	3. In the program	4. Part of a wider change
Pressures for change; goals, vision		❑ ease staff overload ❑ train members to better handle grievances and health and safety ❑ use talents of some bored activists	❑ expand training to more members ❑ mobilize work-places against employer threats ❑ increase member support for the union	❑ mobilize members ❑ mobilize workplaces ❑ spread the work ❑ develop more representative leadership ❑ increase effectiveness in campaigns/lobbying	❑ mobilize members ❑ mobilize workplaces ❑ advance equity in the organization ❑ expand member leadership throughout organization ❑ build capacity to respond to, and initiate effective public campaigns quickly ❑ build better co-ordination between union departments
Top down … bottom up		❑ mostly lecture methods to impart information ❑ occasional training and information sharing with member educators	❑ activist curricula, often based on popular education ❑ some training provided for all worker educators	❑ all courses based on popular education principles ❑ worker educators connected throughout union to support and teach each other ❑ consistent efforts to have cadre of diverse worker educators (gender, race, worksite, age, region, job, disability) ❑ regular training and upgrading programs to build skills of w.e.'s and keep them current ❑ all courses co-facilitated	❑ all courses, meetings, conferences, based on popular education principles ❑ community of w.e.'s throughout union ❑ worker educators representative of workforce ❑ wide variety of educational programs available for all members ❑ regular training and upgrading for w.e.'s ❑ all courses, meetings, and planning sessions co-facilitated ❑ education connected to issues of larger community

Issues	Model	1. On the margins	2. On the move	3. In the program	4. Part of a wider change
Roles of staff		**Delivery/do it** ❏ links to political leadership ❏ staff run all educational programs as part of servicing ❏ designated education staff may also have other responsibilities ❏ w.e.'s seen as assistants to staff	**Training/coaching** ❏ links to political leadership ❏ staff and w.e.'s teach courses ❏ staff still have prime responsibility for revising/developing courses ❏ staff consulted/used as resource in courses taught by w.e.'s ❏ staff occasionally get training to teach	**Building/creating** ❏ links to political leadership ❏ staff are trained to be effective popular educators ❏ used only in courses where w.e's may not have experience – e.g. arbitration; labour law; ❏ train w.e.'s in popular education ❏ do more worksite education with activists – e.g. mobilizing; using collective agreement creatively; campaigns ❏ encouraged to write-up/communicate mobilizing efforts ❏ co-ordinate links between w.e.'s	**Sustaining** ❏ links to political leadership ❏ staff are trained to be effective popular educators ❏ used only in courses where w.e.'s may not have experience ❏ train w.e.'s in popular education ❏ do worksite education with activists ❏ support skill development of w.e.'s to facilitate meetings and other organizational processes ❏ build union links with community organizations ❏ connect work of research, communication, education, organizing for common goals
Desired results		❏ deliver on training promises ❏ activists happy	❏ more members trained ❏ more mobilizing in the workplace ❏ more skilled leadership	❏ increased member influence in union ❏ new leadership, skilled and inspiring ❏ distributed competence ❏ more equitable access to union resources ❏ representative leadership ❏ more effective campaigns and lobbies ❏ more respect from employers	**A union that is:** ❏ a community and home to all members ❏ democratic ❏ class-conscious ❏ equitable and advancing equity as public agenda ❏ capable as an organization of promoting justice ❏ shape public policy ❏ strongly linked to communities

WHY USE WORKER EDUCATOR PROGRAMS?

WORKER EDUCATORS ARE NOT A NEW PHENOMENON. For centuries workers have taught each other, informally, how to do the job, how to read and write, and how to protect their rights and those of brothers and sisters in the workplace.

Worker educator programs in unions are a more recent development. In 1999 the FTQ celebrated twenty-five years of its worker educator program, launched in 1974 as the *Formation des formateurs et formatrices*, explicitly based on popular education principles. Over this time period several other Canadian and Quebec unions have experimented with different ways to involve members in education.

The ever-present pressures on unions have been particularly intense in recent times. In the past decade or so neo-liberal governments across the country have undermined labour legislation even further, making it more difficult than ever both to organize and to maintain certification, as well as more difficult to protect—let alone advance—workers' rights. Bargaining, never easy at the best of times, has become a constant, painful frustration, increasingly requiring strike votes and sometimes necessarily leading to civil disobedience. Few unions have developed mechanisms for formulating quick responses to heavy issues, such as employer and government actions that hurt workers, or built infrastructures that communicate to all members. Union staff and leadership are aging, and stretched to breaking point. Many union staff members have little training and only weak support that would help them meet intense pressures or develop new strategies. Education and mobilization programs reach only a small proportion of the membership; there are huge time lags between requests and response for education and skills development.

All of these constant and common pressures can motivate unions to consider drawing on members as educators and mobilizers. Workers and members have a wealth of knowledge and experience, and the union needs to draw on this knowledge and experience in the service of the union, its members, and the society the union wants to build. Worker educators may or may not have much formal education. But they care about learning—their own and that of other members; and many have talents to inspire other members to learn. Worker educators are often informal leaders, who may or may not be interested in political leadership, but who have capacities that the union needs.

There are other attractions. In the short run considerable initial outlays of time and replacement pay are necessary to develop worker educators. But in the long run worker educators are cost-efficient: they are right there, on the ground, in the local. More members can learn and develop when there are more people teaching.

A worker educator program can tap into a diverse membership, profoundly extending who is involved, who is in a position to support union initiatives, and who is in the upcoming layers of leadership. Members who are reluctant to sit on a bargaining committee or run for election may be attracted to the role of the worker educator as being "less political." Other members who are heavily involved with their families or communities may find a worker educator role more accessible because it does not have to involve significant travel. It may be a more comfortable role because it seems low-profile. In fact, it is precisely this low centre of balance and power that makes the worker educator role so potent.

Increased union education and mobilizing means that the union is in a better position to deliver on organizing promises to new units. In one year, in one local of 15,000 members, using eight worker educators, 1,000 members attended a course of at least one-half day. That number increased to 1,500 members in the following year. The results: those members could better interpret their own collective agreements; they were more likely to support or be involved in worksite actions; and they were better equipped to defend their rights and those of others in the workplace.

In another situation a unionized public-sector employer was hiring lots of part-time workers. The union local had contract language permitting fifteen minutes of union time with each new employee within the employee's first week of work. It negotiated a protocol with the employer, extending the fifteen minutes to one hour, and then used its worker educators to run sessions, paid for by the employer, with every new employee. More new workers signed union cards than ever before, and they started asking to come to union courses. The local started a new two-day course for workers who had been employees for less than three years and who had never attended a union course. This course, called "Rights on the Floor," was also taught by worker educators. Through these two programs, the local increased its support with part-time workers, and identified new potential leaders who were representative of the changing workforce.

Worker educator programs highlight the need to train good facilitators—whether they are worker educators, staff, or elected leaders.

Public Service International

Asia-Pacific Regional Womens' Workshop, Seoul, Korea, 2001.

Education for Changing Unions

STARTING A NEW PROGRAM

Some conditions for starting

There are no perfect conditions for starting a worker educator program. Often the very first condition is a fatigue with what we, a union, have been doing, and a desire and openness to try something new. Every union will offer a different combination of conditions, some of them no doubt beyond our imaginations. But, to begin with, it helps if there is:

- no major internal war that is polarizing sides and absorbing major resources and energies
- a desire/pressures to do things better
- some personal trust of leadership
- a stated commitment of the union to organizing/mobilizing
- a sense that education must contribute to a healthy union
- strong administrative staff
- positive past experiences with worker educators
- Paid Educational Leave (PEL) (in several large Canadian unions, PEL pays for a program taught by worker educators, as well as training for worker educators and new course development; it also covers day care and other supports for members participating in programs)
- a political decision supporting a worker educator program
- interest and support on the part of some staff
- an agreed budget
- expressed interest by members in being worker educators.

Anticipating tensions

The decision to develop a worker educator program can send big waves through the union. It communicates a need for change that will make some people anxious. While that anxiety might make others impatient, it's an anxiety that is loaded with information and needs to be anticipated, and treated with respect. Above all we need to avoid designating as the enemy people who have reflective concerns about a worker educator program. The resistance can take various forms.

"What about education standards?"

Most staff who deliver education programs have themselves never had training in adult education techniques, in popular education, or in many of the content areas they are expected to teach. They've learned on the fly, just the way many members learn their jobs. Still, they have creatively made the best of it, with very little support to do so.

Starting a worker education program provides an opportunity to think through training support for both worker educators and staff in an organizational effort to improve the quality of union education for everyone.

"What about staff?"

Part of the expressed concern about standards may be an unexpressed fear on the part of staff about losing current roles or being inadequate in new roles. For instance, when the education officer in one Canadian union wanted to train some worker educators, other staff stepped in to prevent the program, saying that education was the work of the staff bargaining unit.

Depending on the levels of staff trust for union leadership, staff members may even be fearful about their job security. Involving staff—actively—in the development of new worker educator programs is a key to success. The staff has to feel that it is safe to acknowledge a need for training, and performance evaluation will have to be clearly separated from the development of new programs.

Most union staff are overloaded with work and doing everything they can to react effectively to what is already on their plates. They know only too well that "business as usual" is not taking them as far as it used to. Overload is not the best condition in which to think strategically about a new program that in the short run will take more time. But overload in itself provides the need, and an opening, for finding better ways of doing things.

"We've tried this before and nothing ever came of it"

A certain cynicism about a new program can exist in the very same moment that people proclaim a need for the union to change. It's important to acknowledge that union veterans have seen lots of "new efforts" come and go. Their cynicism isn't stupid; it can be an understandable hedge against further disappointment. We try to ask what worked well, and what went wrong, the last time something new was attempted. Pull the information out of the cynicism to find a place to start, a place in which you can find broad agreement.

"What about the political loyalties of worker educators?"

The political leadership will normally approve the selection of people to be involved, yet may be nervous about the political loyalties of the new worker educators and want to exercise some control over them. A politically accountable culture may regard new horizontal networks with suspicion. Officers or staff may have heard "horror stories" from other unions about worker educators who got supported, then used their contact with members to whip up opposition to the leadership or used their new political base to run against the local president.

Democratizing the union always brings risks to the leadership, but keeping things the same usually carries even greater risks. Most political leaders want their union to be a "player" in the union movement, and in the eyes of the members. Most political leaders also see the need to build a union that actively involves more of the members and uses resources effectively. Union officers have a substantial say over the selection of worker educators, and some officers themselves got their training and worked as worker educators before becoming advocates of worker educator programs.

Examples from different unions

Many unions—in both public and private sectors, large and small—have already begun a process of building worker educators as a strategy for building the union. Although their starting points are different, the following three examples may provide ideas for possible strategies for beginning a program.

AN EXAMPLE: Educating stewards

A local had been receiving complaints about its weak education efforts, but it wanted to maintain strict control of its program. Numerous historical tensions between the central office and the local made joint work difficult but not impossible, as long as the local was getting what it needed.

The local invited the education co-ordinator from the central office to come and outline his new stewards program, which was highly participative and based on popular education principles. The local had heard good things about the program and wanted the education co-ordinator to teach the course to all its chief stewards and later to all its other stewards.

The education co-ordinator explained that doing this with the chief stewards alone would require about eight two-day programs, which would be a large slice of his time. He bargained with the local that they would, in consultation with him, identify eight of the chief stewards through the course of the program who would attend a subsequent worker educator training program; after that they would be able to teach the course to the many stewards of the local.

The education co-ordinator requested that a committee close to the current leadership be part of the planning for the sessions; these members might be potential worker educators and they could get a head start on the thinking of popular education, and how the program worked. He asked that at least one union officer attend each of the training sessions, or at least that an officer would open the training sessions, to demonstrate officer support for the program and answer any political questions that might arise in the training. He stated that he did not want to be in a position of answering such questions on behalf of the local.

The eight two-day sessions were highly successful. The process built a relationship between the education co-ordinator and the officers and staff of the local. Those new educators attended, fully paid, the week-long worker educator training organized by the National Education Department, and then the co-ordinator coached them to begin teaching the stewards programs.

Important factors

- a word of mouth communications process that helps create demand
- the local remains in control of the process
- getting stewards trained as a priority; after meeting that need the local becomes more interested in worker educators
- the impact of experiencing the program in action, as opposed to just talking; officers can see the effectiveness of small groups, more preparation, co-facilitation, different kinds of participation
- central office support for the education officer's time to meet the local's needs, and to develop the worker educators

AN EXAMPLE: Developing a new program

A union with new leadership had a mandate to move towards the mobilizing model. Its locals had little contact with each other, and "education" had been mostly an annual retreat for selected staff and members who did health and safety and handled first-stage grievances. The new education co-ordinator was told to "build an education program," with a budget that was vague, at best.

She started by meeting one on one with all the political leaders and some staff members in the locals to determine interest and support. She asked the locals to name delegates to a two-day working session to establish some principles and priorities for a new education program that would meet the needs of the locals. Then she convened that two-day meeting, which resulted in some guiding principles and an outline of a new union stewards course.

The education co-ordinator documented the meeting and communicated the results to all officers and meeting delegates. She got a couple of delegates released, paid from her budget, to work with her on drafting a new stewards course; and she communicated to all officers that the course was drafted and needed piloting.

The next step was to ask for two more days with the original delegates and anyone else the locals wanted to send for training. Some officers of the locals themselves attended those days, to see what was going on. The course generated excitement and some agreement on the part of five participating locals that a new kind of training to teach this course was required, and that they would each identify a couple of worker educators who would be trained to teach the course in their local.

Important factors

- substantial consultation at the beginning
- meeting the expressed need, which is a stewards course that is more interesting, participatory, and can reach more members
- follow-up with participants to draft a program
- continuous communication with the officers and the participants of the consultation
- officers attending the pilot; enthusiasm spread by word of mouth
- some money to pay for release time

AN EXAMPLE: Changing the organization

The staff of a public-sector union, under a barrage of attacks from government, became exhausted and cynical. Government cutbacks had eliminated jobs through streamlining, privatization, and contracting out. Many members felt intimidated, stressed from work overload, fearful of their uncertain future, divided amongst themselves, and mistrustful and apathetic towards their union. Sound familiar?

The union began an organization-wide renewal process and took a number of steps. To begin, its board crafted a vision of a renewal project, with two priorities: a) win strong contracts; b) build local leadership. A committee proposed a basic framework that linked basic union priorities to a strategy of popular education. The board adopted this plan, taking it for ratification to two conventions, where each time it was supported unanimously by the delegates; and each time it emerged with more clarity through debate and discussion. Still, while there was no disagreement about the vision, considerable resistance was raised to yet another structure that looked participative. The organizers heard familiar refrains: "Training? We've never had training. Here the rule is sink or swim." "You want us to have a strategic conversation? Some of us haven't talked to each other in years!" "There are too many turf wars for us to get together." "I'm too busy. What's this got to do with winning grievances?" "Is this some kind of gimmick to get someone re-elected?"

A strategy evolved that tied together the goals of bargaining, organizing, and shaping public policy. Union activists realized that bargaining could not be conducted effectively in isolation from the effort to mobilize the membership, link with the community, and advocate for broader public policy.

The structure that would implement this change became a steering committee of about thirty members and staff from across the union. The committee organized project teams to co-ordinate the work on the three educational areas: leadership development, member/staff development, and collective bargaining training. The task of these teams was to incorporate popular education into the education in these areas. The union assigned two staff educators to support the committee and project teams.

The education department worked with the steering committee. Together they began with a one-day workshop to look at how popular education might be used to help the union negotiate its (more than five hundred) collective agreements. By the end of the day, the steering committee voted to use popular education as an approach to union renewal that would include the use of worker educators in the process. They introduced first-time, basic, three-day residential training in collective bargaining for all negotiators and other professional technical staff—using popular education and establishing, for the first time, the union's basic standards in negotiation.

They also held leadership development courses for local activists—both veterans and new blood—at the local level. Some two hundred officers and activists attended in the first year, co-facilitated by worker educators and staff. They established mandatory training for all elected bargaining teams, six months in advance of bargaining, using a training program developed by a working group of staff and members and now delivered by field staff.

Part of this mobilizing strategy was to conduct outreach workshops with members of colour. Caucuses of equity-seeking groups, the human rights committee and the women's committee brought forward an "equity framework" to the steering committee. As staff overload increased in the face of further cutbacks and employer intimidation, the roles of member educators became increasingly important in carrying on the education work of this change process.

Important factors

- a critical need—improving contracts and their enforcement
- vision and leadership of the officers
- willingness to try out popular education
- involvement of both staff and members from the beginning
- the development of a structure with wide support to guide the process
- initial skills development integrated into the process of planning and debate, without calling it training
- a willingness to learn and try new things as the process unfolded

Jojo Geronimo

Quebec Popular Summit, April 2001.

Education for Changing Unions

Selecting worker educators

Without a clear process for selecting worker educators, the program can be quickly seen as a dumping ground for political favourites on the part of either the education program or the political leadership. In our experience, the officers of a local make the final selection, no matter what anyone else says. It is essential that the leadership have confidence in the worker educators.

We talk to officers and staff about the benefits of using a worker education program to involve newer members, who can communicate with currently uninvolved, or hostile members. We mention the difficulty of designating already overextended trusted officers or members, who would probably not be able to carry out their educational obligations. We stress the importance of building an overall union leadership with the diverse face of the membership, and we ask for their help. And then we leave it to them, and we work enthusiastically with the people they designate.

We have, then, a number of criteria to aid selection of potential worker educators, and we make these known to officers, relevant staff, and education committees. None of our criteria requires formal educational qualifications or experience.

Our criteria

- careful and open listeners, as well as clear talkers
- activists, willing to fight the boss
- trusted by the leadership
- bored by rivalry
- inspiring and sometimes entertaining
- interested in education, and in genuine participation
- representative—race, gender, region, workplace
- has time to concentrate on the education work

In the end the leadership may still select politically safe, uninspiring people as their worker educators. But effective union educators will nevertheless continue to create conditions for these people to learn and change; they will work to increase the impact of the gifted and committed educators. In practical terms that means including the favourites in all training, pairing them up with your best educators as co-facilitators (see CHAPTER 7) and trying to find different roles for them if they prove disastrous. For example, they might be willing to work on campaign strategy, or review new audiovisual resources. When you are faced with a wall, there is usually a possibility for going sideways.

Assessing your success

It's easy to get discouraged by the amount of work, the resistance of some people, the painfully slow pace of change. But you will know that your worker educator program is having an impact if you see these signals:

- more calls and requests for education programs;
- increased interest in taking courses on the part of women, racialized workers, and others who may have felt "outside" the union;
- members wanting to be educators;
- worksite actions and materials for worksite actions as results of education programs;
- officers asking about the education program;
- excitement—a buzz about education; and
- involvement of worker educators in campaigns, meetings, worksite actions.

DEVELOPING AND SUPPORTING NEW WORKER EDUCATORS

TRAINING WORKER EDUCATORS, like so many other initiatives in union-building, fulfils more than one task at a time.[1] It develops worker educator capacities, yes, but it also:

- builds vision and support for a worker educator program and for the union;
- strengthens connections between worker educators within or between locals;
- provides a forum for prioritizing education issues and shaping the overall education program;
- spawns ideas for new courses and educational initiatives.

There is no one method of achieving these goals through the training of worker educators; rather, there are many possibilities, and here we offer a few ideas for the development of worker educators—ideas developed in collaboration with a number of unions and central labour bodies.

Political planning

In a union that already values education and in which there is broad agreement that educators need training, a week-long training program for worker educators may already have strong support. More commonly, people have learned their jobs on the fly and expect educators to do the same. Before any training for worker educators takes place, important advance work has to be carried out with the political leadership. For doing this work we suggest a number of possible approaches.

- Schedule the training well in advance so that it doesn't conflict with bargaining, conventions, and other important events.
- Make the training open to staff and any officers, should they want to attend.
- Send the proposed program by mail or e-mail and well ahead of time, to the president or designate, and phone to make sure it was received and that the president or designate will be sending worker educators to the program. If you know the names and addresses of worker educators in the local, ask if you can send the material directly to the worker educators as well.
- Schedule a couple of stewards courses right after the training program, using the new graduates as teachers. These new graduates become a tangible benefit that speaks to the value of the program. For example, the worker educator training program might run from Sunday evening until Thursday noon. On Thursday afternoon, teams would take time to prepare to teach a two-day stewards program in a local. On Friday morning, eight participants with one facilitator drive to one location to begin teaching a stewards course from Friday evening to Sunday; eight other participants with a second facilitator drive to a second location, possibly in a second local, to teach another stewards course.

All of this work requires a great deal of organization, but it allows a local (or two) to experience immediate benefits from the worker educator training program. It provides

---

1. We use the word "training" reluctantly because it so often denotes a marching-through-the- manual kind of approach. But the word is widely used in the union movement. We want to stress that training in movement-building is not a mechanical process; even with a manual and detailed facilitator notes, training is different with every group of people. Part of the training of worker educators is to build skills, courage, and the judgement necessary to mobilize energies effectively in different situations.

an immediate application of the training for the new worker educators. It also allows the course facilitators to coach the new worker educators through their first teaching experience.

- Circulate the course evaluations to the officers of the participating locals.
- Phone them afterwards to see what they've been hearing about the training and to ask whether they have any suggestions for the next one.

On the length of training

Some worker educator training programs run one day, and others last two weeks. Sometimes programs last one week, with coaching and practice on top of that. Sometimes there are more sustained programs that, after an initial training period, provide week-long refresher programs every year.

All unions are concerned about money, time off work, and minimizing political opposition to the program. Worker educator training has to balance these bottom lines with a high-quality program that equips worker educators to do their job.

An initial week-long program is best because:

- it allows time to build a group—a community of educators who will be able to support one another after the program;
- it provides time for participants to practise facilitating difficult situations and for them to create new approaches they can use in their locals;
- it ensures that participants have time to absorb the content as well as the methods of a course that they may have to teach; and
- most workers have had little exposure to popular education; it takes time to absorb how it's different, why it works, how to make it your own.

A two-day program, or even less, can be effective if:

- it remains focused on a particular task—for example, facilitating a small-group discussion at a conference; running a half-day session on the collective agreement in the local; co-facilitating a short course that will happen after the training;
- it has clear objectives so that worker educators can see how the piece they're being trained to do fits into the whole; and
- it gives participants time to prepare for the facilitation they'll be doing after the training.

Objectives and content

Whatever the length of the course, the training of worker educators who are learning to use popular education as their framework involves a few essentials:

- ways of creating and sustaining a climate of ease and connection within a group, even when there are tensions and conflict;
- an understanding that popular education is not a set of cute techniques, but an approach to critical thinking and collective action for change in a world of very unequal power relations;
- practice with the spiral model as a tool for planning activist education;
- an examination of equity as a cornerstone of the process;

- some practice applying popular education in "real life," which might include an anticipation of, and practice in dealing with, conflict and power; and
- a grasp of how popular education requires the whole self—brain, heart, creativity, guts.

Our objectives point to process and content. We are working to develop educators who can create conditions for individual and group learning; educators who can help workers teach each other as well as learn from the educator; educators who can build a group conscious of, and able to work with, all its differences; educators who can surface the creativity and the knowledge of workers to build the union.

Methodology

Our most powerful methodology is our belief that workers are smart, that educators have much to learn as well as something to teach. We believe that workers will learn as much about building a labour movement from being respected and seeing their brothers and sisters treated with respect as they will from anything else we do. The spirit that we bring to education work is more important than any technique.

In training worker educators, we:

- spend time on introductory activities and then examine what we did and why, so that new worker educators can think about the experience they've just had and how they can apply what we've done to their own teaching;
- use some version of the "historical timeline" or "helps-hinders" activities (see CHAPTER 6 and the APPENDIX) to identify and share what people already know about effective education; then, in good spiral model practice, we add any points not emerging from the group; and we talk a little about learning from the South and perhaps about the emergence of popular education from the work of Paulo Freire in Brazil and the struggles for justice of peoples in the South (see "PAUSE" after PART I and "Traditions Shaping Our Educational Practice);
- pose direct questions about how "normal" inequities will be reproduced in union courses unless they are anticipated and addressed, and develop a checklist tool to guide our own practice;
- have people apply their learning to education in their own union context—either redesigning and facilitating from selected union courses, or designing and facilitating part of a new course, a strategic planning session, a tricky coalition meeting, or a half-day campaign workshop;
- have participants on their feet from the first hour of the course, with increasingly complex demands to think and to work respectfully with everyone in the room;
- follow practice sessions with structured feedback, so that people learn that critique can be helpful, that it's an important skill in education and movement building;
- work visually as much as possible; we are increasingly aware of how much we still have to learn to reduce the paper and the written word from our work.[2]

---

2. For an outline of a worker educator training program, "Popular Education: Instructor Skills Upgrading Course," contact the Canadian Labour Congress (CLC), Education Department, Ottawa. The course can be adapted to a variety of situations and needs.

SUSTAINING THE PROGRAM

Coaching and support

Too often worker educators receive minimal training and then six months later, when they're finally called to teach, they are terrified to try any of the approaches they have learned, and nobody is around to help them. This is a recipe for the same old lecturing in union courses that everyone complains about. The keys to success for worker education programs are ongoing coaching and support to build skills and improve quality.

Some unions we've been working with have been getting very creative about both providing support to their worker educators and building their education programs. They have tried to do this in a number of ways:

- attach the training program to an immediate teaching experience in the local with coaching built in;
- build a plan into the course schedule for a local, region, or national program to pair up each of the new worker educators with a seasoned popular educator in the local or from outside;
- bring worker educators together for a yearly refresher program, which includes lots of practice teaching;
- bring interested worker educators together to revise union courses, under the supervision of a popular educator who can continue to work on skills while also building in facilitation practice time;
- get release time for a few worker educators to work with a seasoned popular educator on a particular campaign or on conference planning;
- start sending out bimonthly small packages to all worker educators; the packages might include a write-up of a new activity; a popular education brochure on equity or mobilizing on globalization; outlines of new training courses that might be of interest to worker educators; education news from the union;
- make sure that worker educators have each other's e-mails and phone numbers so that they can contact each other for help and support.

Barb Thomas

Michel Blondin, Montreal Labour Educators' Exchange, April 2002.

Worker educator program: Sustainability checklist

Place your tick in the square that best describes where you are right now in answer to each of the following questions:

What have you done about:	Nothing	Just started	Well underway	In place
1. Building an infrastructure that supports the program				
a) Staff with time designated for education?				
b) Education committee, informed and doing the work?				
c) Administrative staff assigned/trained (in smaller unions, is time allocated in education person's job description?)				
d) Effective filing system?				
e) Educational materials organized/accessible?				
f) Up-to-date address/e-mail/phone lists?				
g) Current list of resource people for different aspects of the program?				
h) Current list of suitable facilities?				
i) Current list of all locals, officers, collective agreements, current issues?				
j) Contract language to provide paid union orientation to new members (see example in "Why Use Worker Education Programs")?				
2. Education plan				
a) Have you got one?				
b) Was it developed with an education committee (does it have input from elected officers, staff, worker educators)?				
c) Does it have feasible objectives for the year given your resources?				
d) Does it allocate time to:				
– responding to requests for courses, and initiating courses				
– reviewing and updating current course materials				
– training worker educators				
– using worker educators in education work				
– coaching worker educators				
– working with other aspects of union work, like organizing, research, campaigns				
– building links with community?				
e) Has it got political approval?				

Worker educator program: Sustainability checklist page 2 of 4 **What have you done about:**	Nothing	Just started	Well underway	In place
3. Budget and clarity on who pays for what				
a) Have you got a budget?				
b) Does it have allocations for:				
– travel for staff and worker educators				
– lost time for worker educators				
– facilities and accommodation for training				
– purchase of educational materials				
– resource and outside help for course development, coaching, expertise?				
c) Was it developed with the education committee?				
d) Does it have approval of officers?				
e) Is there clarity on who pays for what?				
f) Have you negotiated a Paid Educational Leave (PEL) clause to provide more money for education?				
4. Selection of and training for worker educators				
a) Have you got a process and criteria for selection of worker educators?				
b) Have you circulated/reviewed selection criteria and process with all officers and/or locals?				
c) Are worker educators representative of the membership?				
d) If not representative, is there a plan for improving representation?				
e) Have officers agreed to send worker educators for training?				
f) Have officers (locals) agreed how to share costs of worker educator training (e.g., travel, lost time, accommodation) and ongoing coaching?				
g) Is there a plan for using trained worker educators?				

Worker educator program: Sustainability checklist page 3 of 4 **What have you done about:**	Nothing	Just started	Well underway	In place
5. Effective use of trained worker educators				
a) Is the union using its worker educators to teach its courses?				
b) Do worker educators feel effectively deployed?				
c) Is the union responding to new education needs of members through initiating new courses?				
d) Is the union using worker educators to revise courses, work on campaigns, facilitate meetings?				
6. Ongoing coaching and support for worker educators				
a) Do worker educators have each other's phone and e-mail addresses?				
b) Can worker educators get help in preparing to facilitate?				
c) Will the union be providing refresher training for worker educators?				
d) Is co-facilitation a policy and practice of the union?				
e) Can people make mistakes and get support to do better?				
7. Working links with the rest of the union				
a) Is education working with one or more other functions of the union in joint projects?				
b) Are worker educators involved?				
c) Do other programs request education's help in their work (e.g., organizing, campaigns, research)?				
d) Does education request help from other parts of the union to carry out its work?				
e) Are education and organizing seen as complementary activities, instead of competing functions of the union?				

Chapter 10   Worker Educator Programs

Worker educator program: Sustainability checklist page 4 of 4 ## What have you done about:	Nothing	Just started	Well underway	In place
8. Building support for the role of education				
a) Working links with officers (of all locals, if there are more than one)?				
b) Working links with staff (at all levels if it's a large union)?				
c) Education on the agenda of executive meetings?				
d) Education involved in planning important union events?				
e) Education active in important campaigns?				
9. Communicating the program				
a) Regular communication to officers of locals?				
b) Regular communication to all worker educators?				
c) E-mail hook-ups between worker educators?				
d) Regular communication to staff about education activities and training of interest to them?				
e) Are people excited about education ?				
10. Drawing on/building links with community				
a) Current list of community and activist organizations in all communities where union exists?				
b) Involvement of community organizations in any union programs?				
c) Use of community/activist resource people in education programs?				
d) Support by education program of community/activist campaigns?				
e) Involvement by education program in equity struggles in community?				

Education for Changing Unions   213

WORKER EDUCATOR PROGRAMS AS PART OF A NEW VISION OF UNIONISM

WORKER EDUCATOR PROGRAMS form a key strategy in building mobilized, democratic unions; and a mobilized, democratic union is a place where workers feel:

- included and involved;
- able to recognize the differing interests of themselves and their employers;
- able to recognize the shared ground that crosses racial and other divides; and
- committed to a common good.

Mobilized, democratic unions are the most effective response to management. As management restructures and downsizes the workplace, the union becomes a stabilizing element. By consciously building community, partly through the use of worker educators, the union can move into the psychological territory that management used to occupy with messages of employee loyalty. At a time when employers are fragmenting national links and encouraging rivalry among workplaces so that traditional co-ordinated structures are threatened, unions can strengthen each workplace by building grassroots leadership... yes, and solidarity across workplaces.

(Left) Nrinder Nann, Regina Labour Educators' Exchange, October 2002. (Right) May Day Parade, Montreal, 2002.

Education for Changing Unions

11. Strategic Planning

CONTENTS

WHAT IS STRATEGIC PLANNING?....216

THE EDUCATIONAL DIMENSION
    The role of the education officer....218
    How to develop consensus: the starting point....219
    Who should be in the room?....221

FOUR APPROACHES TO BUILDING THE PLAN
    Internal linking....222
    Coalition planning....222
    Committee forum....224
    Open space technology....225

TAKING THE PLAN FORWARD....226

F OR UNIONS, THINGS ARE NOW MOVING SO QUICKLY that we can't just repeat what we've always done. Increasingly, union leaders at all levels have to plan more proactively, seeing the bigger picture and monitoring trends. They have to anticipate changes and look beyond the next round of bargaining, the next election, the next organizing campaign. Increasingly, union leaders and activists feel a greater need to sharpen their vision, analyse the broader environment and its impact, and then draw up a plan of action and make it work. Each of these phases has an educational dimension.

The most comprehensive work with a union application in this area—at least that we know of—is by David Weil, working with Elaine Bernard at the Harvard Trade Union Program.[1] Weil speaks of three basic phases of developing, implementing, and monitoring a plan.

The issue for educators is how to go about strategic planning, as an activity by itself, and how to integrate "strategic thinking" into all of our education work, so that the general goals of the organization shape and are shaped by education. Just saying this comes directly up against an assumption amongst some activists that "this democratic popular education stuff" is great for introductory courses but can't work for the big issues facing unions.

---

1. Weil, *Turning the Tide.*

WHAT IS STRATEGIC PLANNING

FOR US, STRATEGIC PLANNING INVOLVES, in essence, the process of "building consensus"—a consensus on what's going on in the broader environment and on the organizational priorities and tasks in the light of that environmental assessment. Given this connection, we face two key questions.

- What can education do to help build that consensus? ("the process"?)
- And *on what* should the consensus be built ("the content")?

Strategic planning—whether done in a one-day workshop or a protracted consultation process that combines data-gathering, analysis, and decision making—is expected to yield a consensus on key strategic questions.

- What is going on in the broader environment?
- What are our major long term concerns?
- What should be our short term priorities?
- What must we do to carry this out?

AN EXAMPLE

Here are the results from a one-day exercise involving the executive board and senior staff of a union.

Deb Barndt

Quebec City, 2001.

What is going on in the "broader environment"?

Strategic planning begins with a discussion of the trends and forces (economic, political, socio-cultural, and ideological) that have an impact on the members and the organization as a whole. In our example, the exercise identified several key themes, including:

- the emergence of the neo-liberal agenda, which is both anti-union and anti- democratic, and the corresponding popular resistance from civil society, including labour groups;
- demographic changes both in society as a whole and within the workforce in particular;
- the tensions and growing coalition between labour and the broader social movement (women, environmental, anti-poverty, anti-racist groups);
- the growing gap between rich and poor, with an adverse impact on women and people of colour;
- technology at the workplace.

Education for Changing Unions

What are the major areas of concern that we need to focus on, in the long term?

Using the data from the environmental analysis exercise, the group focused on these three key organizational areas calling for action:

- organizing
- shaping public policy
- negotiating and enforcing collective agreements.

Working in separate groups, they analysed the impact of the environmental trends they had identified on the members and the organization in these three areas. Each group reported back on four or five strategic issues ("threats" or "possibilities") for each area—the issues with the greatest impact on the members and the organization as a whole. To arrive at these strategic issues, each subgroup assessed what was going on in the workplace, in the light of their understanding of the broader environment discussed earlier in the day. At the end, they lined up the set of strategic priorities from each of the three areas side by side, and identified linkages.

What should be our top priority areas for action in the next two to three years?

The twenty strategic issues identified were grouped into a few broader issues, and then the group as a whole agreed on the "action priorities," using a ranking method. The ranking resulted in a list, prioritized from items one to six, which became the "operational" translation of the strategic issues.

What are the organizational tasks we need to carry out?

For each action priority, the group identified "internal organizational tasks" (for example, financing, staffing, technology, organizational structure) and "basic organizational functions" (for example, how we do bargaining, organizing, research, grievance handling?). The focus of this step was to find the "strategic tasks" needed for each of the action priorities. The group identified milestone activities and placed them on a one-year timeline.

The overall consensus (the three priority areas of concern, strategic issues, and action priorities) served as a "strategic framework" to help the board steer the organization and monitor operational plans and programs.

THE EDUCATIONAL DIMENSION

Learning, as we've already noted, happens in many parts of union life, not just in events announced as courses—which is a crucial point for addressing the educator's role in strategic planning processes. When Michael Newman writes about union education in Australia, he calls his book *The Third Contract*.[2] The three contracts are between the members and the leadership, between the members and the educators, and between the educators and the leadership. All three of these contracts are in effect all the time, in every course or event in which educators participate. In strategic planning exercises the leadership may have a more specific set of goals in mind than they do, for instance, in a stewards course. The structure is more likely to be a working group or committee than a course as such. Nonetheless, the educators need to honour our contracts with the members and the leaders.

The role of the education officer

By the very nature of the exercise, union educators have a supporting role, focused mainly around helping to:

- build a conducive climate, safe enough for people to differ with each other, break out of the present mould, and think "blue sky";
- design a process that leads to a consensus on priorities and plans, rooted in equitable and democratic relations;
- strengthen skills for critical analysis and creative visioning; and
- promote a culture that values the space and time to pause, listen to "far out ideas," and suspend judgement.

In practice, the educator has no direct role in deciding when a strategic planning exercise happens, who participates, and why it should be done. The senior political leadership of the union have the prerogative of deciding on the when, who, and why. It is their role to set strategic directions. Sometimes they turn to the "education or training officer," or sometimes to an outside source, to help them with the "how"—with designing a process that can lead to a consensus on long-term directions and priorities for the whole organization. That is where education staff can find their space, make their contribution to the process: we know a thing or two about developing consensus, is rooted in equity and democracy.

In the implementation phase, it will fall back to educators to ensure that every course is somehow linked to the organization's strategic priorities. In the monitoring phase, educators can be of special value in considering how resistance to change is addressed. In all phases, educational values and the skills brought to this process can make a special contribution.

Formally or informally, educators need to work with a small planning team, shaping a process that is both effective and equitable, from data-gathering and analysis to building consensus on goals. This work involves:

- facilitating the actual process of group analysis and decision-making;
- drawing out the educational implications of both the outcomes and the process of strategic planning; and
- incorporating the results of strategic planning into educational plans and programs.

---

2. Newman, *Third Contract*.

How to develop consensus: the starting point

The spiral model suggests starting with people's experience. In a context of strategic planning, the educator would have to consider whose experience needs to be drawn on. Clearly this goes beyond those who are enrolled in courses, or assigned to teach them. Educators must inquire about the experience of organizers, grievance officers, negotiators, and elected leaders, all busy people. In discussions of future direction, union educators can develop links that will reinvigorate many dimensions of union work. Formally or informally, the educator is "facilitating" not courses, but a wider strategic conversation.

People with a background in corporate strategic planning are often inclined to push organizational change from the top. They consider it a sidetrack to start from people's experiences and the patterns of those experiences. Indeed, some such processes consider history to be an obstacle and organizational structures to be deadwood until proven otherwise. That is how corporations and public employers did their re-engineering through the 1990s.

Myles Horton, the founder of the Highlander Center in Tennessee, gave his long and productive life to grassroots education in the labour and civil rights movements. He said, "Our job as a gardener or as an educator is to know that the potential is there or will unfold. People have a potential for growth; it's inside, it's in the seeds."[3] Leaders in the labour movement, as elsewhere, are at times sorely tempted to stand looking over the terrain, glaring at the seeds as they choose their own time and place for growing. But stubbornly, proudly, workers will insist on learning at their own pace, and in their own direction.[4] In our view, this means starting with the multiple experiences of people involved in the process and then moving to find patterns in the experience and to establish a common vision.

The bottom line for effective strategic planning in unions is that it grow from a desire to change outside practices and power relations while being open to changing internal practices and power relations. Otherwise it is a waste of everyone's time. In turn the bottom line for an educator's contribution to the process is that it enhance democracy and build organizational strength. Those, after all, are two of our key threads.

---

3. Horton, *Long Haul.*
4. One enduring characteristic of adult learning, noted by Alan Thomas during his decades of work, including years of involvement in labour education in the 1950s and 1960s, is that it cannot be coerced. See Thomas, *Beyond Education,* p.14.

AN EXAMPLE

A local union executive meeting was rife with tension. The invitation to the union educator to lead a strategic planning exercise was in part an effort to "clear the air." In the opening discussion of expectations, the educator pushed to get some of the negative energy expressed. Among the expectations that came out:

This session will be a waste of time, futile . . .

Nothing will be resolved . . .

These sessions come and go, and people will return to old behaviours anyway . . .

After "opening" our views, trust will actually decline . . .

Old wounds will be reopened rather than healed . . .

If you speak your mind, it will be held against you . . .

This kind of distrust often pervades meetings that are heading into strategic planning. Beneath the high-sounding discussion of mission and principles, currents of fear, rivalry, and doubt can suck energy out of the process. This is familiar terrain for union educators, who need to have a firm grip on those handy tools for dealing with such climates. Those tools (some of the ones we've already introduced) can help clear the way so that conflict is seen as a source of information, so that discussions of vision and priorities can become productive.

Educators have to consider and address these toxic climates rather than set them aside, even while they are busy discussing the "meta-goals" of social justice and international solidarity, or defining specific priorities in bargaining and organizing. In a healthy union, the courses already underway can help to define goals and further validate the need to create nurturing climates. Education is an incubator for union goals, not just a place where pre-established goals are deposited into members' heads. Union educators, then, should help to build strategic thinking skills within the organization— not just during a formal strategic planning exercise, but all the time. Education can help create a culture receptive to a broader vision for the labour movement, and one valuing the need to pause, listen, reflect, and plan in a way that complements but does not contradict the activist mode.

Most of the available tools draw on the traditions of conservative strategic planning or socialist political planning. At its best, the conservative tradition has aimed to manage change and help organizations survive, while the socialist tradition has aimed to identify openings in the system and maximize the effect of interventions. Most likely, union educators will need to bring a combination of these two perspectives to the planning process.

Who should be in the room?

Whatever approach we take, our planning won't work if the right people aren't present—and having the right people there is a major initial hurdle in preparing strategic planning sessions. Often leaders have dismal memories of work with others outside the union leadership, and the reflex response excludes the outsiders to avoid a repetition of bad feelings. So, for example, one labour council had experienced sharp tensions with a community agency over the issue of workfare. Yet this agency's mandate overlapped with that of two major labour council committees, and excluding its people from the discussion would ensure that any resulting plan would meet with major community opposition. This issue of openness applies as much within the union as outside it. Bad blood with political rivals, memory of times that people failed to deliver on commitments: these past experiences become a reason for not inviting certain people to participate in the process. Even the best tools won't save a process that starts with such narrow thinking.

Assuming that the planning process represents a broad range of people, we believe that union educators can resist top-down approaches. Drawing the six threads through our work, we can use methods such as internal linking, coalition-planning, committee forums, and open space technology.

Public Service International

Asia-Pacific Regional Womens' Workshop, Seoul, Korea, 2001.

FOUR APPROACHES TO BUILDING THE PLAN

Internal linking

One weekend strategic planning activity we participated in involved several bargaining units that faced a well-networked public-sector employer. The units themselves were divided by geographic locations, traditions, and personalities. The educator was brought into a co-ordinating meeting of twenty people, a meeting that was often a place for working out rivalries. Rather than engaging in "conflict resolution," the educator decided to move directly into strategic planning and to work through the divisions as an integral part of that broader process.

After much discussion, the participants expressed the goals for the session as:

- deepen our critical appreciation of who we are as bargaining units and as a union—our shared history as well as the diversity that makes up our membership;
- analyse what's going on in our workplaces, specifically anti-union management techniques and the employer's agenda;
- develop an overall activity plan linked to the sector's timeline of activities; and
- develop a back-to-the-workplace strategy to involve members in all phases of the activity plan.

Using several of the activities outlined in this book, the session then went a long way towards pulling people together for concerted action based on a shared strategic plan. In other words, a group of twenty people were able to work out their differences as part of a comprehensive strategic planning process. The approach, following the spiral model, started from the experience of division, worked through the patterns in that experience, introduced ideas around how management benefited from those divisions, and ended with a commitment to work together in certain specific areas. The process was intricate, demanding all the craft of which the educator was capable. The attention to building community early in the weekend was of decisive importance in moving towards the ambitious goals that strategic planning processes typically set.

The immediate results included a consensus on the issue that would take priority throughout the sector (workload); priorities for each local within the context of bargaining, organizing, or public policy; a strategy of co-ordinated bargaining, despite different expiry dates; and linking plans, from local to sector to local.

Coalition planning

The labour council executive had voted to engage in a strategic planning exercise, and set one evening date for it, to which community partners might be invited. Two union educators were brought in to facilitate the session. Their first phone conversations with the labour council president helped to determine key issues and current thinking about the format and focus of the meeting, as well as about who was coming and who else needed to be invited. Given the time of day, it was important to arrange for food to encourage people to come directly from work and to get an early start.

The educators also met with the labour council executive, at which they explored:

- where the labour council was already working with community groups and where they wanted to expand;
- the key issues people wanted to address in the coming year;

- what the executive members were afraid would go wrong in the meeting; and
- where action ideas would go, so that energy wouldn't dissipate through fuzzy follow-up.

Based on this meeting, the educators had some sense of the five priority areas for labour council work over the coming year.

For the meeting itself, the educators then set three specific objectives: to strengthen the labour council's links in the community; to identify common interests and possible joint actions for the coming year; and to agree on a firm follow-up for joint work.

This specific meeting opened with a solidarity bingo (see CHAPTER 6), and other activities that encouraged people to see the meeting as a source of rather than a drain on energy. The educators tried to give everyone a sense of who was in the room, so that participants would feel seen and excited, part of something lively and interesting. In that climate it became easier to focus people's attention on the work to be done together.

At this point the working proposal from the labour council came up. In the flow of the spiral model, this was the point for introducing new ideas. The educators presented five flip charts, each with the title of an action area as identified by the labour council executive. Each flip chart included some specific action ideas, with each idea written on a separate card taped to the flip-chart paper so that it could be moved around. The meeting broke into small groups, each with at least one labour council and one community person. The participants discussed what they found interesting in the five areas, what else needed to be added, and which proposed actions were too ambitious or perhaps better handled by someone else.

Gradually through the evening the participants amended the list, adding more detail to the ideas. People divided up again, according to the idea that most interested them, and developed a SMART plan (Specific, Measurable, Action-oriented, Realistic with the resources available, and Time-specific with some deadlines). In the end they had a list of nine action areas, which they labelled as:

- actions for which the labour council should take the lead
- actions for which the labour council should share the lead with one or more community groups
- actions for which a community group should take the lead, with specific ideas for support by the labour council.

Again in keeping with the spiral model, the process wound up in action-planning. This kind of experience encourages us to think that participatory processes for strategic planning can be highly efficient as well as energizing.

Committee forum

The federation of labour had a wide range of committees, some more active than others. Each tended to push for resources and attention to their specific area of work, and union officers managed their priorities with little involvement of the executive board. The federation organized a weekend "think-together," with all the committees to meet first, followed by a one-day session of the executive board to deal with the results. The federation leadership set clear goals for the session:

- to develop committee work plans that would advance the general federation agenda;
- to link work plans to mobilizing efforts in the locals, affiliates, and the federation as a whole; and
- to build a work plan for the federation for the coming year.

These three goals also provided the sequence for the event. The first goal showed some faith in the committees themselves: that their members would try to think beyond their immediate tasks to consider the general needs of the federation. The second goal tried to ensure that committees did not work in a vacuum—that their activities connected to concrete interest and support within the locals and affiliates of the federation. The third goal was for the executive as a group to consider the results of this work, to consider the needs and priorities involved, and to provide the necessary support and leadership. This sequence is the precise opposite of what traditional managers do in re-engineering strategies, which are controlled from the top by a small group of people.

Again, the opening of the session was carefully designed. It moved quickly into building a portrait of the political landscape in which people worked. Members of small groups wrote on small cards the elements of an agenda for four distinct groups: employers, government, members, and affiliates. As these items were pasted on a large wall sheet, and links were drawn graphically, a general picture emerged, a more shared sense of context than is the case in most environmental scans.

Based on this shared picture, the committees began their own planning work for the coming year, each noting down activities, according to month, on long, narrow strips of paper. When they placed these strips of paper on the wall, one above the other, everyone in the room could see the connections and overlaps, conflicts and duplications. By working through the similarities and variations, and then leaving the results of their "committee forum" on the wall, they prepared the ground for the executive board itself to do its job on the next day.

In the next step a second spiral began, as the executive board looked at the patterns on the wall, compared them with the patterns in their own experience, and undertook to move the federation towards co-ordinated action—towards a strategic plan for the organization as a whole.

Open space technology

This approach is most useful for unclear situations in which the leadership is willing to experiment by pulling a wider range of people together to figure things out. It is a variant of the "search conference," a tool developed by Eric Trist and others in the Tavistock Institute in the United Kingdom. Their "socio-technical systems" (STS) approach to workplaces combines the social dimension of organizational values, norms, and behaviours with the technical dimension of tasks, technology, and organizational structure. Without adopting the whole STS package, unions can benefit from open space technology, which opens the floor to a broad range of people involved in the situation. The approach trusts them to identify the key issues for a future plan, to facilitate the discussion of those issues, and to translate the results of that discussion into accessible written form. The tool is most helpful in the initial phase of developing a plan, but it may also foresee some of the issues likely to emerge in implementation and evaluation. (For the basic outline of the activity itself, see CHAPTER 6.)

The process is rigorous, despite the spontaneous climate it creates. If the leadership is open to new ideas and new blood, the process will help to sustain a healthy, participatory organization.[5]

Unions' hesitation in taking up this tool has largely been because it is difficult to predict and control the outcomes of such processes. In one group we worked with, the educator was assured that the leadership was fully open to new ideas. The activity worked beautifully, to the point that a group of twenty-five people produced a twenty-page document, collectively ranking suggestions for the future of the organization. In the closing plenary the leadership addressed the top three suggestions in turn, carefully explaining why none of them could be implemented. The educator suffered in silence as the results of a successful process were apparently flushed down the drain.

But, as it turned out, no confrontation was necessary. The leadership was shaken in its convictions, and in its own time conducted an internal consultation that led to significant changes along lines that could not have been predicted at the time of the session. Interestingly, that group subsequently produced a full-scale strategic planning document and is on better terms than ever with the educator. We love it when scary stories have a happy ending.

In the above examples of approaches to strategic planning, four of our six threads come into high relief.

- The educators took time to build community, before rushing into action planning.
- The participants were screened in terms of equity, so that a broad range of voices would be heard.
- In each case the elected leadership participated directly in planning the session, strengthening their capacity for the future by reviewing what makes such sessions work.
- The design allowed people to modify and add to proposed ideas, rather than trying to sell them a prepackaged plan. The climate is one of contextualized creativity: the past is linked to the present; the local is linked to the central; and the union is linked to the broader community and the larger movement for social change.

---

5. See Owen, *Open Space Technology: A User's Guide.*

These four approaches go some distance towards building consensus both on the key challenges facing the union and the priorities for action in response to those challenges. The implementation phase, though, generates still more educational challenges. Sometimes people need new information, skills, and attitudes to play a constructive role in the process.

TAKING THE PLAN FORWARD

ANY GOOD PLAN in the labour movement takes account in the initial environmental scan of where management is and where management is going. In developing implementation and monitoring a plan, the widespread course "Facing Management" has helped many unionists. A further development of that course, "Union Judo," emphasizes the importance of balance in conflict, as articulated centuries ago by Sun Tzu in *The Art of War*. As the term "judo" suggests, the approach works to sense the direction and speed of employer initiatives in order to use their momentum against them. Here, to provide a flavour of the course, we present an excerpt from the Sun Tzu text (taking up the principles involved), followed by what we see as its relevance for union work.

Principle no. 1: "To fight a hundred battles and win them all is not really good strategy. The best strategy is to render other armies helpless without fighting."

Union note: For many of our members, joining the union was not enrolling in a battle. They are willing to fight when necessary, but hesitant to trust a leadership that is constantly battling. When goals can be achieved without unnecessary fighting, their loyalty is strengthened.

Principle no. 2: "So it is said that if you know others and know yourself, you will not be imperilled in a hundred battles; if you do not know others but know yourself, you win one and lose one; if you do not know others and do not know yourself, you will be imperilled in every single battle."

Union Note: Sometimes we become so absorbed with management's tactics that we lose a sense of ourselves, of the union culture. In that case, we are in danger. But if we can keep a solid sense of our identity, and adapt our tactics with an updated and accurate knowledge of management's moves, we will achieve effective and contemporary union representation.

This kind of thinking works by analogy, as developed in the literature of creative thinking. It is the third in a four-step process of "integrated thinking." First, union values need to be articulated, followed by an analysis of the situation. The third step is creative exploration, which enriches the final step of strategic planning. Our point is that there are many ways in which unions can approach a strategic plan. Creative and participatory education can reinforce the process of internal change.

David Weil's work is particularly valuable on the point of what must happen *after* a strategic planning session in order for a plan to be implemented and monitored. There is a tendency in unions (and perhaps elsewhere) for people to think that once they have reached a policy consensus the results will automatically follow. In part this hiccup reflects an unwillingness to manage the union as an organization, which is an unfortunate and widespread tendency among activists and leaders who have spent much of their lives fighting management. Whatever the reason, poor management within the union is the cause of many failed strategic plans.

In implementing strategic plans, union educators sometimes need to play a role that seems strangely conservative. By insisting that people have the time to learn new skills and habits, educators may seem to be slowing things down. By asserting union values and stopping to take a look at our history, educators may be challenging fads for a "quick fix." By promoting the need to pause and reflect on the bigger picture, we might seem too "theoretical" or "academic." All of these possibilities can lead to renewed, or increased, tensions——but, most importantly, they work to ensure that a part of organizational life that is often presented as technical and top-down is addressed in creative and participatory ways.

Paul Keighley, CEP

Rally organized in support of CEP's fight for pay equity, Ottawa, November 1996.

12. Staying the Course

CONTENTS

MOVING THROUGH HEARTBREAK....229

BUILDING SPIRIT—THROUGH WORKERS' ARTS AND HERITAGE....234

STAYING GROUNDED....237

"This is the road. We need faith, vision, enthusiasm. Maybe we will not see results. Maybe our children or grandchildren will see them. The important thing is that we make the road.
—Fernando Cardenal of Nicaragua, in Barndt, *To Change This House*

Deb Barndt

Quebec City, April 2001.

IT'S GREAT TO INFLUENCE THE UNION MOVEMENT, and to make some contribution to the greater good, but not if it comes at the expense of burning out ourselves and those around us. How do we keep engaging, with this level of intensity and caring, year after year? At some point, union educators also need to find some compassion for ourselves, some protection from the drive towards breakdown and/or addiction that awaited many of those who have gone before.[1]

This mission—to sustain our emotional and psychological health in union educational work—is delicate, and highly personal; the tensions, again, cannot easily be resolved, but they can be explored. One way of doing this is to look at the ways of moving through heartbreak; another is to consider the idea of feeding the spirit, specifically through workers' arts and heritage initiatives.

---

1. Our friend Adriane Paavo, a Saskatchewan labour educator, is exploring this issue in depth in her M.A. thesis, to be completed in late 2002 at the Ontario Institute for Studies in Education/University of Toronto.

MOVING THROUGH HEARTBREAK

PEOPLE WHO APPLY FOR THE JOB of union educator had better be ready for some heartbreak. It is part of the job description, right there in the small print. We are expected to sustain the passion of a social movement, while leaving undisturbed the internal bureaucracies and political turf of an institution. To fall for the idea of labour unionism often involves a large dose of unrequited love. To commit to the values we promote in this book— especially of equity, democracy, and community—means running up against structures that many people still conceive of as being largely economic and functional.

The hazard may lie above us, in the senior elected leadership, beside us, in our colleagues, or around us, in the broader membership. There's a lot of pain in the working class and its institutions, much more than can be fixed by educational interventions, however skilled and sustained. Educators don't have easy access to the sources of people's hurt or anger or caution, but the scars are on display in classes, in meetings, and in the corridors of the union bureaucracy. No doubt the origins of these conflicts lie in the subordination of workers and their organizations, in what Michael Lerner calls "surplus powerlessness," how people hurt in the hierarchies of our society turn those familiar weapons on one another.[2]

The heartbreak itself, then, should come as no surprise. Some critics may wonder why we keep coming back for more. What's in it for us? Well, for one thing we tend to be filled with a passionate determination that the employers won't outwit us. Then there's the warmth and fun of being inside the circle of union activists; and the opportunity to carry out Brecht's version of the radical vision: "to comfort the afflicted and afflict the comfortable." These are all great reasons to keep going, so long as we are ready for our hearts to be broken from time to time.

The weapons used on activists

Let's explore the weapons themselves: the ways in which employers and their allies in the media portray union activists in order to break our spirits. Our friend the Chinese worker educator Rita Hoi Yee Kwok provides a neat summary, the "five D's":
- **D**ivide (splitting up the members to weaken our ability to mobilize)
- **D**elay (postponing decisions in the hope that activists will forget or disappear)
- **D**iscredit (suggesting that unions have a hidden agenda, or that their representatives have difficult personalities, rather than addressing the pertinent issues themselves)
- **D**istract (raising irrelevant matters to divert attention from concrete issues)
- **D**emoralize (intimidating and isolating union activists, to the point where they just give up).

These are weapons of the owning class, turned upon those in the working class who dare to defy their rule. Still, over the centuries of building workers' organizations, activists have learned to identify these weapons, to deflect them, to mock them. The problem really gets serious when the labour movement itself picks up and brandishes these same familiar weapons. Once activists start using them on each other, the weapons do much deeper damage than they could in the hands of a nasty manager or

---

2. Lerner, *Surplus Powerlessness*.

unscrupulous newspaper columnist. Anyone who has lived through a bitter union election knows the wounds that can be opened.

Most of our course participants, colleagues, and national officers have been hurt somehow along the way, and our events often provide occasions for them to vent their pain. We just get sprayed with that pain. If our programs become a terrain for battle among different political tendencies or cliques, the spray is directed against anyone who isn't on their side. Precisely by not taking sides, educators may be targeted for one or more of the "five D's." No matter how polished our course manuals may look on the surface, at these personal and political levels we are vulnerable. When an educator gets hit, it is often in public, in front of others.

Responding when we get hit

We need first of all to be in good shape emotionally and psychologically for our work. The heart is a muscle. Like any muscle, it requires exercise and strengthening and rest, and the union culture offers little space for this. If we arrive tense, tired, and defensive, we're in no shape to teach. We need to deal with our own pain and frustration, or we won't be able to deal with the pain and frustration around us.

AN EXAMPLE

In the course a union steward talks of being "held hostage" by two employees who are always in trouble on issues of work performance. They aren't careful; their fellow workers have to cover for them. The supervisor complains publicly that the steward keeps defending those employees while making no effort to document the problems or follow the proper steps of progressive discipline. As a result, the steward feels undermined by the supervisor, manipulated by the two "problem" employees, and misunderstood by the other members.

When this situation is brought up, one co-facilitator is really triggered. He identifies with the steward's frustration because he feels the same way about two colleagues on the union staff who he thinks do much less work than he does. Nobody higher up in the union seems to notice or care about this unfairness. So he wades right in with the course participant, identifying with her frustration. In the process he implicitly joins in bashing both the members for their apathy and the leadership for their indifference. While the bond between the facilitator and this one participant grows, the rest of the class picks up a broader message—that union activism is a useless and thankless enterprise.

Of course, that's not the conscious intent of the facilitator, but it is the result of limited self-awareness. When one of us has a hot button pushed by a participant, or when tension in a group builds to the point of being almost unbearable, we need to be in shape, emotionally balanced to deal with it. Without a sensitive and alert co-facilitator, this union course could actually demobilize the participants.

This is particularly important when the dynamics of our work often limit our links to communities outside our union. Many of us travel a lot. We work a lot of evenings and weekends and commit most of our time outside the job to a small circle of intimate people or to just plain resting. Like many of our members, who toil in workplaces now built for continuous operation and overtime, we find that synchronizing moments for collective celebration and relaxation is less easily done than in an earlier age. When we come into conflict in our union life, we have fewer supports and alternative recourses than we need. We're sitting ducks for heartbreak.

The role of union politics

A staff person in a union might be assigned, for instance, to work with a particular officer. As a result that officer's opponents will presume that the staff person will take the officer's side in a forthcoming election. Despite meticulous neutrality, this staff person's competence starts to come under fire immediately before the union convention. Suddenly, the person's capacity to make educational change in the union is broken.

Elections are not the source of the problem; but electoral democracy is demanding, and it can cause frustration. We need techniques for venting such frustration in ways that don't undermine the specific educational program. As educators, we need to be in training, to find the strength and balance required for healthy educational leadership within the union.

It is this capacity—to anticipate heartbreak, breathe through it, and recover to engage once again—that sustains transformative work in union education.

We carry on these discussions in education committees, where we can compare notes across regions and affiliates. We get together in "instructor meetings" at major courses across the country. And in the time-honoured way of the labour movement, we gather informally in corridors and cafés, in doughnut shops and bars, in pauses during union conferences, to support and challenge one another.

Responding with humour

Our efforts to stay whole parallel those of the members with whom we work, and often take the form of humour. An example of such effort comes from a group of janitors at a U.S. university. Most of them were long-service workers, people who took pride in their keen knowledge of their jobs. One week they were issued a diagram outlining the proper procedure for cleaning a classroom: "1. Open door. 2. Turn on lights. 3. Check lights. 4. Are lights out? If yes, report that lights are out. If no, continue to next step."

Within a couple of days, alternative procedure diagrams began appearing in the buildings, left in strategic places where management would find them. One of them looked like this, although we have toned down the language:

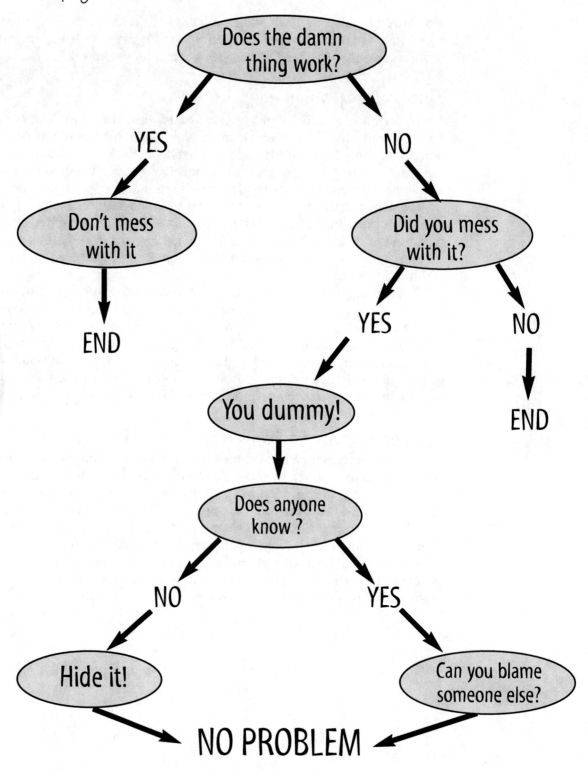

This was the response of one group of workers to the degradation of their job. Some of the gallows humour in discussions among union educators has a similar edge to it.

Our own survival tips

Often our brightest ideas in life come to mind after the fact, much as we dream up the smart rejoinder in a debate the morning after it's over. Likewise, most of our survival tips were developed after we needed them most. We could really have used these ideas at the time.

Tips for survival

† When you are punished for doing good work, pause before hitting back and marginalizing yourself further. Sometimes no action is the best action.

† When you are punished for poor work, try to separate out what you could have changed and what was beyond your control or capacity to change. Then "fess up," at least to yourself, for the part that is your own.

† When you've pushed too hard, consider what the price would have been of not pushing the limits in this situation, for you and for the others involved.

† When all you can see is those arrayed against you, consider who you met during this process who wishes you well, and contact them for personal (and perhaps confidential) support.

† When you become impatient, consider whether what you are doing is really a "false start," a first try at something that could well succeed at a later point when the balance of forces has shifted. Then you are laying the groundwork for later progress, however much you're smarting at the moment.

† Consider whether you got carried away in this process, even arrogant or judgemental, and what useful personal learning comes from this setback.

† While grieving the loss, avoid a self-righteous and self-pitying stance that isolates you from possible support.

† When things are going really well, and you are making great gains, remind people and yourself that it can't continue forever in any organization, and don't be surprised when resistance suddenly surfaces.

Above all else, these tips represent a start to a broader conversation about possible tactics for survival when you and others are working against the grain of organizational life.

The tips remind us that we need to know how to lose in a society that mostly values winning. Often we labour under the delusion that dedicated and honest work will be rewarded. More likely such virtue is its own reward, and in organizational life good work can provoke envy, resentment, and defensiveness. When we are punished for doing what we said we would do, it is easy to get caught up in anger about the injustice and hypocrisy of the situation. It is also a waste of time. At those times we need to reach into our emotional reserves, exercise our heart muscles. We need to step back, to acknowledge and process our sense of loss, and to figure out how to get back into action.

When the door slams on us, we need to pause and then look for an open window.

BUILDING SPIRIT— THROUGH WORKERS' ARTS AND HERITAGE

MANY OF US KEEP OUR EMOTIONAL STRENGTH up by engaging in activity outside the labour movement. Bonds with family, friends, and community can bring strength, perspective, and comfort during hard times. For ourselves and for participants in our programs, doing labour arts and heritage activity is another way of recharging our spirits and linking us to wider communities.

Many of the week-long courses run in each region by the Canadian Labour Congress commit one evening to a professional arts performance of some sort, usually poetry readings or plays.[3] The event's theme addresses workers, their unions, and their politics in some way, and the form is often challenging. In this way unionists experience the sense of dignity that comes from seeing themselves reflected, without being patronized, in the arts.

Sometimes a course commits a second evening in the week to the other end of the arts labour bridge: workers directly engage in a creative expression rather than just being mobilized as an audience. Classes compete in writing and performing a song. These instant "class choirs" usually address a political theme in a slapstick style. The performances usually involve hamming it up, with costumes, choreography, and sound effects, often with a raucous audience response—a practice that is now being debated. Some participants find the competition and self-ridicule to be a hallmark of old-style old-boy unionism. Others see choir night as innocuous working-class humour.

Whatever the outcome of this debate, some form of arts expression by workers seems to be a logical extension of union education. Participation as performers and as audience represents more than a change of pace; it is integral to the education process in residential union courses. Increasingly, this practice extends to union conferences and campaigns, often through the initiative of people who have experienced a lift of spirit and imagination in courses. We might find a choir at conventions of the Saskatchewan Federation of Labour, or at events of the FTQ, an award for labour arts and union banners at conventions of the Ontario Federation of Labour, and everything from puppets to street theatre at major public demonstrations.

These activities have enriched union education with information, insights, confidence and skill that a more inward turned and cautious didactic approach could not have achieved. In turn the events help union educators to take care of themselves by feeding the intuitive and creative side.

That doesn't mean it is always easy. Developing a union education sufficient to the challenges of a media-saturated society is a big challenge. The work requires curiosity, a willingness to risk, and respect for difference. This is a small gesture, a squeak of defiance perhaps, in the face of the arts, media, and publicity machinery of the employers. There is a long way to go for it to mature. As one of our readers observed, unions still treat artists in much the same way as the Medici rulers of Florence did: unions expect flattering portraits.

Courses and workshops for rank-and-file poets, musicians, theatre performers, and visual artists have been conducted as a part of union education programs, strengthening labour's claim as a vehicle for creative expression by the membership. When a professional artist works "in residence" as a part of such programs, a collaborative link of workers and artists is modelled, and the educational impact is multiplied. In such

---

3. Examples are "Highball," "Union Made," "St. George/ The Dragon," "Life on the Line," "Free Trade Zones," "Glow Boys," and "Working Peoples' Picture Show."

work, other dimensions emerge in people, so that playfulness or imaginativeness or a talent in cartoons or photos or music comes to the fore. At another moment in union life, when disagreements come up, these other points of human connection turn out to be critically important. These other layers of solidarity can help to carry us through the hard times.

Labour arts and heritage work develops workers' energy and skills for communicating the metaphors of their own culture. Indeed, the labour movement is full of "closet artists." "Amateur" storyteller John Kelly talks about a day he remembers in his youth, coming home from school: "I walked into the house and saw my Dad sitting at the table, which was an unusual thing at that time of day. I'd never seen my Dad home at four o'clock in my whole life. That was my first introduction to the words 'plant closure' and 'layoff'."

From this simple introduction, Kelly sketches the history of his family and four generations of plant closures. In the process he shows the harshness and tenderness of working-class life, so far from the negative stereotypes of beer bellies and domestic violence. He also contributes to the process whereby workers can reappropriate their own imagery. Public storytelling is one mode through which this can occur.

For most union women, poetry is more likely to be the form of expression than storytelling. The union poets are overwhelmingly women. They maintain the "right brain" record of union life.

Deb Barndt

Quebec City, April 2001.

A poem by Mary Rowles addresses another part of the union culture that rarely speaks directly—the staff rep, or employee of the movement. Usually, union staffers craft words for the elected officials to whom they report, and these officials in turn speak for the membership. Wistful and ironic, Rowles speaks for the "go-betweens" for leaders and members, the staff. When her union decided to run a public campaign and put her in charge of it, her summer vacation was cancelled and she hit the road:

> Summer hurtles down highways
> is faint through the car exhaust
> seen retreating down runways
> as we lift and touch down
> lift and lift
> over lakes that ache and sparkle.
>
> Are there truly emergency exits
> located for our convenience
> over each wing?
> Can we grasp our complimentary
> rye and peanuts
> in each fist
> and plunge down
> into the black water
> of a Muskoka adolescence?
> No, we must sit obedient
> shuffling through papers
> and join the pinstriped conga line
> snaking through the terminals
> of fourteen cities.[4]

As the labour movement engages in this work, it will begin stretching the limits of what is defined as "art," and a "labour aesthetic" will begin to influence wider public discussion of culture. In some circles, cooking is regarded as an art. What about ship models, model railroads, union jackets? In what sense can certain parts of work be considered in the same light? How can the material of daydreams on the job be captured and showcased? These questions move us far from the techniques of workshop design and facilitation, yet they remind us of the broader culture in which the labour movement is located. They also draw out the need we have to sustain our imaginations as well as our physical health if we are to try to change the movement in positive ways.

On occasion this chemistry is broadened into public education. The most sustained union effort in this regard has been the Mayworks Festival of Working People and the Arts. This series of events across the country began in Toronto in May 1986, co-ordinated by Catherine Macleod.[5] A similar festival emerged in Vancouver shortly afterwards.

---

4. Excerpted from Mary Rowles, "Passed by Seasons," unpublished, read at the Mayworks festival, Toronto, 1988.

5. See Catherine Macleod's article, "Mayworks Festival of Working People and the Arts," in Beveridge and Johnson, *Making Our Mark*, pp.21-25.

Since then Mayworks festivals have been organized in Edmonton, Moncton, Winnipeg, Windsor, and London, Ontario, with the most recent additions being in Saskatoon and Regina. The first week of May has become a showcase across the length of Canada: there have been murals painted, street banners mounted, performances of classical music in workplaces, and dances, film showings, and other celebrations of the union culture and its artistic strengths. Unionists act on what they learn. Their learning about the arts will necessarily move outside the union classroom, and even outside union-sponsored events such as Mayworks, into the public arena, the wider politics of perception.

In the meantime, labour educators can turn to labour-positive artists and arts-positive union activists as allies in the task of building community, equity, and democracy inside our unions and in society as a whole. Here is a source of personal strength and spirit to sustain this work over the long haul.

STAYING GROUNDED

Humour helps, and the arts help, but neither is a substitute for self-care in our daily lives. Beyond events and activities, educators need to invest time in rest, reflection, and intimacy, so that we bring the best of ourselves to the activists we work with. In the educational work itself, the source of stamina has to be the joy of accompanying workers. Like the close link between laughter and tears, this joy is enhanced when we accompany workers who need help.

Deb Barndt

Quebec City, April 2001.

AN EXAMPLE

The strike for a first contract was among a group of low-paid workers with militant leaders but little union experience. The employer's reaction was ferocious. It brought in strikebreakers and videotaped and charged picketers to provoke incidents and win an injunction against the union. The first few skirmishes convinced the strike leaders of the need for in-depth training of the members, and they scheduled a full-day session—and then called a union educator, who had less than a week to prepare. He pasted together existing material around three themes: your rights on the job; your rights in the union; and your rights in the society.

The "rights course" opened with discussion of a collective agreement, its meaning and legal weight in a workplace, and a review of the key provisions that the employer had refused to grant in bargaining. The group then moved to an analysis of the union constitution and a discussion of how their local structure and strike committee related to that constitution. The final third of the day dealt with the labour laws, including a discussion of the police presence on the picket line, and hence zeroed in on the political dimension of union work. The focus was on encouraging people to get to know their individual and collective rights and to exercise them effectively.

The course was a tremendous spirit-raiser, and the result was a more orderly and more solid picket line. After that the union held sessions every month, releasing strikers from picket duty so they could attend them. All the sessions used the basic structure of three levels of rights as the frame, which not only gave people a sense of familiarity but also provided a basis for encouraging less active strikers to participate. By the end of the eleven-month struggle, nearly every member of the unit had attended a session, and many attended several. This simple educational intervention deepened the learning of workers in their battle, making the learning more systematic, more collective, and more durable.

The course was valuable, but it wasn't the key. The decisive teaching took place one evening two months into the strike. Outside the main work location, a bus filled with strikebreakers pulled up to the picket line. An aggressive driver sat behind the wheel. He raced the engine. He leaned on the horn. He edged the bus forward, bumping into picketers. They wavered, uncertain of their rights, intimidated by the hostile driver and demoralized by the power behind him.

Having signed up most of the picketers himself, the union organizer could see that this first contract strike might be broken by brute force. He shouted that he wanted the driver's ID, so that he could lay assault charges against him. Then he simply lay down in front of the bus. The only way into that workplace would be over his dead body, literally.

In a mix of awe and fear, the other picketers stepped back. The driver honked some more, backed up a bit, and then raced the engine as he inched forward. The organizer simply lay there. Police came, an ambulance came, and he refused to move until the driver was identified. Finally, whether from impatience or fear of being charged, the driver backed up and drove away, swearing loudly. The picketers cheered.

That night they phoned their friends, and in the morning the picket line was back up at full strength. It held for another nine months, until the employer fired its most abusive managers and signed its first collective agreement.

A decade later, that group of workers has a reasonable boss, a safe and productive workplace, and a habit of turning up to union conferences and supporting other people's picket lines.

The organizer got no award, no raise, no promotion. In fact, a decade later, he is doing the same job, organizing new groups of workers. He and others have inspired us to keep loving and building the labour movement, despite its many problems.

Formal courses will never replace the raw courage of union activists. We know that the basic lessons of community and democracy, of equity and class-consciousness, of organization building and the common good, are mostly learned through action, without skilled facilitators or careful course designs. They can be learned in a flash of brilliance on the job, in a meeting, through a struggle.

Between those flashes of brilliance come our chances to promote thoughtful activism. As educators, we stretch the learning workers do year after year when they or their co-workers act for justice. We provide time, space, and energy for people to sort out the learning points generated in the heat of the moment. We help extend flashes of learning into changed ways of looking at events, relating to people, and going into action. We try to model consistency, to suggest strategies, to offer tools and a helping ear.

In the spirit of rising up through solidarity, we offer this song to the tune of the Johnny Cash classic, "I Walk the Line":[8]

Deb Barndt

Quebec City, April 2001.

We are women, hear our voices roar
Social justice is what we're fighting for
We are sisters united in the cause
This Union's mine, we WALK the line.

CHORUS:
 We stand together and we do just fine
 Union strength is always on our mind
 It's through our struggles that we all are tied
 The Union's mine, we ARE the line.

Our labour holds up half the global sky
We have less pay, pension, benefits, ASK WHY?
Sisters and brothers around the world combine
This is the time, let's FORM a line!

(CHORUS)

6. This was composed and performed by the Popular Education Class (Instructor Training, Level 2), led by Jojo Geronimo and Barb Thomas at the CLC Winter School, co-ordinated by Winnie Ng, February 2001.

More of Our Favourite Union Education Activities

CONTENTS

MORE OPENINGS AND CLOSINGS
Building participant guidelines....242
Class contract....243
Table stand-ups....244
Songwriting....245

MORE TOOLS FOR ANALYSING EXPERIENCE
Puzzles as a way of introducing equity/the triangle tool....246
"Stickies": factors in effective bargaining....250
The Wall: doing a gender analysis of the economy....252
A political weather report....254

MORE TOOLS FOR LINKING NEW INFORMATION TO WHAT PEOPLE
ALREADY KNOW
Active listening: interactive presentation....256
Listening self-assessment tool....258
Jeopardy....259

MORE TOOLS FOR PRACTISING NEW SKILLS AND STRATEGIC
PLANNING FOR ACTION
Pepperpot....262
Case study roleplays to develop facilitator skills....264
What's happening.....268

MORE ENERGIZERS LINKED TO COURSE CONTENT
Union workout (political exercises)....269
Pass a gesture....272

BUILDING PARTICIPANT GUIDELINES FOR PARTICIPATION AND RESPECT

Why use it?
- to develop a safe place for learning and discussion (in a meeting, for example)

Time it takes
- 15 minutes

What you need
- a set of draft guidelines written on a flip chart. Here is one example:

Draft Guidelines for Participation and Respect

- Everyone will participate in all sessions.
- No cell phones will be used during class.
- We will all come on time and end on time.
- We will all value our differences and diversity.
- Everyone will avoid side conversations.
- Everyone will have the opportunity to speak or pass.
- We will all respect confidentiality of what is shared in the room.
- We agree to listen to each other with respect.
- Participants will take care of themselves and ask for what they need.

How it's done

1. Explain that we want to agree to some guidelines for participation in the course. Ask: "What do you hope people WON'T do in this course? (Things that block your participation.)" If you have time, do a round so that everyone gets to contribute.
2. List points on the flip chart.
3. Review the draft participation guidelines that you have written on the flip chart. Ask if there are any we need to change/add given the discussion.
4. Note changes on the list. Get agreement on the guidelines by a show of hands.
5. Post the list where it can be seen and leave it up for the duration of the course.

Variations
- Spend more time for longer courses (see the next activity, "Class contract").

Challenges
- You don't want this to take up a lot of time. On the other hand, you want people to consider the guidelines seriously and take ownership of them.
- Using the set of draft guidelines does mean that there is less buy-in than if participants generate the list themselves.

Building in equity
- Be sure to discuss differences that emerge. Doing a round ensures that everyone gets a chance to speak to the guidelines.

Source
- This version was suggested by Jackie Larkin of the B.C. Nurses Union.

CLASS CONTRACT

Why use it?
- to develop a safer place for learning in a longer course

Time it takes
- 30 minutes

What you need
- coloured cards and a marker for each participant
- masking tape and a section of blank wall for posting that everyone can see, headed "Class contract."

How it's done

1. Introduce the activity briefly by saying that to learn together, we need to create a learning space in which people can take risks. For that reason we need to know what each person needs to create a safer climate. Review the question on the flip chart: "What behaviour do you need from others to help you learn." For example, you may want people to avoid side conversations, or jokes at people's expense.

2. Each person makes a card, using a marker and coloured card, which says what behaviour most helps them learn. They sign their name to it.

3. Each person sticks their card on the wall where the facilitator has placed the title "Class contract,"and says a few words about their point. Each succeeding person clusters their card with like-minded cards before them. Stress that people don't have to make a new point. They can have the same point as someone else. If there are lots of people who have the same point, we get a sense of how important it is to the group. Some examples of points people might make are: no interruptions; one speaker at a time; no cross-talking; humour; mutual respect.

4. Review key points on the cards. Ask if there's anything important that's missing. You might ask, for example, "What about pagers and cellphones?" if no one has mentioned it. Make cards for any other points. Say that not everyone has to agree to all points. If the point is important to one person's learning, then we all need to try to abide by that, as long as it doesn't hurt anyone else.

5. Clap on the contract. A way that Nigerian popular educators use to show agreement on something is to ask if people are ready to clap on it. If people signal, yes, count to three and everyone claps loudly. It's a deal.

Variations
- Where you have less time, consider using the "Building Participant Guidelines" activity on the previous page.

Challenges
- It is always difficult for some people to get up alone in front of the group early in a course. If you anticipate this as a major problem, you could have people work and report in pairs.

Building in equity
- It is important to establish that the contract needs to respect differences among participant needs.

Source
- the authors

TABLE STAND-UPS

Why use it?
- as an energizer and a way to learn participant names in the second session of a course

Time it takes
- 15 minutes

What you need
- people sitting at separate tables

How it's done
1. Each table has thirty seconds to look at the people sitting at the table on their RIGHT (make sure each table knows which table they will be introducing). In the thirty seconds, the table prepares to introduce each member at the assigned table.

2. As each person is introduced, they are asked to stand up.

3. Applause after each table introduces their partner table.

Variation
- If people are not sitting at tables, you could form random groups and then proceed as above.

Challenges
- none we can think of

Building in equity
- If in doubt, check to make sure that all names are said (and learned) correctly, particularly those that originate in other parts of the world.

Source
- the authors

Education for Changing Unions

SONGWRITING

Why do it?
- to use as a closing activity

Time it takes
- 30 minutes

What you need
- a chorus you have written to the tune of a song everyone will know; the words should say something about the course, and if you can use a well-known union song, so much the better
- flip-chart paper and markers for each group
- optional but nice: participants with musical instruments

How it's done
1. Explain that in this exercise, people are invited to say something about the course in music.
2. Introduce the song and have everyone sing it if there is anyone who is not familiar with the tune.
3. Divide participants into groups of three to four. Each group is to write one verse and put it on a flip chart so it can be read easily. (Note that there are no marks for rhymes!!)
4. Have groups post their verses and the facilitators post their chorus.
5. Do a rousing rendition as a closure to the event.

Variation
- Introduce songwriting on the first evening and have participants write a verse at the end of each day.

Challenges
- Because it is the end of the session, some people may be reluctant to do the activity, mainly because it sounds difficult. To anticipate this problem, you might talk with several "musical" participants in advance and ask them to assist with the activity. Sing the prepared chorus with some enthusiasm, because this also helps drum up energy.

Building in equity
- If you have several people from a different language group in the room, encourage them to write a verse in their own language.
- Don't assume everyone knows the tune you've picked.

Source
- the authors

Appendix

MORE TOOLS FOR ANALYSING EXPERIENCE

PUZZLES AS A WAY OF INTRODUCING EQUITY/ THE TRIANGLE TOOL

Why use it?
- it's an energizer which also forms new groups
- starts from participant experience and knowledge of inequity in the world around us
- invites a second critical look at everyday forms of unequal power relations that look normal
- can show visual connections between different kinds of inequity
- can act as a bridge for examining inequity in the workplace and/or union

Time it takes
- 60-75 minutes

What you need
- one to four pictures/ads that show inequitable relations, copied so that every-one in the group can have a copy or copies. (See our example here, "Columbus and the Slave Girl.")
- a hat or basket for passing the puzzle pieces around
- the questions for small groups on flip-chart paper, covered

How it's done
1. Before the session cut up each picture into three or four pieces so that it forms a kind of puzzle. Fold the pieces, mix them up, and put them in a hat or basket. If you have sixteen participants, and four pictures, you'll cut each picture into four pieces to have a total of sixteen pieces so that each participant can pick one; if you have twenty participants, you'll cut the same four pictures into five pieces each, and so on.

2. Pass the hat or basket with the puzzle pieces folded and mixed. Ask participants not to show their piece to their neighbours just yet.

3. When each person has a puzzle piece, give the instructions: tell them that there are four pictures, and that each person has a piece of one of the pictures; they must find the other people who have the pieces to their puzzle, and form a new group with them; when they've found their group, they should tape the pieces of the puzzle together, using masking tape, so that they can see the whole image.

4. Participants then go to find each other, and tape their puzzle together. Show people where each new group will work.

5. Give copies of the complete image to each group. (You can give each person a copy of all four puzzles at this time, or only the puzzle they are working on to keep the focus.)

6. Reveal the questions below that you want them to work on for fifteen minutes in their small groups, and ask them to record their comments on the flip-chart paper provided:

246

Education for Changing Unions

- What messages about white people, Aboriginal people, people of colour, men and women, do this image and text convey?
- Who has what kinds of power? How do you know?

7. Small groups work, recording their comments (15 minutes).

8. Reporting, Discussion, Analysis: start with the group who examined the image (in this case of Christopher Columbus and the Slave Girl). Ask them to report their findings. This image is a good one to start with because it's familiar, the oppressive relations between men and women, and Europeans and Aboriginal peoples, are obvious, and participants can start seeing that these old relations are still with us in more current images. Press the group to get as specific as possible about the messages conveyed (see triangle analysis for examples).

Option one   At this point, you can introduce the triangle tool to analyse the drawing. Simply follow the first few steps outlined for introducing the triangle model (CHAPTER 6) and then apply what they've said to the model. For example, one group we worked with came up with this analysis:

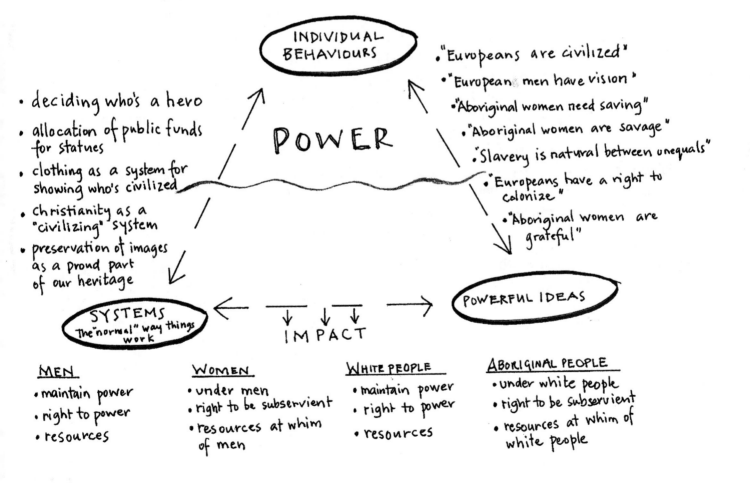

INDIVIDUAL BEHAVIOURS

POWER

- "Europeans are civilized"
- "European men have vision"
- "Aboriginal women need saving"
- "Aboriginal women are savage"
- "Slavery is natural between unequals"
- "Europeans have a right to colonize"
- "Aboriginal women are grateful"

- deciding who's a hero
- allocation of public funds for statues
- clothing as a system for showing who's civilized
- christianity as a "civilizing" system
- preservation of images as a proud part of our heritage

SYSTEMS
The "normal" way things work

IMPACT

POWERFUL IDEAS

MEN
- maintain power
- right to power
- resources

WOMEN
- under men
- right to be subservient
- resources at whim of men

WHITE PEOPLE
- maintain power
- right to power
- resources

ABORIGINAL PEOPLE
- under white people
- right to be subservient
- resources at whim of white people

Option two
- Don't use the triangle tool here. Simply press the first group to be as specific as they can about the ideas that this statue promotes.
- Continue with each group's report in turn, challenging each group to be as specific as possible about what assumptions/powerful ideas underlie their image. Even if these statements are offensive to say out loud, they are an important part of what's under the table.

Synthesis
- After EITHER option one or two, summarize key points from the exercise.
- We are surrounded every day by images of unequal relations between men and women, white people, people of colour, and Aboriginal people. They are so normal, we often don't even notice them.
- Our past history of colonialism in Canada (and in other countries) is an important base for current everyday inequities.
- When we talk about inequity, we are talking about more than offensive individual behaviour; we are talking about the normal, everyday ways we do things.

Variations
- You can use the puzzles purely as an introductory activity, using different images and different questions. (See *Educating for a Change*, "Starter Puzzle," p.83.)

Challenges
- Give equal time to each reporting group.
- Keep it moving, while probing for details.
- Don't use more than four pictures, because the debriefing will take too long; if you have many participants, break each image group into two so that you have two groups talking about the same image.

Building in equity
- Choose images that connect to a broad range of workers, so that all the work of analysis doesn't fall to workers of colour, or women.
- Although there may be text with some of the images, reading is not a requirement for active participation in this activity.

Source
- the authors with Tina Lopes

Deb Barndt

Columbus and the Slave Girl

"STICKIES": FACTORS IN EFFECTIVE BARGAINING

Why use it?
- to equalize participation, especially early in a session
- to collectivize different experiences; develop consensus
- to track visually how ideas are connected and to group ideas into common themes

Time it takes
- 15 to 60 minutes

What you need
- markers for everybody
- several packages of large multicoloured sticky notes or cards (3"x 5") and masking tape
- the task—as a handout or on flip chart

How it's done

1. Hand out the stickies and markers to everybody.

2. Pose the question for discussion. For example, "What are the factors or conditions essential for effective contract negotiation?"

3. Review the task:
   - Write one idea on one sticky note (very important!).
   - Use two or three words per idea (as in a brief heading).
   - Write big and bold for everyone to see, using markers.
   - Submit as many ideas as you can generate in three minutes.

4. Call time. Then ask for one sticky note as a starter. Have the author read it aloud, then post it in front of the class. Then ask for other stickies similar to the first one. Once that first "cluster of ideas" has been completed, begin a new cluster using the same process.

5. After all the stickies are on the board, ask everybody to step back and now review all the clusters of stickies. (Usually four to eight major clusters emerge from twenty participants.)

6. Ask all contributors to a cluster to start elaborating on what they wrote. Move the stickies from one cluster to another as necessary to ensure that similar ideas are in one cluster. (Do this quickly, but make sure the group, not you, is deciding on what goes where.)

7. After all the clusters have been formed, label each one to reflect its major theme.

8. At the end, synthesize. For example: "Here's a snapshot of what our group thinks are essential conditions or factors for successful bargaining. We seem to agree on four or five major key themes, reflecting our different individual bargaining experiences or roles."

9. People can now form into different subgroups to further discuss each theme or cluster; or develop recommendations/solutions relevant to the theme.

Variations
- Work in pairs or small groups rather than individually.
- After ideas have been generated, each pair or group reports, and subsequent groups cluster their sticky notes near similar points already posted.

Challenges
- People write too small, or want to elaborate fully on their ideas too early in the process.

Building in equity
- This exercise creates a "level playing field." Each person gets her or his turn to post, and each idea is used as a building block in creating collective knowledge.

Source
- the authors

Barb Thomas

Regina Labour Educators' Exchange, October 2002.

THE WALL

This methodology uses the image of a stone wall to build a gender analysis of today's economy or a particular aspect of it. The wall image provides an opportunity to analyse changes in the economy over the past ten years or so, and to consider what those changes mean for women. The handbook *Starting with Women's Lives* outlines in detail how to do a one-two day workshop using this method. Below is an adapted, four-hour version.

Why use it?

- to do a gender analysis of the economy or a sector of the economy in a visual way
- to identify strategic actions that women in the union movement can take

Time it takes

- 4 hours for this version

What you need

- See *Starting with Women's Lives* (in "Resources and Sources"), which details the materials and supplies you need to prepare.

How it's done

1. **Introductions**—to participants, the Wall, and the workshop

2. **The top of the Wall.** Participants identify key changes to jobs and social programs over the past ten years. In groups, they share how these changes have affected them at home, in the community, in the workplace, and in the union. Points are written on paper stones and posted on the Wall. Patterns are identified.

3. **The work women do: the triple role exercise.** Each person picks a scenario from a hat and is asked to act out the scene with gestures, no words. Groups form around the same scenario, which is then acted out for the other groups. Participants identify paid and unpaid jobs in the role plays and review statistics to show how women's work is traditionally undervalued, underpaid, or unpaid. Participants name marginalized groups in their communities/countries and these are noted on the Wall with a few statistics to show how some women are hurt more severely than others.

4. **Gains women have made.** The group discusses the gains women have made to achieve equality and get their work valued, and these are recorded on the Wall.

5. **The causes.** Participants discuss why this is happening (the causes), and these points are recorded on the Wall, with notes on the connections and links among the causes identified.

6. **Naming our power and our allies.** Everyone is given a card with the name of an individual or institution on it and asked to line up across the room according to how much the person on her card benefits from the Wall. Discussion follows in the lineup about who benefits, what power different women have, and where their power comes from. The group is asked to identify allies who might work with them in changing the Wall. The facilitator asks, what would happen if all of us women were to withdraw our labour tomorrow? Answers are recorded on the flip chart.

7. **Moving to action**. Participants identify changes needed to get women's work valued and paid fairly, and these are recorded on the Wall. Then they identify signs of hope, actions that have already begun with the power to change parts of the Wall. These are written on the plants growing on the bottom of the Wall. In small groups, participants discuss action ideas, relevant to the group. These are summarized on paper women and posted on the wall. Next steps are identified if appropriate.

8. **Evaluation and closing.**

Variations

- See *Starting with Women's Lives* for a longer version of the workshop and several adaptations for different circumstances.

Challenges

- You need to make sure enough time is available to move through the analysis to action-planning.
- The methodology was developed for use with women. Adding men to the workshop requires adaptation.
- The preparation of the visual aids is time-consuming.

Building in equity

- This workshop focuses on gender by looking at how women's experience is different from men's.
- The activity identifies differences in women's experiences due to race, class, age, or disability, for example.

Source

- adapted by the authors with Suzanne Doerge

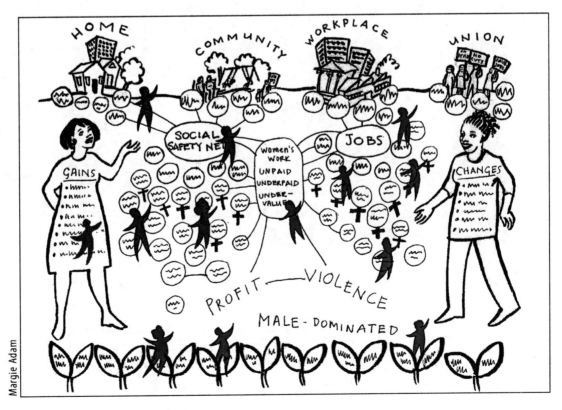

Margie Adam

A POLITICAL WEATHER REPORT

Why do it?
- to identify forces working for and against us specific to one critical issue common to the whole group, prior to developing a strategy
- to learn to think "dialectically"—to see the contradictions and tensions in relation to a specific issue

Time it takes
- one hour

What you need
- sticky notes
- wall chart
- markers, glue stick, or tape
- task sheet

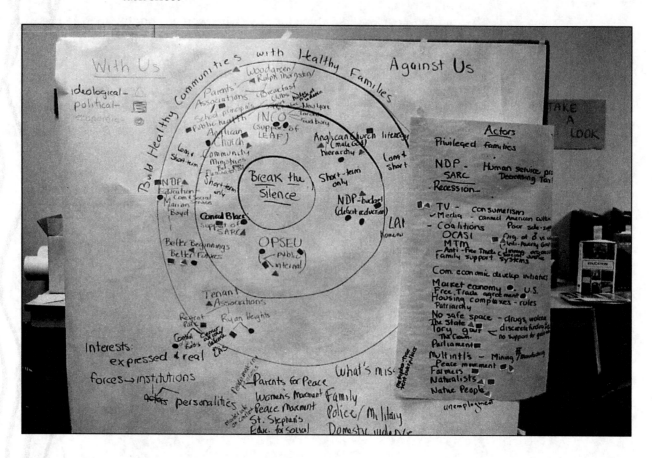

How to do it

1. **Select the issue.** As a full group, select one critical issue common to all or most participants. (Example: workload.)

2. **Set goals.** In groups, participants draft goal statements on the issue for: i) a demand setting or bargaining situation. (Example: negotiate better client ratio by hiring more full- time staff); ii) a public policy campaign situation; iii) an organizing situation.

3. **Identify forces for us, against us, and undecided on this issue**. Ask groups to identify the key forces both "inside and outside" the workplace. Forces are "key actors" who have an influence on this issue or on the members. They should consider: "inside/internal forces"—for example, middle management, contract workers, or younger/less senior staff who joined in the last three years; "outside/external forces"—any institution (for example, media) or other constituency groups (for example, labour councils, women's coalitions). Be specific. For example, don't just say "media"; specify which newspaper or radio station, or even the columnist/reporter/radio host. Note that one newspaper might be "against" an issue, but one particular writer could be tilting towards "forces for."

   Decide whether these forces are for us or against us on this particular issue. (Note: a group that might generally be against labour could in fact be on our side on one particular issue. These are your "tactical or temporary allies.")

   Then consider the "undecided" forces—the "swing votes" that can be persuaded one way or another.

4. **Locate forces on the chart**. Groups headline the forces on sticky notes. These are posted on the wall chart.

5. **Analyse**. After all groups have reported back, analyse the forces.
   - What are the specific interests of these forces in relation to your issue? (For instance, part-time workers have no problem with workload, it gives them more hours.)
   - Who/where is your main base of support among all the identified forces?
   - Where are the key tension points among the membership? What are the points of convergence, or alliances, for or against the issue?
   - Where would management drive a wedge to divide the membership on this issue?
   - What's the relative strength of these forces? Which ones are soft, and could shift? Which ones are firm and can be expected to hold in face of management's tactics?

6. **Summarize**. Your mobilizing strategy will be to make a choice: hold the ground, consolidate the forces for, hold off the forces against, or win over undecided forces. A focused strategy will help you conserve your resources.

Variations
- You can use "forces" simply as an event, strengths or weaknesses, or actions that can influence an issue.

Challenges
- There might be a tendency to generalize what the "forces" are—to see them as homogeneous groups.

Building in equity
- The exercise should highlight how the issue can hurt marginalized groups; it can make visible certain groups of members who would otherwise be invisible.

Source
- Barndt, *Naming the Moment*; adapted by the authors

MORE TOOLS FOR LINKING NEW INFORMATION TO WHAT PEOPLE KNOW

INTERACTIVE FACILITATOR PRESENTATION OR "RANT" ON ACTIVE LISTENING

Why use it?
- to add some theory on active listening

Time it takes
- 20 minutes

What you need
- three levels of listening written on cards
- two examples with questions about them written on flip chart:
  - key content
  - feelings
  - intentions
- sample questions on flip chart
- active listening graphic on flip chart
- group to have completed the "Listening self-assessment tool"(see page 258)
- a listening practice exercise to follow the presentation (we use a version of the "Triads" activity outlined in CHAPTER 6)

How it's done

1. Based on the self-assessment tool, ask for any contributions from pairs about:
   - how we like to be handled by others; what drives us crazy
   - our own behaviour patterns
   - what interferes with and helps our own listening?

2. Introduce the levels of listening. When we listen, we're not just trying to hear the speaker's key points. It's on this level that we have many of our disagreements. The other information we get from listening relates to the person's feelings (anxiety, fear, excitement, whatever), and her or his intentions, values, or what's important to that person. For facilitators it is critical to listen at all three levels—key points, feelings, intentions/values. (The three levels of listening should be noted on cards, to be stuck up as each is mentioned.)

3. Review the following examples and ask people to discuss the questions. (The examples and questions are written on a flip chart.)

Example one

"The local president is out to get me. What he said at that meeting proves it. He's purposely undermining a year of work I've been doing with that local."
- What do you know for sure (facts/key points)?
- What might be the feelings of the speaker?
- What seems to be of importance to the speaker?

Example two   "I think we need to define more clearly what racism really is. I've been in a situation recently where someone accused me of racism and that's the last thing I meant. Let's not get too sensitive about this whole thing."

- What do you know for sure (facts/key points)?
- What might be the feelings of the speaker?
- What seems to be of importance to the speaker?

4. Introduce open-ended and closed questions. (Write the examples on the flip chart.) Questions are very important in inviting and acknowledging information. What kind of information and reactions do these pairs of questions invite?

(i)   After he did that, did you call the steward?
(ii)   After he did that, what did you do?

(i)   Do you think maybe you overreacted?
(ii)   You mentioned earlier that "maybe you raised your voice." Can you tell me some more about that?

- Note that question (i) in each pair is closed; it calls for a yes or no answer; and they might be experienced as a judgement about what to do;
- Question (ii) in each pair is open-ended; it invites more information and keeps the conversation focused on the speaker, and not on the questioner's agenda.

5. Return to the two examples from "Levels of Listening" (step 3) and brainstorm some open-ended questions for each.

Variations
- You might ask participants to read out loud the examples and questions.

Challenges
- The facilitator needs to link the new information to what people already know about active listening.
- Don't drag it out so that the presentation is boring and/or too long.

Building in equity
- The questions and materials are read out loud as well as posted on flip chart or cards.
- One example incorporates a discussion of racism.

Source
- the authors

LISTENING SELF-ASSESSMENT TOOL

These two questions ask us to think more carefully about listening. This first question is about when we feel listened to; the second is about listening to someone else. Rank your top-five, most likely responses, where 1=most likely, 2= second most likely, and so on.

1. When **someone disagrees with me**, I respond best when they
   - roll their eyes and wait for me to finish ❏
   - furrow their brow and wait for me to finish ❏
   - do something else while they wait for me to finish ❏
   - interrupt me to set me straight ❏
   - ask me questions if they don't understand what I'm saying ❏
   - change the subject and keep their ideas to themselves ❏
   - cite authorities I don't know to prove I'm wrong ❏
   - patiently explain why I'm wrong ❏
   - explain why they disagree ❏
   - identify where they think we're in agreement and where we differ and ask some questions about why I feel that way ❏
   - other? (specify) _____

2. When **I disagree with someone**, I'm most likely to
   - furrow my brow and wait for them to finish ❏
   - drum my fingers and wait for them to finish ❏
   - roll my eyes and wait for them to finish ❏
   - plan what I'll say when they finish ❏
   - interrupt to set them straight ❏
   - ask questions to clarify what the person is saying and why ❏
   - change the subject and keep my ideas to myself ❏
   - cite authority to prove I'm right ❏
   - make sure they know why they're wrong ❏
   - explain my point of view and ask the other to do the same ❏
   - ask some clarifying questions to find out what motivates their opinion ❏
   - other? (specify) _____

Note: Probably all of us use all of the responses possible here at one time or another, depending on the situation. However, think about your top-five most likely responses.

Education for Changing Unions

JEOPARDY

Why use it?
- as an energizer and as a creative way of linking course content or adding more or new information; the activity is a takeoff on the television game show *Jeopardy*.

Time it takes
- 30 minutes

What you need
- five to eight categories written on paper or cards
- corresponding statements to the categories you have chosen
- space enough to form two lines of participants

How it's done
1. Decide on the categories and corresponding statements, drawing from the material that is being covered in the class. For example:
   - "Job crisis" is the sample category;
   - The corresponding statement might be: "The Canadian company that sold off 2,500 phone operator jobs to an American call centre."
   - Answer: Bell Canada
   (See the other sample categories and questions listed here.)

2. Post the category title sheet on the wall; place all the corresponding statements underneath that category. Tape each sheet so that they can be easily peeled off to expose the next statement under that category. Each category should have the same number of questions underneath the category title sheet. Facilitators should have the answers.

3. Participants form into two teams and then into two lines. The teams will take turns giving the answer to the statement. The participant at the front of the line chooses a category and then makes a buzzer noise, which indicates they have the answer within an agreed upon time frame. Once the answer is given they go to the end of the line and the next person chooses the category when it is their turn, and so on. The team members can assist the person at the front of the line with the answer.

4. Facilitators act as the judges and announce how much time is permitted for an answer to each question. Once the time is up, the other team is given the opportunity to answer the question. If neither teams knows the answer, the facilitators give the correct answer and the same continues with the next member of the appropriate team.

5. Have Fun!

Variations
- Facilitators could use this as part of a closure exercise and have one category as "Stars" or "Personalities" and choose a positive, recognizable quality of each participant, or something inspiring they said or did, and use those features as the corresponding statement under the category. For example, if one participant shared with the class that she was so inspired that when she returned she intended to run as a steward in her department, the statement could be "The inspiring woman who didn't want to be involved with the union, who will now be running as a steward."

Challenges
- Participants will want to keep playing.
- The "game" can become more important than the content.

Building in equity
- Line up two rows of chairs for each team.
- Be sure to include statements of equality issues to elicit discussion and thought.

Source
- Deena Ladd

THE QUIZ

BACKLASH	GETTING ORGANIZED	EQUALITY IN JEOPARDY
? He suggested that school breakfast programs were necessary because women weren't staying home and cooking hot breakfasts.	? One out of every three workers in Canada belongs to one of these.	? Only one level of government in Canada has passed a law challenging systemic barriers to equality in employment.
? Includes members who believe it is an employer's right to keep Black or gay workers out of sight, as a business decision.	? In the private sector, women represent this percentage of Canada's workforce.	? The Canadian company that sold off 2,500 phone operator jobs to an American call centre.
? The opposite of the democratic principle that one should be paid for one's labour.	? In the public sector, women represent this percentage of Canada's workforce.	? Workers for this employer fought for pay equity for fifteen years.
	? This legal document is the most effective guarantee of rights and conditions at work.	? This was the first piece of legislation repealed when the Ontario Tories came to power.
	? The fastest way to shrink the pay gap for the lowest-paid workers in Canada.	? Most growth has been in these kinds of jobs. More and more workers are turning to this kind of work, nicknamed after the world's largest fast-food chain.

THE ANSWERS

A. The Premier of Ontario, Mike Harris

A. The Canadian Alliance Party

A. "Workfare"– the Tories' concept of criminalizing and stereotyping the poor by forcing them to work for their welfare regardless of their circumstances and without providing any support systems such as affordable child care or transportation means

A. A union

A. 23.8 per cent

A. 64.3 per cent

A. A collective agreement or a contract

A. Unionizing

A. Employment equity in the federal government

A. Bell Canada

A. The Public Service Alliance of Canada

A. The Ontario Employment Equity Act

A. McJobs

MORE TOOLS FOR PRACTISING NEW SKILLS/STRATEGIC PLANNING FOR ACTION

PEPPERPOT

Why use it?
- to practise "sticky moments" in facilitating

Time it takes
- 60-90 minutes for twenty participants

What you need
- at least ten "sticky moments" written on small pieces of paper (these can be from facilitators and/or the participants; see "Sample Scenarios" below)
- a hat or box to put the "moments" in

How it's done

1. **Introduce the exercise.**
   (a) Explain the purpose: to practise dealing with difficult moments that come up in social change education.
   (b) Ask people to choose a partner. (It's less threatening to work in pairs.)
   (c) Explain that each pair in turn will pick a situation from the hat. They will read the situation and then have a minute to talk about how to deal with it; then they role play their best response with the facilitator playing the role of "problem participant."

2. **Do the exercise.**
   (a) The first pair picks from the hat, reads out the situation and prepares briefly (one minute). Other participants should be encouraged to talk about what they would do as well.
   (b) One of the participants or a facilitator plays the role of the "problem partici-pant." The other facilitator guides the process.
   (c) The pair role plays their response. The other participants can jump in to help the pair find effective responses.
   (d) The second facilitator times the role play for three minutes.

3. **Discussion**
   (a) Briefly review the most effective responses (maximum 2-3 minutes). Record these with the title for future reference. It is important to keep this moving along.
   (b) Continue until each pair has had a chance to role play.

Challenges
- A level of trust needs to be established in the group so that people will feel able to take the risk of trying to handle a difficult situation on their feet in front of their peers.
- The facilitator needs to be sure that main points are made about how to deal with each situation while guarding against leaving some participants feeling less confi-dent than before.

Building in equity

- All of the pepperpot situations outlined in "Sample Scenarios" deal with equity issues.
- Participants are working in pairs, which helps if one person has difficulty reading.

Source

- the authors

Sample Senarios for the Pepperpot

- On the first day of a one-week human rights course, the participants in targeted groups (women, or people of colour, for instance) decide to caucus. While you are sure that participants from the dominant culture (white males) feel threatened by the decision, they don't say anything at the time. On day three the situation blows up. The white men say they are being left out, and that it is not proper for special groups to meet without their participation. They are angry and there is a lot of tension in the room.

- In a discussion about Aboriginal peoples' rights, a Caucasian brother decides to be the spokesperson for Aboriginal people. There is an Aboriginal sister in the class who is new to the union and thus very shy to speak. The brother tries to badger her to support his position on what terminology to use—Aboriginal, Native, or First Nations peoples.

- One woman of colour is a participant in a class of white, able-bodied men. Someone says that neither racism nor sexism really exist; there are just misinformed individuals. Your co-facilitator is a white able-bodied male, who is uncomfortable with the statement, but not sure what to do.

- You are co-facilitating a course. Your partner does not challenge a homophobic comment made by a participant when he is facilitating. In fact, he tells the participant, encouragingly, "That's a good point."

Deb Barndt and Cathy Lang,
The Moment Facilitation
Training, Toronto, 1992.

unknown

Education for Changing Unions

CASE STUDY ROLEPLAYS TO DEVELOP FACILITATOR SKILLS

Why use it?
- to understand the basic principles of different facilitator skills
- to practise building equity into union facilitation
- to develop new, creative approaches to routine tasks

Time it Takes
- 1.5 to 2 hours

What you need
- a small-group activity sheet (see sample on next page)
- coloured paper, scissors, markers, flip-chart paper, and other supplies

How it's done

1. Divide participants into four groups.

2. Review the activity sheet and assign each group its task (a different task to each group).

3. Small groups prepare (about forty-five minutes).

4. Group one actively presents its work in a way that involves the other participants. After their presentation, group one summarizes the three to five things to keep in mind to do their task well.

5. The course facilitator asks questions to pull out additional points. (See "tip sheets" in CHAPTER 5, which were produced using this activity with different union groups.)

6. Repeat for each of the other three groups.

Variations
- The format of this activity, with an adapted activity sheet, could be used to practise skills in dealing with member complaints and/or grievances, dealing with a health and safety problem, dealing with harassment, running a meeting, or building links with community, among other things.

Challenges
- It encourages participants to try something new, while at the same time they recognize what already works well, and why.
- Make sure that the challenge to each group is relatively equal.

Building in equity
- Read activity sheet aloud to everyone.
- In the short discussion after each group, keep asking how the group tried to keep equity in mind in developing its approaches.

Source
- the authors

Education for Changing Unions

ACTIVITY SHEET

PRACTISING FACILITATOR SKILLS

General Instructions

You are teaching a stewards course with the topic "Supports and Obstacles to Member Participation." Participants are primarily new stewards, along with some veterans who never got the training. All of the veterans are white men and most of the new stewards are white women, though they also include two Aboriginal women. There are no participants with visible disabilities. Your group should:

- review how you've seen the facilitators perform your assigned task over the past few days in this course;
- refer to any relevant reference materials;
- keep in mind how you will ensure equitable participation;
- prepare to demonstrate your task using the rest of us as your "participants";
- at the end of your facilitation, summarize three to five things to keep in mind to do your task well.

All groups have forty-five minutes to prepare.

Group one: dividing into groups

Develop three ways in which you can divide participants into groups to deal with the topic ("Supports and Obstacles to Member Participation"). Prepare any materials you need to demonstrate these three methods, using the rest of the group as participants. After your demonstration, summarize the three to five points to keep in mind when dividing participants into groups.

Group two: giving clear instructions

Adapt the "Helps/Hinders" exercise[1] to the theme "Supports and Obstacles to Member Participation." Identify what you need to say to give clear instructions to pairs and prepare any materials you need. You will be demonstrating your clear instructions using the rest of us as participants. After your demonstration, summarize the three to five points to keep in mind when giving clear instructions.

Group three: taking up small group reports

Outline two ways to take up small group reports of discussion on the theme of "Supports and Obstacles to Member Participation.

After your demonstration, summarize the three to five points to keep in mind when taking up small group reports.

Group four: leading effective large-group discussion

You are leading a full group discussion on the topic "Supports and Obstacles to Member Participation." Anticipate where discussion might get off track or overheated. Demonstrate, with us as participants, how you would guide discussion in such moments. After your demonstration, summarize the three to five points to keep in mind when leading a large-group discussion.

---

1. See Arnold et al., *Educating for a Cha nge*, p.85, for an outline of this exercise. We often use it as one of the early activities in a facilitator training program.

Appendix

TAKING A STANCE ON DIRECT ACTION

Why do it?
- to name our different assumptions about violence
- to create a safer space where people can engage in critical debate about violence
- to develop a common framework of values and concepts on violence
- to develop a set of guidelines for a strategy of direct action

Time it takes
- 30 to 60 minutes depending on the size of the group

What you need
- a roll of masking tape

How it's done

1. Using a strip of masking tape, draw a straight line on the floor, indicating that one end of the line represents one position ("The use of violence can <u>never</u> be justified") and the other end the opposite position ("The use of violence can <u>sometimes</u> be justified").

2. Ask people to line up, depending on how they relate to these two positions. Say that "violence" is left to one's own definition.

3. Once everyone has taken a position on the line, ask people to share why they took that position on the lineup.

4. Summarize the key themes that emerge from what people said. These themes, plus those you want to raise, will be the focus of a conversation following the exercise. (For example, there are different forms of violence: from physical, to psychological, to economic; personal, institutional, or state violence; poverty is violence; assumptions about violence: religious/moral, philosophical, and pragmatic elements; concept of self-defence, non-violent active resistance.)

5. After listing the key themes, ask for comments on the range of positions in the group—spread out, polarized, or concentrated on one point? Ask, "What's our comfort level in speaking to the question of violence?"

6. Synthesize/debrief by reviewing the purpose of the exercise. (See "Why do it?") We hope that as a result of the exercise people will agree that violence is more than just an act at the individual level, but is also a system that operates at various levels of the power structure.

Variations
- The process we describe here is introductory. To further explore direct action, you can use a matrix instead of a line. In the matrix variation, there are two questions to explore. The horizontal axis will explore the question, "What's my comfort level with using direct action that can unintentionally lead to violence?" The vertical axis will ask, "Is non-violent resistance/direct action an effective means to achieve our goals?" People will then position themselves in one of the four quadrants defined by these two questions. There will be four possible positions to choose from.

266

Quadrant 1:	Quadrant 2:
"I'm not personally comfortable with using direct action; but I think direct action can be an effective strategy or tactic for our campaign."	"I'm not personally comfortable with using direct action; and I also think direct action is not an effective strategy or tactic."
Quadrant 3:	Quadrant 4:
"I'm fairly comfortable with using direct action; and I believe direct action can be an effective strategy or tactic for our campaign."	"I'm comfortable with using direct action; but in this case, I don't think direct action is an effective strategy or tactic."

Challenges
- People might not feel safe to participate because of personal experience with violence (for example, victims of police brutality or sexual assault).
- People might start with already polarized positions.

Building in equity
- Members of some groups (refugees, people of colour, people with disabilities, younger or older people) are more vulnerable to violence during direct action, and the planning should not unfairly expose them to becoming targets.

Source
- the authors (for the CLC winter school, 2002)

The Combined Disabilities Association
AGM, Kingston, Jamaica, 1989.

Barb Thomas

WHAT'S HAPPENING

Why use it?
- as a quick visual way to share a lot of information
- to encourage people to locate their own situations in comparison to those of other people
- to generate material for strategic planning

Time it takes
- 1-2 hours

What you need
- a blank wall (on which it's okay to stick things), lots of index cards (preferably four different colours), markers, and masking tape
- a prepared flip chart with the instructions and the colour code for the index cards

How it's done
1. Explain to people that we will try to quickly build a shared picture of the context in which we are working. Divide people according to who sent them to this course or event (union local, affiliate, provincial federation, labour council, for example).

2. Reveal the colour codes for the four types of index card:
   - within your union organization
   - within the labour movement
   - in the political arena
   - in our communities

3. Ask people to identify and discuss in their groups the top three concerns that workers face in each of the four dimensions. Mark each concern on a separate card, following the colour codes.

4. In plenary, move quickly around the room, asking each group to put up one card in the first colour; each card should identify a different concern than the cards already on the wall. In the second round, they can place a check mark on another group's card if they strongly agree with it, and can place another card of their own. Continue until all the cards in that colour are up, and then discuss what is there.

5. Move through the other three colours in the same way, and sum up.

Variations
- Depending on time available, you can vary the number of cards per group, the number of groups, and the number of card colours used. This works best as part of a strategic planning sequence, and it provides a kind of environmental scan.
- For more elaborate visual tools along the same line, see "A political weather report," p.254, and "The Wall," p.252.

Challenges
- It can drag on and become boring if too much detail is allowed in the explanations.
- It can generate a massive amount of information, which people will have difficulty assimilating.

Building in equity
- Make sure that people with limited eyesight or hearing are placed near the wall where material is being posted.

Source
- Saskatchewan Federation of Labour and the authors

Education for Changing Unions

MORE ENERGIZERS LINKED TO COURSE CONTENT

UNION WORKOUT (POLITICAL EXERCISES)

These exercises go particularly well with discussions about facing management—for example, Quality of Work Life (QWL), bargaining, and grievance handling. You can create these exercises according to whatever you are dealing with at the moment. The movements can draw on karate, tai chi, dancing, whatever. The "text" is humorous, helps people laugh at workplace craziness, and reminds them of what they're fighting and what they're trying to build. Alternate the action instructions with sample text while you demonstrate the exercise, with people doing it with you. After the initial one, and the laughter, people should repeat it several times, saying the punch lines together to get a bit of exercise. Here are some examples.

Why use it?	• to give people some energy
Time it takes	• about one minute each exercise
What you need	• space for each person to move around • a short text (written or in your head) to lead the movements
How it's done/ variations	

Up with the Union

Action

Sample Text

Stand with feet comfortably apart, knees bent, arms out a bit in front with palms facing down.

Slowly straighten legs, breathing in deeply through the nose, palms turning to face up and coming out to the side in open gesture.

It's important to keep our balance, to keep breathing, keep centred when we're dealing with management.

Up with the union.

Breathe out slowly, as you bend knees, slowly bringing hands in and turning palms to face down.

Down with management.

Repeat at least ten times, with class saying "Up with the union, down with management" as they do so.

Source • Cliff Cheung of CUPW, adapting Tai Chi exercises for CUPW classes

Education for Changing Unions

Who's Responsible

Action

Stand straight, arms loosely at sides. Shoulders begin rising to ears, hands begin rising, palms turning slowly to face the ceiling.

Palms spread at shoulder level, elbows bent, chest out, face turned up to one side, mouth in an "O," eyebrows arched, chin pushing out.

Sample Text

It's hard to relax at work; we're always having to question the way management does things

Even when you, yourself, witness something that management has done.

Even when you have other witnesses that management has made the mistake, management will still ask: "Who's responsible?"

Repeat a few times, saying "Who's responsible?"

Source
• the authors

Pass the Buck

Ask people to hold a piece of paper in their right hands for this exercise.

Action

Stand straight, arms out to the side, right hand holding the paper.

Raise your arms slowly, and turn your head to the left, hands meet over your head.

The paper passes from your right to left hand as arms lower, and face swivels to the right.

Sample Text

This is something we see management do all the time.

It takes some co-ordination, and occasion-ally we see unionists who are adept at this exercise.

At no time should your eyes meet the paper as you "pass the buck."

Source
• the authors

Education for Changing Unions

Downsize

Action

Stand relaxed and begin shaking hands as though flicking water from them.

Shake the head, shake one leg, then the other, then the whole body.

Then stand and lift each knee a few times as in a march, slowly, then stop.

Legs apart, bend your knees, keeping back straight, and slowly lower your body as far as it's comfortable.

Source   • the authors

Sample Text

We've been through a lot of meetings and we need to shake out the tensions.

Shake out the tensions of too many quality circles, too many pictures of (president/ manager) posing as a worker.

Yes, lift your knees, and get ready

and down, down, down, downsize.

Quality Circles

Participants stand in a circle, with enough room to hold their arms out on either side.

Action

Marching on the spot, slowly at first then a bit faster, starting to march in a small circle on the spot moving faster, stepping higher in the circle.

Moving slower, shaking body a bit from side to side, coming to a halt and crouching, arms out towards the people on either side of us.

Source   • the authors

Building in equity   • As written, these require movement.
However, most can easily be adapted to sitting in chairs.

Sample Text

Lift your knees, get your heart into it

because we need careful movement into a circle.

not just any circle, but a quality circle, enough of those and you have a runaround.

A management runaround; as a union we need to stop and think, get our balance, create our own circles—**union circles.**

PASS A GESTURE

Why do it?
- to energize people and link to the theme of listening or non-verbal communication

Time it takes
- 5–10 minutes

How it's done
1. Ask participants to stand (or sit) in a circle. Explain that we'll be practising non-verbal communication, the kind of communication we often use unconsciously.

2. Pick a theme—for example, a motion they do at work; how the morning session went; how people are feeling at the moment about the course.

3. Each person, in turn, will use a gesture to communicate their feeling about the theme. Stress that only a non-verbal gesture can be used—no words. Illustrate by making a gesture (for example, holding an imaginary telephone, washing imaginary dishes), and then pass to someone else by pointing at the person and saying their name.

4. That person says your name, plays back your gesture to you, and plays a gesture of their own to someone else. Continue until everyone has had a chance to receive and send a gesture.

Variation
- The activity can also be used to evaluate the day or to lead into a discussion of health and safety.
- The whole group repeats the name and gesture of each person.

Challenges
- Some individuals may find the exercise "silly." Linking it to the concept of non-verbal communication helps this problem.

Building in equity
- This exercise can be done from a standing or seated position.

Source
- Sandy McIntyre, adapted by the authors

Resources and Sources

ABOUT POLITICS

Barndt, Deborah, ed. *Women Working the NAFTA Food Chain: Women, Food and Globalization.* Toronto: Second Story Press, 1999.

_____. *Tangled Routes: Women, Work and Globalization on the Tomato Trail.* Aurora, Ont.: Garamond Press, 2002.

Bellman, Geoffrey. *Getting Things Done When You Are Not in Charge.* New York: Simon and Schuster, 1992.

Betto, Frei. *Fidel and Religion: Talks with Frei Betto.* Havana, Cuba: Publications Office of the Council of State, 1967.

Bishop, Anne. *Becoming an Ally: Breaking the Cycle of Oppression.* Halifax, N.S.: Fernwood Publishing, 1994.

Clarke, Tony and Sarah Dopp. *Challenging McWorld.* Ottawa: Canadian Centre for Policy Alternatives, 2001. See web site <www.policyalternatives.ca>.

Common Frontiers. *Free Trade Area of the Americas (FTAA) Kit: Building a Hemispheric Social Alliance.* Toronto: Common Frontiers. See web site <www.web.ca/comfront>.

Galabuzi, Grace-Edward. *Canada's Creeping Economic Apartheid.* Toronto: Centre for Social Justice, 2001.

Gramsci, Antonio. *Selections from the Prison Notebooks.* Ed. Quintin Hoare and G. Nowell-Smith. New York: International Publications, 1971.

Gutierrez, Gustavo. *A Theology of Liberation.* Maryknoll, N.Y.: Orbis Books, 1973.

Kuyek, Joan Newman. *Fighting for Hope: Organizing to Realize Our Dreams.* Montreal: Black Rose Books, 1990.

Lederer, William and Eugene Burdick. *The Ugly American.* New York: Fawcett Crest, 1960.

Lerner, Michael. *Surplus Powerlessness: The Psychodynamics of Everyday Life . . . and the Psychology of Individual and Social Transformation.* Oakland, Cal.: Institute for Labor and Mental Health, 1986.

Lorde, Audre. *Sister, Outsider: Essays and Speeches.* Freedom, Ca.: Crossing Press, 1984.

Maquila Solidarity Network (MSN). *Stop Sweatshops: An Education/ Action Kit.* Toronto: MSN. See web site <www.maquilasolidarity.org>.

Monture-Angus, Patricia. *Journeying Forward: Dreaming First Nations Independence.* Halifax, N.S.: Fernwood Publishing, 1999.

Ollman, Bertell. *Dialectical Investigations.* New York: Routledge, 1993.

Robin, Jacques. "Les contours d'un autre monde: Cette grande implosion de l'an 2002." *Le Monde Diplomatique*, March 2002.

Sun Tsu. *The Art of War.* Trans. and Intro. by Samuel B. Griffith. Oxford: Oxford University Press/UNESCO, 1963.

Swanson, Jean. *Poor Bashing: The Politics of Exclusion.* Toronto: Between the Lines, 2001.

Swift, Richard. *The No-Nonsense Guide to Democracy.* Toronto: Between the Lines and New Internationalist, 2002.

Wildavsky, Aaron. *Speaking Truth to Power: The Art and Craft of Policy Analysis.* New Brunswick, N.J.: Transaction Publishers, 1987.

Yalnizyan, Armine. *The Growing Gap: A Report on Growing Inequality Between the Rich and Poor in Canada.* Toronto: Centre for Social Justice, 1999. See web site <www.socialjustice.org>.

ABOUT ADULT, SOCIAL CHANGE EDUCATION

The theory

Brookfield, Stephen D. *Understanding and Facilitating Adult Learning.* San Francisco: Jossey-Bass, 1988.

_____. "Unmasking Power: Foucault and Adult Learning." *Canadian Journal for the Study of Adult Education,* vol.15, no. 1 (May 2001).

Foley, Griff. *Strategic Learning: Understanding and facilitating organizational change.* Sydney Australia: Centre for Popular Education, 2001.

Freire, Paulo. *Pedagogy of the Oppressed.* New York: Continuum, 1970.

Gadotti, Moacir. *Reading Paulo Freire: His Life and Work.* Trans. John Milton. Albany: State University of New York Press, 1994.

Hart, Mechthild. *Working and Educating for Life: Feminist and International Perspectives on Adult Education.* London: Routledge, 1992.

hooks, bell. *Teaching to Transgress: Education as the Practice of Freedom.* New York: Routledge, 1994.

Horton, Myles. *The Long Haul: An Autobiography.* With Judith Kohl and Herbert Kohl. New York: Doubleday, 1990.

Horton, Myles and Paulo Freire. *We Make the Road by Walking: Conversations on Education and Social Change.* Ed. Brenda Bell, John Gaventa, and John Peters. Philadelphia: Temple University Press, 1990.

Kolb, David A. *Experiential Learning: Experience as the Source of Learning and Development.* Englewood Cliffs, N.J.: Prentice-Hall, 1984.

_____. *The Learning Style Inventory Technical Manual.* Boston: McBer and Company, 1976.

Livingstone, David W. *The Education-Jobs Gap: Underemployment or Economic Democracy.* Toronto: Garamond Press, 1999.

Mayo, Peter. *Gramsci, Freire and Adult Education: Possibilities for Transformative Action.* London: Zed Books, 1999.

Newman, Michael. *Defining the Enemy: Adult Education in Social Action.* Paddington, NSW, Australia: Stewart Victor Publishing, 1994.

Thomas, Alan M. *Beyond Education: A New Perspective on Society's Management of Learning.* San Francisco: Jossey-Bass, 1991.

The practice (tools)

Arnold, Rick, Deborah Barndt, and Bev Burke. *A New Weave: Popular Education in Canada and Central America.* Toronto: CUSO and Ontario Institute for Studies in Education, Adult Education Department, 1985. See web site <www.catalystcentre.ca>.

Arnold, Rick, Bev Burke, Carl James, D'Arcy Martin, and Barb Thomas. *Educating for a Change.* Toronto: Doris Marshall Institute and Between the Lines, 1991.

Barndt, Deborah. *Naming the Moment: Political Analysis for Action—A Manual for Community Groups.* Toronto: Jesuit Centre for Social Justice. See web site <www.catalystcentre.ca>.

_____. *To Change This House: Popular Education under the Sandinistas.* Toronto: Between the Lines, 1990.

Doerge, Suzanne and Beverley Burke. *Starting with Women's Lives: Changing Today's Economy—A Facilitator's Guide to a Visual Workshop Methodology.* Ottawa: Women's Inter-Church Council of Canada and Canadian Labour Congress, 2000.

GATT-Fly. *Ah-Hah! A New Approach to Popular Education.* Toronto: Between the Lines, 1983.

Kivel, Paul. *Uprooting Racism: How White People Can Work for Racial Justice.* Gabriola Island, B.C.: New Society Publisher, 1995.

marino, dian. *Wild Garden: Art, Education, and the Culture of Resistance.* Toronto: Between the Lines, 1997.

Marshall, Judith, with Domingos Chigarire, Helena Francisco, Antonio Goncalves, and Leonardo Nhantumbo. *Training for Empowerment: A Kit of Materials Based on an Exchange among Literacy Workers in Mozambique, Brazil and Nicaragua.* Toronto: International Council for Adult Education and Doris Marshall Institute, 1990. (To order: <jmarshall@uswa.ca>.)

Owen, Harrison. *Open Space Technology: A User's Guide.* Potomac, Md.: Abbott Publishing, 1992.

Spencer, Bruce. "Workers' Education for the 21st Century." In *Learning for Life: Readings in Canadian Adult Education.* Toronto: Thompson Educational Publishing, 1998.

Walters, Shirley and Linzi Manicom, eds. *Gender and Popular Education: Methods for Empowerment.* London: Zed Books, 1996.

ABOUT UNIONS

Beveridge, Karl and Jude Johnston. *Making Our Mark: Labour Arts and Heritage in Ontario.* Toronto: Between the Lines, 1999.

Brecher, Jeremy and Tim Costello. *Building Bridges: The Emerging Grassroots Coalition of Labor and Community.* New York: Monthly Review Press, 1990.

Briskin, Linda and Patricia McDermott. *Women Challenging Unions: Feminism, Democracy and Militancy.* Toronto: University of Toronto Press, 1993.

Canadian Labour Congress (CLC). *Notes on Unions,* nos.1-9. Ottawa: CLC.

Gagnon, Mona-Josée, ed. "Un syndicalisme en crise d'identité." *Sociologie et Société.* Les Presses de l'Université de Montréal, vol. XXX, numéro 2, 1998.

Heron, Craig. *The Canadian Labour Movement: A Brief History.* 2nd ed. Toronto: Lorimer, 1996.

Kaminski, Michelle and Helena Worthen. *The Regina V. Polk Fund & Labor Union Activism: Confidential Survey.* Chicago: Labor Education Program. February 2001.

Melksins-Wood, Ellen, Peter Melksins, and Michael Yates. *Rising from the Ashes? Labor in the Age of "Global Capitalism."* New York: Monthly Review Press, 1998.

Piotte, Jean-Marc. *Du Combat au Partenariat: Interventions critiques sur le syndicalisme québécois.* Montréal: Éditions Nota Bene, 1998.

Rinehart, James W. *The Tyranny of Work: Alienation and the Labour Process.* 3rd ed. Toronto: Harcourt, Brace and Company, 1996.

Rouillard, Jacques. *Histoire du Syndicalisme Québécois.* Montréal: Boréal, 1989.

Yates, Michael D. *Why Unions Matter.* New York: Monthly Review Press, 1998.

ABOUT UNION EDUCATION

Bernard, Elaine. "Education vs. Propaganda." *Our Times*, September/October 1997.

Canadian Labour Congress (CLC). *Anti-Racism Integration Guide*. Ottawa, 2002.

_____. *Seeds for Change: A Curriculum Guide for Worker-Centred Literacy/Semer Pour L'Avenir: Guide d'élaboration de materiel d'alphabetisation axé sur les travailleurs et les travailleuses*. Ottawa, 2002. <clcliteracay@clc-ctc.ca>.

_____ *Toolbox for Global Solidarity*. Rev. ed. Ottawa, 2002.

_____. *Making it Clear: Clear Language for Union Communications/Ecrire pour Agir: Guide syndical de communications claires*. Ottawa, 2000 <clcliteracay@clc-ctc.ca>.

Cohen, Marcy, Denise Nadeau, and Nancy Pollack. *The Workplace Anti-Stress Guide*. Vancouver: Hospital Employees' Union, 2000. (For information on workshops with Denise Nadeau and HEU using the guide, visit <www.heu.org> or <dnadeau@look.ca>.)

Delp, Linda, ed. *Teaching for Change*. Los Angeles: UCLA Labor Centre, 2002. (Order book and other materials from <www.labor.ucla.edu>.)

International Confederation of Free Trade Unions (ICFTU). "Education Policy Action Programme." Reprinted for Educ-action Conference, UCLEA, Toronto, 1999.

Gereluk, Winston, Derek Briton, and Bruce Spencer. *Labour Education in Canada Today*. Athabasca, Alta.: Athabasca University Centre for Work and Community Studies, 2001.

Martin, D'Arcy. *Thinking Union: Activism and Education in Canada's Labour Movement*. Toronto: Between the Lines, 1995. See web site <www.thinkingunion.net>.

Nadeau, Denise. *Counting Our Victories: Popular Education and Organizing*. Vancouver: Repeal the Deal Productions, 1996.

Newman, Michael. *The Third Contract: Theory and Practice in Trade Union Training*. Sydney, Australia: Stewart Victor Publishing, 1993.

Spencer, Bruce, ed. *Unions and Learning in a Global Economy: International and Comparative Perspectives*. Toronto: Thompson Educational Publishing, 2002.

St-Amour, Johanne avec le service d'éducation de la FTQ. *Guide de méthodes pédagogiques utilisées par la FTQ, ses syndicats et conseils de travail*. Montreal: Fédération des travailleurs et travailleuses du Québec, 1998.

Taylor, Jeffery. *Union Learning: Canadian Labour Education in the Twentieth Century*. Toronto: Thompson Educational Publishing, 2001. See specialized web site at <http://unionlearning.athabascau.ca>.

Thomas, Barbara and Charles Novogrodsky, Charles. *Combatting Racism in the Workplace: A Course for Workers*. Toronto: Cross Cultural Communication Centre, 1983.

Weil, David. *Turning the Tide: Strategic Planning for Labor Unions*. New York: Macmillan/Lexington Books, 1994.

Education for Changing Unions

Appendix

WEB SITES Canadian Centre for Policy Alternatives. A progressive think-tank, linking researchers inside and outside the universities. <www.policyalternatives.ca>.

Canadian Labour Congress (CLC). News in English and French from Canada's central labour body, including its educational initiatives. <www.clc-ctc.ca>.

Catalyst Centre. A Toronto-based popular education group, with an excellent on-line bookstore. <www.catalystcentre.ca>.

Centre for Research on Work and Society (CRWS). Research centre at York University, Toronto, which concentrates on sociology and economics, and runs an on-line magazine, *Just Labour*. <www.justlabour.yorku.ca>.

Centre for Social Justice. A research organization with good material on economic and racial inequality. <www.socialjustice.org>.

Centre for the Study of Education and Work (CSEW). Research centre at the University of Toronto, which concentrates on learning issues and occasionally runs exchanges among North American labour educators. <www.csew.oise.utoronto.ca>.

Fédération des travailleurs et travailleuses du Québec (FTQ). News in French from Quebec's largest union central, including its educational initiatives. <www.ftq.qc.ca>.

Highlander Center. The long-standing centre for progressive adult education in the Southern United States. <www.hrec.org>.

Labour Start. Daily updates on labour-related news, in a variety of languages. <www.labourstart.org>.

Labor Notes and New Labour Forum. Two forums for discussion among union democrats and radicals in the United States. <www.labornotes.org>. <www.qc.edu/newlaborforum/>.

Our Times magazine. Independent, sympathetic coverage of unions in Canada. <www.ourtimes.org>.

Rabble, on-line news with a progressive perspective. <www.rabble.ca>.

Turtle Island Native Network. The site has educational material as well as many other interesting resources. <www.turtleisland.org>.

United Association for Labor Education. Brings together union educators with those based in colleges and universities who teach workers. <www.uale.org>.

United for a Fair Economy (UFE). Network of progressive economists in the United States, which produces lively popular economics material. <www.ufenet.org.>